TAKING THE HEAT

TAKING THE HEAT

Women Chefs and Gender Inequality in the Professional Kitchen

DEBORAH A. HARRIS AND PATTI GIUFFRE

RUTGERS UNIVERSITY PRESS
New Brunswick, New Jersey, and London

Library of Congress Cataloging-in-Publication Data
Harris, Deborah Ann.
    Taking the heat : women chefs and gender inequality in the professional
kitchen / Deborah A. Harris, Patti Giuffre.
        pages cm
    Includes bibliographical references and index.
    ISBN 978–0–8135–7126–3 (hardcover : alk. paper) —
ISBN 978–0–8135–7125–6 (pbk. : alk. paper) — ISBN 978–0–8135–7127–0
(e-book (web pdf))
    1. Women cooks.   2. Food service.   3. Women in the hospitality
industry.   4. Women in the food industry.   5. Sex discrimination against
women.   I. Giuffre, Patti, 1966–   II. Title.
HD6073.H8.H37 2015
331.4′816415—dc23

                                                                2014035985

A British Cataloging-in-Publication record for this book is available from the
British Library.

Visit our website: http://rutgerspress.rutgers.edu

Manufactured in the United States of America

We would like to dedicate this book to
Ella Harris and Tim Paetzold

CONTENTS

Acknowledgments   ix

Introduction: "There's a Girl in the Kitchen?!":
Why a Study of Women Chefs   1

1   Home versus Haute: Gender and Status in the
Evolution of Professional Chefs   17

2   From Good to Great: Food Media and
Becoming an Elite Chef   43

3   Fitting In and Standing Out: Entering the
Professional Restaurant Kitchen   84

4   Bitches, Girly Girls, or Moms: Women's
Perceptions of Gender-Appropriate Leadership
Styles in Professional Kitchens   130

5   Challenging "Choices": Why Some Women Leave
Restaurant Kitchen Work   162

Conclusion: Where Are the Great Women Chefs?   189

Appendix: Methodological Approach   203
References   213
Index   223

ACKNOWLEDGMENTS

We wish to thank the thirty-three women chefs who agreed to participate in our research. We are in awe of the women chefs and their strength, dedication, and passion for cooking. They generously shared personal details about their work and family lives, and this book would have been impossible without their help. We would also like to thank our editor at Rutgers University Press, Katie Keeran. We are extremely grateful for her support and excitement about the project. Thanks also go to Leslie Mitchner and Nicole Manganaro at Rutgers University Press for their help finalizing the book.

This book has been a work in progress for a few years now, and several people gave us feedback and support along the way as we formulated different aspects of the book as conference papers and articles. Several graduate students helped us find literature and data. We thank Raul Casarez, Jamie Hornbuckle, Kelley Russell-DuVarney, Whitney Harris, Alyssa Powell, and Tracy Quiroz. We thank Deborah's friend who "fancied up" Figure I.1, Suzanne Daniels. We are grateful to friends and colleagues who commented on the proposal, previous articles, papers, or chapter drafts: Kirsten Dellinger, Christine Williams, Dana Britton, Patricia Richards, Gretchen Webber, Ellen Slaten, Jessie Daniels, and Vanina Leschziner. We would like to thank John Bartkowski for his suggestions about precarious masculinity. Thanks to our colleagues at Texas State University including the Department of Sociology (particularly Dr. Susan Day, our department chair, and Tina Villarreal, who assisted us in some of the technical aspects of producing the book), College of Liberal Arts (particularly Dean Michael Hennessy), and the Office of Academic Affairs (particularly Associate Provost Cynthia Opheim), whose financial support for subvention costs made this book a reality.

We also offer more personal thanks to our dear friends and family members who provided us with emotional support over the duration of this project. Deborah would like to thank her mother, Ella Harris, for demonstrating what tenacity and verve look like. She would also like to thank her sisters, Gwen Gibbs, Angela Stanford, and Susan Williams, for all their love and support. Several friends have provided encouragement and counsel during this process. Kristi Fondren, Diana Bridges, Aerin Toussaint, Maggie Schleich, and Jamie Smith have all heard more about women chefs—and the process of writing about them—than anyone should ever have to hear. You can all expect copies of this book and Deborah really hopes they aren't immediately thrown in a paper shredder. Deborah would also like to thank the supportive ladies from the Feminist Kitchen Book Club, particularly founder Addie Broyles, for their enthusiasm and interest in studying women chefs. She would also like to thank Virginia Wood for her helpful comments early in the planning of this project.

Patti would like to offer her utmost gratitude to Tim Paetzold, whose confidence in her never wavered. This book would not have been possible for Patti without Tim's love, faith, and support. She would also like to thank her dear friends and colleagues, Kirsten Dellinger, Christine Williams, Julie Winterich, Ellen Slaten, Jeff Jackson, Michelle Reese, Michelle Roebuck, Steve Roebuck, Beth Bertin, and John Baker who read drafts, offered suggestions and insight, made her laugh, required her to dance occasionally, and always offered a bright light in her life. Finally, she would like to thank Ginger and Neil Whitesell, Perry Giuffre, and Pat Paetzold for supporting her academic work for many years. Patti is eternally grateful for her friends and family who are constant reminders of what is important in life.

We thank Emerald Publishing and Springer Publishing who gave us permission to include some of our work from previously published articles. Portions of chapters 3 and 4 were based upon some ideas in our 2010 article, "Not One of the Guys: Women Chefs Redefining Gender in the Culinary Industry," *Research in the Sociology of Work* 20:59–81. Portions of chapter 5 were based on our 2010 article, "'The Price You Pay': How Female Professional Chefs Negotiate Work and Family," *Gender Issues* 27:27–52.

TAKING THE HEAT

INTRODUCTION: "THERE'S A GIRL IN THE KITCHEN?!"

Why a Study of Women Chefs

For the past three years, champagne maker Veuve Clicquot has sponsored a World's Best Female Chef Award. When the company announced that the 2013 winner was Italian chef Nadia Santini, the praise for Santini, who was the first woman ever awarded three stars by the prestigious Michelin Guide, was tempered with criticism about the merits of singling women out for a special award. Anthony Bourdain, the chef-turned-television host, asked via his Twitter account, "Why—at this point in history—do we need a 'Best Female Chef' special designation? As if they are curiosities?" Other chefs and influential food writers have also commented on having separate designations for men and women chefs and suggested doing away with woman-centered awards. They argued that reserving a special award for women is divisive and implies women have to be evaluated differently, and, it is often suggested, less stringently, than their male peers.

These remarks are just part of a larger discussion about women's place in the (professional) kitchen. Underlying these responses, however, is the fact that women chefs *are* sometimes regarded as curiosities, much like women in many male-dominated careers. While there are several rock star men chefs so famous even the most casual foodie knows who they are by first name alone (Emeril, Mario, Wolfgang), lists of accomplished women chefs are harder to provide. As gender scholars who focus on the role of work in perpetuating and challenging gender inequality, we were fascinated by the case of women professional chefs and the numerous contradictions they face in their work lives. How is it that women—the gender most commonly associated with food and cooking—have lagged so far behind men in professional kitchens?

We soon discovered that answering such a question was more difficult than originally thought. Understanding the gendered nature of the culinary world involves examining the history of professional chefs, the influence of cultural intermediaries such as food critics and writers who are tasked with evaluating and promoting food created by chefs, and the experiences of women chefs working within male-dominated workplace cultures. When examined together, these conditions can tell us something about how certain jobs become coded as masculine and feminine and, therefore are perceived as men's or women's work. Studying women chefs can also help identify the mechanisms and processes that allow these gender disparities within occupations to continue and highlight strategies that allow more gender integration to occur.

WHERE ARE THE WOMEN CHEFS?

Before continuing, we wanted to make clear what we mean when we refer to someone as a "chef." Due to the increasing attention to the career, just who is a chef is an issue of debate within the field (Ruhlman 2007). All restaurants employ cooks; however, higher-end restaurants and upscale hotels employ both cooks and chefs. Chefs are the "chiefs" of the kitchen and they are expected to manage both the kitchen and its staff, as well as hold creative control over the kitchen. While many chefs have attended culinary school, others have learned their skills working in various restaurants through on-the-job training. In general, a head/executive chef, also known as a *chef de cuisine*, heads more upscale, or fine dining restaurants. Immediately under the head chef is the role of *sous chef*, who works closely with the head chef and is often responsible for the day-to-day running of the kitchen, including supervising the various *chefs de partie*. These chefs work as line cooks responsible for individual stations such as *saucier*, entrée/grill station, *poisonnier* (fish), and *garde manger* (salads and cold appetizers). Some restaurants may also employ one or more pastry chefs and cooks to provide desserts and other baked goods for the restaurant. Particularly large or elaborate kitchen setups also employ *commis*, who are there to assist and learn each station.

According to data from the U.S. Bureau of Labor Statistics, in 2013 only 20 percent of chefs and head cooks in the culinary industry were women. Starchefs.com, an online magazine dedicated to the occupation, conducted an industry survey in 2005 and reported that 89 percent of executive chefs, 82 percent of sous chefs, 66 percent of line cooks, and 60 percent of management positions were held by men (Marcus 2005). The only area where women hold a higher percentage of positions is in the pastry department where 80 percent of bakers, 77 percent of pastry chefs, and 84 percent of the cooks who work in pastry beneath them were women. Examining some of the most elite kitchens, Bloomberg News analysts found that women held only 6.3 percent of the 160 head chef positions within the fifteen top U.S. restaurant groups (Sutton 2014). To give some comparison, there has been a lot of attention given to women's under-representation in the corporate world, where women currently make up about 24 percent of CEOs (U.S. Bureau of Labor Statistics 2013), meaning that women have actually found greater success in the boardroom than the professional kitchen.

Why have women lagged behind men in the chef occupation? Despite the growing popularity of the culinary world, there has been little research conducted on professional chefs. While some works have examined the history of the gastronomic field (Ferguson 2004) and how particular restaurant kitchens operate as successful teams (Fine 1996b), little sociological research has focused on the stark gender disparities within professional kitchens. In describing women's lack of parity, some cite the difficult conditions in professional kitchens and suggest that women do not have the physical and emotional strength needed to work as chefs. However, other demanding careers, such as law, finance, and the military, have become more gender integrated in recent years (see, for example, Britton 2003; Denissen 2010a, 2010b; Levin 2001; Pierce 1995; Roth 2006; Williams 1989; 1995; Williams, Muller, and Kilanski 2012; Yount 1991; Zimmer 1987), suggesting that demanding work conditions alone are not enough to discourage women's participation. Others propose that the rise of feminism worked to move women out of the kitchen and, as a result, few women have wanted to pursue cooking as a career (Ruhlman 2007). It's true that feminists have had somewhat of a complex relationship with domestic cooking (Brundson 2005; Hollows 2003), but to describe feminism's stance toward cooking as a cultural monolith would be inaccurate. Some feminist writers have argued that women could find personal satisfaction and even power through cooking for the family (de Beauvoir 1953). The arguments that it was feminism that kept women away from professional kitchens also rely upon "rhetorics of choice" and suggest that inequality, particularly gender-based inequality, is a result of men and women merely making different choices that result in differing occupational outcomes. This focus on choice ignores both structural inequalities in the workplace and the reality that the majority of positions in low-paying, low-status occupations in food preparation (e.g., cafeteria worker) are held by women. It is primarily the more high-status jobs like head or executive chef that are male dominated.

Data on the demographic makeup of culinary school attendance suggest that women have shown interest in the culinary world. According to the U.S. Department of Education, in 2007, 47.2 percent of students receiving a bachelor's degree in culinary arts/chef training in the United States were women. This represents an almost 6 percent increase in less than five years. Even the most highly regarded culinary school in the United States, the Culinary Institute of America (CIA), has seen an increase in women's attendance and its 2012 graduating class was composed of 36 percent women (Moskin 2014). These numbers suggest that something must happen between the time when women enroll in culinary school and when promotions to high ranks in the kitchen are given that sets them on a different career path.

GENDER INEQUALITY AND PROFESSIONAL CHEFS

So why study women professional chefs? Examining the difficulties faced by women in the culinary industry can be helpful in learning more about the mechanisms and processes that allow gender disparities within occupations to continue. Cecilia Ridgeway (2011) points out that gender inequality in the workplace is important because it is through work that men and women gain access to both material resources and positions of power. Occupations are highly gendered (Acker 1990; Britton 2003; Britton and

Logan 2008) and gender segregation at work has been found to be the most significant explanation for the wage gap between genders (Britton 2003; Reskin and Roos 1990; Williams 1995). Occupational segregation refers to the fact that men and women are concentrated in different jobs. With few exceptions, the jobs that are male-dominated pay more than jobs that are female-dominated. Even within the same occupation, such as chef, men and women are concentrated in different specialties. While these jobs may not be all that dissimilar technically, these positions carry different levels of pay and different opportunities to progress up the organizational hierarchy.

Numerous studies have examined single mechanisms of gender work inequality such as hiring discrimination, gendered evaluations of employees, and male-dominated work cultures. In this book, we use the occupation of professional chef as a case study to take a closer look at the many ways gender inequality is created, maintained, and sometimes even challenged and transformed at work. By focusing in depth on a specific occupation, we are able to examine the way that gender inequality has been manifested historically as well as in current workplace structures and interactions.

What can studying women chefs provide students and scholars of gender inequality in the workplace? First, studying chefs helps illustrate how the gender coding of jobs (whether particular work is labeled as masculine or feminine) is socially constructed and how these constructions are used to deny opportunities to women within an occupation. Men who cook are doing what is generally considered women's work (Beagan et al. 2008; Bugge and Almas 2006; DeVault 1994), but in the context of professional kitchens, cooking has been transformed into a high-status, masculine pursuit. Research like ours helps illustrate how even women's work, under certain conditions, can ultimately prove to become a site in which men prove their dominance. Therefore, we need a more thorough understanding of how this gender coding has been altered to define professional cooking as masculine and the processes through which this coding is upheld even when women enter these jobs. Doing so can help us understand the entrenchment of gender as a status characteristic at work.

Second, chefs are an ideal occupation to use in studying gender inequality among creative careers. The chef occupation is in a period of transition (Rousseau 2012; Ruhlman 2007) as chefs have transformed from members of the servant class to being hailed in the pages of *Time Out New York* as "the new rock stars." Part of the new cultural status of chefs is due to their recasting from blue-collar production work to being part of the creative economy, where innovation is rewarded and old divisive elements such as sexism and racism have been replaced by work cultures marked by meritocracy (Castilla 2008; Florida 2002). With this new focus on professionalism, if the ability to produce new, exciting food is a marker of success and provides chances for promotion, why are head and executive chefs still primarily male? Our study challenges the claims that talent is always the primary determinant of success in creative careers and addresses how status characteristics like gender can impact occupational success even within creative fields.

WOMEN, THE GASTRONOMIC FIELD, AND GENDERED ORGANIZATIONS: A THEORETICAL FRAMEWORK

In order to examine how gender inequality is created, maintained, and even sometimes challenged among professional chefs we utilize two different theoretical concepts, Pierre Bourdieu's notion of fields and Joan Acker's work on gendered organizations. Occupations do not exist in a vacuum but are situated within fields composed of various actors, rules, and norms that can affect occupational outcomes. Bourdieu's work allows us to examine how various elements of the field, including how the "game" is set up, the rules of the game, and the interactions between players all work together to create the positions available for women in what is known as the gastronomic field. While the use of fields can be useful in understanding how certain cultural domains arose and provide historical context concerning the conditions that shaped these arenas, these approaches can ignore how status characteristics like gender can operate and constrain the options available to agents within the field. This can be particularly important in studies of creative careers, like chefs, where too often these positions are presented as meritocracies when, in reality, gender and other forms of inequality can be prevalent (Ridgeway 2011). Incorporating the gendered organizations research of Acker (1990) and others helps us examine the ways components of the field may be influenced by gender in ways even unknown or unquestioned by actors within the field. As Acker notes, all organizations (also all occupations) are gendered because each reproduces and maintains ideas about masculinity and femininity, as well as notions about which groups of workers are ideal for the job at hand. Gendered organizations theory can help explain how the rules of a field are developed and enacted in ways that can disadvantage women and how women can challenge or bypass certain rules of the game in order to win and succeed as a chef. Taken together, the use of both of these concepts will allow us to discuss 1) how chefs arose as a male-dominated occupation; 2) how the gendered nature of the occupation is maintained by current conditions; and 3) how these gender divisions can be challenged and even transformed.

Pierre Bourdieu argued against acontextual studies of cultural production and suggested that items considered to be art are never created within a vacuum. Instead Bourdieu stressed that cultural production should be conceptualized as a social activity. He introduced the concept of fields to emphasize the dynamic and relational nature of cultural production and to describe the process through which cultural products are created and how these products and their producers earn status and prestige. In *An Invitation to Reflexive Sociology* (1992), Bourdieu and Wacquant describe a field as a distinctive social microcosm with specific practices, rules, forms of authority, and standards of evaluation. Bourdieu provides the metaphor of a game to describe cultural fields. In the game, there is struggle and competition to be seen as legitimate cultural producers and to earn status and capital (economic, social, human, and cultural). This capital will allow a player to move up into higher positions within the field and earn the power to influence how the game is shaped.

The notion of fields allows researchers to study the historic forces that shape the development of these fields of cultural production. Studies of specific fields also give attention to the numerous agents within the field including cultural producers, artistic critics, and audiences and the ways in which they interact to shape the field and the outcomes of those within it. When cultural tastemakers, such as critics, provide legitimacy to cultural producers, this can lead to the artists earning more forms of capital, described by Bourdieu as "tokens" in his game metaphor. Only a few players can ever reach the highest levels of the game where they and their work become consecrated. This rarity of elite artists helps reinforce their status as being unparalleled within the field, as well as uphold the power of the legitimizing institutions and cultural tastemakers.

Building upon this concept, Priscilla Parkhurst Ferguson (2004) examined the rise of French haute cuisine and suggested that there exists a gastronomic field composed of chefs, audiences, and culinary elites. Ferguson argues that the reification of French haute cuisine, with its specific rules and standards of evaluation, has established this gastronomic field. Chefs operate within this field and compete for attention and capital. The gastronomic field includes the historical forces that guided how chefs established themselves as an occupation, rules of the field such as commonly shared beliefs regarding the role of a chef and what career paths a chef should take, and unique cultural tastemakers like food critics and culinary organizations who confer status on chefs' cultural products.

Ferguson believes the United States does not possess a gastronomic field due to its less established and uniform culinary culture. However, the term can still be useful in understanding today's interconnected gastronomic world in which there is a distinct culinary hierarchy in which chefs compete to gain recognition and status. Another way today's culinary world fits with the notion of fields includes the importance of cultural tastemakers and critics in legitimizing certain chefs and their cooking and awarding status. A broader use of the concept also recognizes that the gastronomic field is no longer bound to one geographic location. Elite chefs travel all over the world to train alongside chefs from other countries or to expand their culinary empires.

In our study, we use the concept of gastronomic field to illustrate the historical context and current institutional mechanisms that have prevented women from advancing within the occupation of professional chef. Figure I.1 presents our theoretical model describing the gastronomic field and the entities that shape chefs' placement within the field. At the base of the model is the historical process through which professional chefs arose as an occupation. We begin by focusing on the history of professional chefs and how early chefs created occupational norms and institutional arrangements that disadvantaged, and sometimes even excluded, women. Because the work of chefs is closely linked to cooking, which is generally considered a feminine activity, the occupation was faced with a feminization threat in which their work was constantly in danger to be defined as a feminine endeavor. Once work is defined as feminine, there is the chance it will become devalued, and numerous researchers have reported that the higher the percentage of women in an occupation, the lower the pay (Cohen and Huffman 2003; Mandel 2013; Reskin and Roos 1990; Tomaskovic-Devey 1993). For jobs that ᴇ as male-dominated but become female-dominated over time, such

GASTRONOMIC FIELD

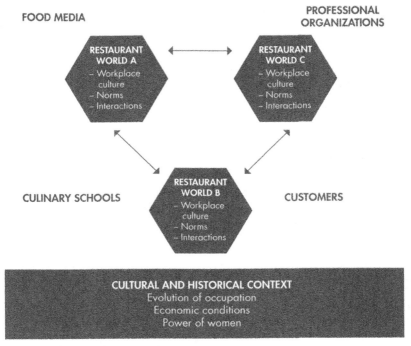

FOOD MEDIA

PROFESSIONAL
ORGANIZATIONS

RESTAURANT
WORLD A
– Workplace
  culture
– Norms
– Interactions

RESTAURANT
WORLD C
– Workplace
  culture
– Norms
– Interactions

CULINARY SCHOOLS

RESTAURANT
WORLD B
– Workplace
  culture
– Norms
– Interactions

CUSTOMERS

CULTURAL AND HISTORICAL CONTEXT
Evolution of occupation
Economic conditions
Power of women

FIGURE I.1. Theoretical Framework

as in elementary school teaching, these positions even experience a decline in earnings. According to Paula England and Nancy Folbre (1999), a major explanation for this gendered pattern in pay is the devaluation of femininity. Carework performed in the home and viewed as an expression of caring about others is given less value than outside-of-home work performed for a wage (England 2010; England and Folbre 1999).

For chefs, this masculine, professional activity is always at risk of comparison to the unpaid, nonprofessional cooking of women in the home. Feminization threat leads to a sense of insecure and unstable masculinity amongst men in jobs requiring them to perform female-coded tasks—a term we refer to as precarious masculinity. To neutralize feminization threat and prevent men workers from experiencing precarious masculinity, several actions can be taken including emphasizing the masculine nature of their work (e.g., focusing on the military background of their occupation) while deemphasizing skills or attributes that could be considered feminine (e.g., caring for others). Early chefs were aware of this feminization threat and purposefully distanced their work from the activities of women home cooks by excluding women from influential institutions within the gastronomic field, such as cooking schools and high-status restaurants. This process allowed men chefs to gain status, legitimacy, and compensation and firmly entrenched the notion of the chef occupation as a masculine pursuit.

Our model acknowledges that the chefs themselves are not the only actors within the gastronomic field that shape the occupation. Several important actors within the American culinary scene exert tremendous influence on the chef occupation as a whole and the success or failure of individual chefs (Davis 2009). Elite culinary schools, food writers, food critics, and industry organizations such as the James Beard Foundation are all examples of current legitimizing forces in the gastronomic field. Food writers and critics can be especially influential in shaping the discourse around chefs and helping define whose efforts are valued and rewarded within the gastronomic field. As media attention is becoming more important for chefs (Rousseau 2012), it is vital to examine the role media representation plays in women chefs' ability to progress.

Over time, the dominance of men chefs has created organizational norms and arrangements that benefit men while excluding women. These norms and arrangements take place within the various restaurant worlds that are part of the gastronomic field. Restaurant worlds operate as social spaces in which a network of people produces a defined product (Ferguson 2004). These spaces of production are not gender neutral, as Joan Acker's (1990) theory of gendered organizations maintains that masculinity and femininity are institutionalized in all organizations (or industry, or occupation). Restaurant worlds are no different and contain work arrangements and interactions that reproduce the gendered aspects of professional cooking (Ferguson 2004; Fine 1987; Fine 1996b). This can include the structure of culinary careers (e.g., long hours, little upward mobility) and daily work interactions between culinary professionals (e.g., harassment, discrimination). Because gender segregation can preserve men's interests, men in workplaces often attempt to shore up masculinity (Bird 1996; Dellinger 2004; Martin 2003) and resist gender integration. This manifests itself in workplace cultures that are hypermasculine and unwelcoming to women to enter such jobs. For men chefs, this can include fostering male-dominated workplace cultures that are aggressive and competitive and resistant to change when women chefs integrate restaurant kitchens (Fine 1996a).

Acker (1990) emphasizes that gendered organizations value masculinity in both subtle and overt ways. One way organizations remain gendered is through the reproduction of gender stereotypes that helps advantage the current male job holders by defining men as more productive, better leaders, and with greater commitment to work. For women chefs, these stereotypes include claims that women are physically incapable of completing tasks associated with restaurant work and that they have poor leadership and business skills (Bartholomew and Garey 1996; Cooper 1997; Swinbank 2002). Such beliefs help ensure that being a chef remains seen as "men's work" and makes it difficult for women to advance within traditional kitchen hierarchies.

STUDYING CHEFS: A QUALITATIVE METHODOLOGY

To better understand how the gastronomic field operates and influences the position of women chefs, we combined content analysis of chef-focused media with in-depth interviews with thirty-three women in central Texas who had experience working as professional chefs. The appendix details our methodological approach and provides further details on our data, sampling, and analytical approach.

Our media data included over 2,200 restaurant reviews and chef profiles published in well-known newspapers (the *New York Times* and *San Francisco Chronicle*) and national food magazines (*Food & Wine* and *Gourmet*) published between 2004 and 2009. Food-centered media has been growing and remains a powerful influence in the gastronomic field. This material helps represent the gastronomic field at a national, and even international level, and provides a glimpse into who are considered the most noteworthy and accomplished chefs. We analyzed these articles to learn more about how important tastemakers in the gastronomic field—food writers and critics—evaluate and assign accolades to these chefs. We wanted to understand if men and women chefs were evaluated and described in different ways and, if so, in what ways were they described differently. The media representation of chefs can help perpetuate men's dominance, particularly in

TABLE I.1 Description of Participants

Pseudonym	Current position	Line or pastry	Years in industry	Age	Race/ethnicity	Marital status	No. of children	Culinary school
Alexandra	Events planner at a restaurant	Line	22	36	Asian	divorced	0	Yes
Amber	Owner, meal delivery service	Line	10	34	White	married	1	No
Anna	Executive chef	Line	17	40	Hispanic	married	1	Yes
Brenda	Owner, pastry shop	Pastry	18	54	White	single	0	Yes
Camille	Executive pastry chef, restaurant	Pastry	12	32	White	married	2	Yes
Candace	Pastry chef, restaurant	Pastry	6	39	White	engaged	0	No
Cathy	Chef, owner of restaurant	Line	25	60	White	married	2	Yes
Chelsea	Culinary instructor, pastry chef	Pastry	15	34	White	divorced	1	Yes
Christine	Culinary instructor, pastry chef	Pastry	7	31	White	married	1	Yes
Dana	Executive chef	Line	7	24	White	single	0	Yes
Elisa	Executive chef, owner	Line	3	46	Hispanic	married	2	Yes
Ellen	Culinary instructor, pastry chef	Pastry	28	42	White	divorced	3	Yes
Erin	Chef de cuisine	Line	22	37	White	married	1	Yes
Gloria	Owner, upscale catering	Line	25	57	White	married	1	Yes
Jane	Culinary instructor, pastry chef	Pastry	20	35	White	married	0	Yes

Name	Job Description	Type	Years	Age	Race	Marital Status	Children	Yes/No
Jill	Chef, restaurant	Line	10	36	White	married	0	Yes
Joan	Selling manager, upscale grocer	Line	26	42	White	married	3	Yes
Karen	Executive pastry chef, hotel	Pastry	16	32	Hispanic	single	0	Yes
Kate	Owner, business end of restaurant	Line	32	49	White	married	0	No
Lisa	Culinary instructor, upscale grocer	Line	30	49	White	single	0	Yes
Lyndsay	Pastry chef, upscale grocer & café	Pastry	10	26	White	partnered	0	Yes
Marisel	Chef, restaurant owner	Line	25	45	Hispanic	married	4	No
Melissa	Owner, pastry shop	Pastry	12	36	White	single	0	Yes
Michelle	Executive chef, owner	Line	15	52	Black	married	0	Yes
Monica	Sous chef, upscale grocer & café	Line	3	25	Hispanic	married	0	Yes
Natasha	Chef de cuisine, bistro	Line	8	31	White	married	0	Yes
Patricia	Executive chef, owner	Line	25	59	White	divorced	2	Yes
Rose	Culinary instructor, pastry chef	Pastry	25	43	White	married	2	Yes
Sara	Culinary instructor	Pastry	9	25	White	married	1	Yes
Sharon	Culinary instructor, pastry chef	Pastry	12	47	White	married	0	Yes
Shelly	Executive chef, owner	Line	21	43	White	single	0	Yes
Susan	Pastry chef, owner of pastry store	Pastry	6	28	Asian	married	0	Yes
Tabitha	Pastry chef, upscale restaurant	Pastry	18	34	Black	married	0	No

the upper echelons of the gastronomic field by assigning greater status to the work of men chefs while devaluing the work of women chefs.

All of the thirty-three women we interviewed had worked at jobs that fit our working definition of a "chef"—their positions included both some degree of creative control over the food served at their restaurants as well as managing a staff. Chefs working on the "hot" side of the kitchen preparing appetizers and entrees were included, as well as pastry chefs who work on the "cold" side of professional kitchens. We also talked with women who had left chef jobs to learn more about what factors influenced their career changes. During the interviews we asked the women to talk about their motivations for becoming a chef, educational and training backgrounds, experiences working their way up the kitchen hierarchy, decisions regarding work-family balance, and general views of the place of women in professional cooking. Our use of semi-structured interviews allowed the women to speak in their own words and link together events and reactions in ways that best reflected their own lives.

Our combination of data allows us to examine the intricate ways occupational arrangements disadvantage women in the workplace. We can discuss historical forces that have shaped certain jobs to be labeled as men's or women's work, as well as look at current conditions within restaurant worlds that make male-dominated fields more or less available for entry by women. Using both media data to represent conditions at the national level and local data from women chefs can help us examine gendered patterns in different areas of the field.

CHAPTER OVERVIEWS

In the following chapters, we examine how the arrangements and norms within the gastronomic field work to disadvantage women professional chefs. We focus on the evolution of professional kitchens in the first chapter and discuss how chefs arose to form a legitimate occupation. We argue that gender and occupational status has always been intertwined in the gastronomic field and detail how the early exclusion of women was fundamental to the establishment of a professional identity due to feminization threat. A historical look at major trends among chefs and cooking styles is used to illustrate how gender still remains prevalent in professional cooking arenas.

Chapter 2 is devoted to examining the role of media attention and professional accolades in earning status and comparing the way men and women chefs are discussed in the media. We argue that the process of evaluating chefs has a gendered component and that these different ways of assigning titles of greatness to chefs may play a role in women chefs' ability to earn high levels of prestige in the field. This includes the framing of successful men chefs as provocateurs who challenge traditional cooking while women obtain more accolades when they are good girls who stay firmly within culinary boundaries, perhaps by relying on family or cultural traditions. We discuss what these differences mean for women attempting to advance within the gastronomic field and within individual careers.

In the third chapter we examine the process of becoming a chef and how women chefs attempt to enter and become accepted members of professional kitchens. We discuss the pressure to fit in at the same time that their gender causes them to stand out within professional kitchens. There is a long process of proving oneself as a professional chef and we illustrate how women can be disadvantaged due to their designation as "others" invading all-men workplaces. We also discuss the pervasive references to gender neutrality—the insistence by our participants that, as a chef, gender doesn't matter. This focus on gender neutrality helps highlight the importance of fitting in to professional kitchens while providing some insight into how hypermasculine workplace cultures continue to thrive even after women have entered these spaces.

Chapter 4 is used to examine the role of gendered leadership styles in professional kitchens and draws from in-depth interview data to discuss how women chefs view the options available to them when they lead. According to the majority of the chefs we interviewed, women in professional kitchens often choose to be "bitchy" by adapting a masculine style of management or "girly," which was used to describe women who relied heavily on their femininity in order to get what they wanted. Neither of these routes guaranteed the respect of coworkers and there were downsides to both. Several of the women reported taking a third route: that of "mom" or "big sister" to their male coworkers. We discuss the implications of these limited choices and the impacts they have on women workers who may feel that, in order to be taken seriously in professional contexts, they must act in ways that feel inauthentic.

We examine women who have left jobs in traditional cooking outlets for other employment in the fifth chapter. Among our in-depth interview participants, seventeen of the women had left kitchen work by the time of our interviews. The main reason given for their exit was the incompatibility of restaurant work with family lives. The long hours, little time off, and lack of health benefits made it difficult for mothers to remain in the field. We discuss some of the alternative jobs held by women who leave professional kitchens. Among women who stay in these jobs, we discuss what resources were needed for them to successfully combine work and home.

The concluding chapter provides a summary of our major findings about how gender influences women's place in the gastronomic field. Historical trends, legitimizing agents that favor men chefs, hypermasculine workplace cultures, gender stereotypes about leadership, and workplace arrangements that make combining work and family responsibilities difficult all work together to disadvantage, not only women professional chefs, but also women in a number of male-dominated fields. We examine the commonly held belief that chefs are a different breed of worker and their workplaces are unique cultures that would be difficult to alter. We conclude with a discussion of changes that can be made within the field and larger society in order to make professional cooking (and other male-dominated jobs) more gender inclusive.

1 · HOME VERSUS HAUTE

Gender and Status in the Evolution of Professional Chefs

In 2013, the ABC television network debuted its new competitive cooking program *The Taste*. The competition featured a variety of amateur and professional cooks whose dishes were blind taste-tested by four judges, chefs Anthony Bourdain, Ludo Lefebvre, and Brian Malarkey and cookbook author/cooking show host Nigella Lawson. *The Taste* promised to truly democratize cooking contests. No longer would the winner be predetermined by who had the most years of experience working as a chef or who had won the most professional accolades. On this cooking show, the winner would be decided solely by—as the name of the program promised—the taste of the cook's dish. To this end, the show began with contestant hopefuls preparing a small tasting portion of their signature dish, which was then served to the four judges who ate each bite without seeing who had prepared it. Contestants ranged from stay-at-home moms to professional chefs, and the show emphasized how this blind taste-testing would level the playing field to allow home cooks to compete with professionals.

However, as the first episode of *The Taste* progressed, a pattern emerged. After tasting each dish, the judges would discuss their responses to what they just ate. Several times this talk would turn to whether or not something about the dish served as a "tell," or marker, that the food was prepared by either a professional (meaning a chef or someone employed in the culinary field) or an amateur. Presentation styles, perceived sophistication of the ingredients, and the skillfulness of the technique used to prepare the food were all cited by the judges as ways to differentiate types of contestants. Often the origins of a particularly good dish were discussed with a knowing smile that "of course" this dish was the work of a professional. At the end of the discussion, the cook would be revealed to the judges.

The judges' commentary helps illustrate the long-held division between home cooking done by nonprofessionals and the food produced by those within the culinary industry. Their discussion was based on the underlying assumption that professional cooking experience would undoubtedly be represented in the dishes of chefs and this food would be superior to the efforts of those who cook at home. While such responses could seem antithetical to the purpose of the show, which was to democratize cooking competitions, they highlight an enduring hierarchy in which cooking performed at home is seen as less than the cooking carried out by professionals.

Much of this hierarchy derives from the fact that chefs have traveled a long road to arrive at the professional status they receive today. For much of their history, chefs have been seen as a form of blue-collar manual labor. It has been quite the journey from the "chef as servant" mentality to the idea of "chefs as the new rock stars," complete with television shows, lucrative product lines, and international restaurant empires. Michael Symons notes how, historically, "Cooks have been publicly ignored, privately humiliated, ordered to eat last, and not paid any income" (2000, 173). Only in the last few decades have we seen the mass movement of chefs into the public consciousness.

While there can be many factors influencing this transition in the status of professional chefs, we are using this chapter to discuss the gendered history of the occupation. We wanted to know how the occupation of professional chef became identified as men's work. As no jobs are intrinsically "men's" or "women's" work, we have to examine how certain occupations became coded as masculine or feminine pursuits. Part of this answer can be found in the origins of professional chefs and how the concepts of feminization threat and precarious masculinity were major influences during the establishment of the occupation. The exclusion of women was integral in raising the status of the occupation. By performing this boundary work, men chefs were able to control access to resources and opportunities and aid in the overall professionalization of chefs (Lamont and Molnar 2002).

This chapter begins with a discussion of the public and private divides in men and women's cooking. Then we skip ahead to the establishment of the first professional chefs in France during the 1700s and changes to French cuisine during the nouvelle cuisine movement of the 1960s and 1970s. We then describe the development of the American gastronomic field during the twentieth century, and we document the rise of celebrity chefs in American culture and what this has meant for women's place in professional kitchens. Throughout our discussion we highlight ways in which women were formally excluded from the gastronomic field and, more recently, how women's participation and influence has been marginalized and downplayed. Our main purpose is to illustrate how the exclusion of women and the maligning of women's cooking has been an integral part of the establishment of professional chef as an occupation, particularly in its journey toward becoming a high-status pursuit. This information sets the stage for the current gender relations in professional cooking and provides context for the entrenchment of men's continued dominance of the chef occupation.

GENDER, COOKING, AND SEPARATE SPHERES

Gender and cooking have been intricately linked for much of human history. This has usually taken the form of women's cooking being associated with routine maternal care work that nourishes family members. In contrast, men's cooking has long been viewed as more high status and important. Some of the first men to cook publicly were men working for ancient Egyptian royalty (Swinbank 2002). This form of cooking was professionalized via the priest class, who engaged in animal sacrifices to their gods involving the preparation and cooking of meat. These priests were able to link their food handling and preparation to the divine and garner powerful positions in society. Therefore, their cooking was given special status and was elevated above the ordinary, everyday cooking of women (Pollan 2013).

This example illustrates how part of the different statuses afforded to men and women's cooking can be traced back to the public or private nature of cooking. This was particularly true following the spread of industrialization during the late 1700s to early 1800s, and the rise in what came to be known as the "separate spheres" for men and women (Crittenden 2001). Historically men's public agricultural work was seen as more important than the home-oriented cooking of women (Symons 2000). According to Ann Crittenden (2001), when men began to work for wages in this new cash economy, women remained in the bartering family economy. During this period, men were moving into the public realm through paid work, politics, and other areas of public life. Women, in contrast, were relegated to the private sphere of the home where they were tasked with domestic duties, such as cooking, cleaning, and childcare. Because it did not receive a wage, unpaid labor in the home became defined as unproductive. Women's family labor (particularly that of middle- and upper-class women) became defined as a labor of love as men withdrew from the home. Women were encouraged to create citizens of the new republic (Crittenden 2001) and take care of the emotional needs of the family.

The separate spheres ideology helped institutionalize power in the hands of men as they were the gender associated with positions of influence in business, law, and politics (Crittenden 2001). Women lacked legal rights to participate in many realms of public life, which further cemented the ideas that men and women were simply better at different things. The different tasks aligned with the two spheres became hierarchically arranged with the paid labor of men done in public seen as much more valuable than the unpaid labor of women done within the home.

These gender divisions also relate to cooking and many are still in practice today. While men have been taking on some of the sharing of cooking tasks, they still cook much less often than women. In Marjorie DeVault's (1994) study of men and women's domestic foodwork she found that women not only do most of the actual cooking, but also most of the other food-related labor, such as organizing and meal planning. Foodwork is such an everyday event, and it received little attention and became a form of invisible labor for many women. Because women's cooking is performed in the home as unpaid labor, it is automatically given less importance than both the general work done by men outside of the home for a wage and, in particular, the professional cooking performed by men chefs (Shapiro 2001; Swinbank 2002).

FROM CARÊME TO ESCOFFIER: THE BIRTH OF FRENCH HAUTE CUISINE AND PROFESSIONAL CHEFS

It took more than the rise of separate spheres for the burgeoning chef occupation to become established as a masculine field. First, cooking had to be unified and codified into a particular form—French haute cuisine. Haute cuisine (or high-status cuisine) was developed in France during the seventeenth century and was founded as, and continues to be, food of the elites (Trubek 2000). The early chefs who created these dishes were often selected out of the military. In fact, the position known as *chef de cuisine* originated from the military title *officer de cuisine* (Ferguson 2004). Chef positions at this time were very competitive and characterized by a closed ranking system and a high level of hierarchy due to their military history. Having one's own personal (male) chef was seen as a sign of status and early chefs were called upon to create large, decadent feasts to showcase their employer's wealth. Dinners were elaborate and required a large staff, sometimes numbering into the hundreds, which also helped symbolize the employer's status (Pinkard 2009). Despite their skills in cooking, organization, and management, as well as the artistry displayed by chefs, they were still seen as a class of servants with no more acknowledgment than any other hired help. Many chefs, understandably, grew tired of this lack of recognition. Early chefs sought to differentiate their work from the low-status cooking of homemakers and untrained domestic staff. Yet, even if chefs were able to demonstrate the special type of ingenuity they claimed elevated their efforts above *la petite cuisine* prepared by women in the home, most still toiled for years in obscurity because their creations were seen as belonging to their employer (the person presenting such elaborate food) rather than an expression of their own creativity and taste.

The first chef to garner major attention on his own was Marie Antoine Carême (1784–1833). During his lifetime, Carême would become known as the "King of Chefs" and become the first celebrity chef whose influence extended beyond individual kitchens to shape the larger gastronomic culture (Ferguson 2004). While it could be argued that there were other chefs who had garnered some form of renown within culinary circles, Carême is credited with radically changing what it meant be a chef and his influence is still evident today, particularly in traditional French kitchens.

Carême was one of twenty-five children and was abandoned by his parents in Paris during the height of the French Revolution in 1794 when he was only ten years old. This time period became known as the Reign of Terror due to the vast numbers of bodies lining the streets of Paris due to extreme poverty, hunger, and widespread massacres (Kelly 2003). Carême was extremely lucky to be rescued by a cook, who offered him work at a pastry shop and, as a young man, he exhibited an early talent for elaborate sugar and pastry work. Over the course of his career, Carême cooked for numerous members of the nobility and for other wealthy patrons. Ian Kelly (2003) describes how a typical feast prepared by Carême could include eighteen choices of dishes per each of the twelve guests. Such dinners would take days to prepare and require numerous assistants and underchefs.

Carême had a grand vision of the role of chefs in the French culinary world. He believed that chefs should be seen as a legitimate occupation and emphasized the role of chef as "the scholar, the scientist, and the artist" (Ferguson 2004, 57). Part of Carême's influence came in his abandonment of traditional dietetic or medicinal modes of cooking. At this time, many early restaurants bore little resemblance to what we call a restaurant today. Restaurant proprietors aligned themselves with medical practitioners and sold mainly curative broths at their establishments to elite members of society. By the 1700s, the burgeoning medical profession was emphasizing their specialized knowledge and separating itself from cooks who were seen as a more manual trade (Spang 2000). Carême's cooking shed the old linkages to food as medicine and emphasized a "pure gastronomic aesthetic" and the view that food could serve as art for art's sake (Fantasia 2010, 30). One of his great accomplishments was his ability to employ cooking methods that allowed the natural flavors of his foods to be showcased while, at the same time, using them in visually stunning showpieces that married culinary taste with art (Kelly 2003).

Some of Carême's other accomplishments involved systemizing the principles of post-revolutionary cuisine through publishing works that outlined his theories and methods of French cuisine (Rao, Monin, and Durand 2003). These cookbooks gave one of the first behind-the-scenes views of cooking for some of French society's most elite diners, as well as encouraged other cooks to replicate his ideas (Kelly 2003). Carême is also credited with helping develop what came to be known as the French mother sauces (*béchamel, espagnole, velouté, hollandaise,* and *tomate*), turning the focus toward the freshness of the food prepared, and emphasizing several new sanitation practices. It is also Carême who was responsible for designing the white jacket and toque (pleated hat) still worn by professional chefs today to mark their status (Ferguson 2004). These sartorial choices were meant to elevate the position of chef away from manual labor to more professional and respected standing. For example, the longstanding myth that the 100 pleats on a toque represent all the ways chefs know how to prepare an egg helps highlight the knowledge and training needed to be considered a true chef.

Carême's publication of *L'Art de la Cuisine Française* (1833–1834), a three-volume set focusing on French cuisine, helped cement his reputation as a culinary master and his legacy as the first celebrity chef. While Carême was not alone in publishing books on French cuisine, his work was particularly wide-ranging, covering not only the history of French cooking but also notes on food preparation. This time period also saw the creation of culinary journals that featured well-regarded chefs. The movement of Carême and his chef contemporaries into publishing had ramifications beyond just the careers of individual chefs. According to Amy Trubek, "The written word helped chefs move from being anonymous domestics in the homes of the nobility to being experts for the public because now their knowledge could be spread everywhere" (2000, 29). These writings helped underscore the professional nature of chefs by codifying and standardizing French cuisine. Just as medicine had to move towards standardized texts and training in order to be seen as a legitimate profession, the writings of early chefs helped provide a sense of legitimacy to their work. These writings also served the purpose of reinforcing the dichotomy between the elevated, rational cuisine of men—who were teachers—and the simple, maternal cooking of women—who could be educated by the books of these accomplished men chefs.

The concept of men professional chefs as educators of women home cooks was not new. Even prior to the Revolution, men like François Marin and François Menon were capitalizing on the decline in large noble houses with extensive staff by publishing books aimed at smaller homes where the cooking was performed by women (Pinkard 2009). The status of men as the source of cooking information was further established because of women's lesser status in book publishing at this time. The loudest voices producing culinary knowledge were men, and the contributions of women to French gastronomic culture were stifled. Similarly, gender norms at the time also precluded women from engaging in the newfound restaurant culture, reaffirming that cooking in the public sphere was the realm of men.

The French gastronomic field was further refined through the work of Georges Auguste Escoffier (1846–1935). Escoffier was a chef and writer whose *Le Guide Culinaire*, published in 1902, is still referenced by some chefs today. Prior to the Revolution, chefs worked primarily in the houses of the nobility. The public places where food was available included taverns, inns, and cookshops, which were seen as low status, and businesses known as a *tables d'hôte*, or host's tables, which were large public eating houses where patrons were seated at a large communal table and served food selected by the owner, or host (Gopnik 2011). Another option for food was in businesses run by caterers (*traiteurs*), who were part of a restricted guild allowed to cook for those without kitchens. The strict rules of the guilds and the laws guiding them meant that there were few places outside of the homes of nobility for chefs to work.

Following the Revolution of 1789, these restrictions were overturned and chefs who had worked primarily in the houses of the nobility moved into the public realm to work in restaurants (Rao et al. 2003). This change was instrumental in the development of the gastronomic field as more consumers equaled new places of support for cultural creators, which resulted in a more autonomous environment in which to create (Bourdieu 1993). Chefs who moved into restaurants were able to exercise more control than when they worked primarily for the nobility. Escoffier was no different and, in 1889, he helped open the Savoy Hotel in London. Working with a hotel developer is seen as commonplace among today's well-known chefs, but Escoffier's work at the Savoy was unusual at the time and helped move haute cuisine from private, upper-class households to public restaurants (Fantasia 2010).

The movement from noble houses to public restaurants marked a turning point in French culture and the occupation of professional chef. At the Savoy, Escoffier pulled from his time as an army chef and reorganized his restaurant kitchen into the more standardized, station-oriented hierarchy that it is today. No longer did individual chefs craft dishes from start to finish. Instead, kitchens were manned by a number of cooks who each contributed a different element to a dish. For example, one cook may be tasked with cooking a piece of fish while others are responsible for making the sauce that goes on top of the fish or the vegetables that are served alongside it. Breaking up tasks in this way greatly increased the efficiency and speed with which cooks were able to prepare food.

Escoffier implemented several other influential changes to haute cuisine, including á la carte ordering, reducing the number of courses offered in a meal, and eliminating many of the fussy displays and garnishes that had marked fine dining during Carême's time (Rao et al. 2003). He replaced the traditional French, or banquet style of eating, that required all the food to be placed on the table at once, with a Russian service in which courses would be served one at a time in an order chosen by the host or his chef (Gopnik 2011). Escoffier also emphasized the scientific aspects of professional cooking with particular focus on the ability to create recipes that could be replicated and produced for large numbers of diners each night. Through these efforts, Escoffier was able to save labor and streamline the production of food. The modern concept of a restaurant that can serve hundreds of diners a night would be inconceivable without many of these systems and arrangements put in place during Escoffier's time in the kitchen.

During this time, there was pressure to engage in social closure practices within the occupation. Rick Fantasia (2010) details how the relatively closed European markets were suddenly threatened by American agricultural production following a European agricultural depression in 1873. According to Fantasia, European agricultural producers and chefs were concerned that the entrance of American products and American ways of food production would sully the well-respected French gastronomic field. Chefs were anxious that the American model emphasizing efficiency, high volume, and standardization would lead to a deskilling of the occupation. They feared this dumbing-down process would erode some of the newfound credibility of being a chef. In order to combat this threat, chefs created trade union associations that emphasized the training and specialized skill sets of French chefs.

Women were not allowed in these associations and they were still unwelcome in professional kitchens during this era. Cultural norms surrounding the appropriate social spaces for men and women left many women out of the early restaurant culture developing in Europe at that time. Some explained women's exclusion by citing beliefs that women's presence would distract from the food, which should be the true focus of dining (Spang 2000). Another reason according to Priscilla Ferguson (2004) was that many women lacked the funds needed to be a true gastronome and participate in restaurant culture. Even among women of financial means, restaurants, and their locations in urban centers, were tinged with "inherent promiscuity" (Why else would a woman go into a city to dine?) that provided restaurants "an uncertain moral status" and, therefore, dissuaded women from entry (Ferguson 2004, 93).

Women were also excluded from working in such venues. While women cooks could be found within country inns or more humble establishments, women chefs were unheard of within French gastronomy at this time. Escoffier himself unfavorably compared the detailed cooking and plating of men chefs with women cooks who had to work with the (often meager) ingredients available and who needed to measure everything (Trubek 2000). For Escoffier, the difference in the two cooking styles (and the people carrying them out) was clear.

This commentary on women's inferior cooking was bolstered by policies that banned women from competing in culinary competitions and enrolling in culinary schools. The 1800s were marked by culinary expositions where chefs competed to showcase their cooking techniques and presentations. Women were not allowed to compete in these events, and the expositions' focus on the more technical aspects of cooking helped further distance professional cooking from the taste- and nurturing-focused home cooking of women (Trubek 2000). These competitions, as well as other systems of awarding accolades to chefs, also helped to establish the rarity of truly great cooking. By limiting the number of those allowed to compete, and awarding honors to a select few, these competitions suggested that, while cooking may be common, true culinary artistry was rare and valuable.

Women were also excluded from early culinary schools. These schools actually arose in part as a means of drawing boundaries around the chef occupation in order to establish it as a profession (Trubek 2000). Early chefs learned their trade through apprenticeships or while in the military, but with increasing standardization of recipes and expectations that chefs should be knowledgeable about certain core techniques, more education was needed (Ferguson 2004). This emphasis on the specialized skills needed to be a chef and the institutionalization of the transmission of this knowledge capital through the establishment of elite culinary schools helped chefs to be seen as a legitimate profession. Culinary schools allowed graduates to claim credentials that would be above and beyond those possessed by non-graduates (including home cooks), further emphasizing the occupation's legitimacy.

NATURAL DIFFERENCES AND THE RESULTS OF EXCLUSION

The end result of these exclusionary tactics was that women had little presence in the world of haute cuisine for many years. We want to be clear that we are not arguing that women were not cooking during this time or creating recipes and texts. However, much of this work was seen as lesser status (if it was seen at all) within the gastronomic field at the time. According to Ferguson, "Confined to the home kitchen, excluded from the public culinary life of the professional kitchen, and, for that reason, excluded from the cultural space occupied by culinary texts, women's cooking/ *cuisine de femmes* was long absent from the prestigious culinary-cultural space of professionalized haute cuisine" (2004, 132). While men chefs have always drawn from the recipes and techniques of women, including their own mothers and grandmothers, women were rarely given any credit for this work (Swinbank 2002). Such arrangements further cemented the differentiation between men and women's cooking and served as a means of protecting the new status of professional chef from feminization threat. By casting men and women cooks as operating in distinct venues (restaurants vs. homes), with different levels of skills (professional vs. amateur), and with very dissimilar goals in mind (expression of creativity vs. caring for the family), the separation of men as the professional chef and women as the amateur cook could be upheld. If men and women's cooking were merely seen as different, issues of inequality would not occur. It was when the cooking of men was seen as superior to that of women chiefly because it was produced by women that issues of gender inequality resulted.

An example of the separation of professional and home cooking, as well as the different status afforded to both forms is found in the work of Alexandre Balthazar Laurent Grimod de La Reynière (1758–1837), widely recognized as the first food critic. He is given credit for coining the term "gourmand" to refer to someone who gains great pleasure from food. In his work, he wrote about the importance of keeping the kitchen and dining room separate because in order to find food to be good one must not see it being made (Spang 2000). Grimod de La Reynière's statements refer to the unpleasant work that often occurs in food preparation, particularly as it was done during his time. In order to truly enjoy a dish, one needed to be separated from the original product. This can also be applied to the different views of men and women's cooking. Professional cooking in restaurants separates the kitchen (referred to as "the back of the house") from the dining room (the "front of the house"). Diners often see little of the work that is done in the back of the house in order to create the dishes they consume. Even in some of today's open kitchen arrangements in restaurants, cooking becomes more a type of theater than a true representation of raw ingredients and hard labor that goes into professional cooking (Pearlman 2013).

In addition to hiding the unpleasant aspects of food preparation, the work of men chefs also highlights the magic of cooking. A dish is ordered and it appears in front of the diner from out-of-nowhere. For food cooked in the home, it is very different. There may be little to none of the spatial separation of dining from the kitchen. This close proximity of the ingredients and act of cooking, and its role as part of a family's daily routine, means that women's home cooking lacks the magical appeal of men's professional cooking. The hard work and mess of daily cooking is on display, removing some of the mystery of cooking and devaluing the skill it takes to provide food for a family day after day.

Beyond the spatial differences in men and women's cooking, women experienced difficulties in moving into the culinary field because these perceived contrasts between men and women's cooking became accepted as natural. When cooking is done by a woman it was seen as a "'natural' and unconscious extension of their biological capacity to nurture their young . . . when cooking [was] done by a man it [was] seen as a manifestation of reason and consciousness, and therefore, as an expression of culture" (Swinbank 2002, 472). From this perspective, women's attempts at cooking derive from an innate need to provide for others, such as their children and husbands. While women may be the natural cooks, their efforts are simple and represent a fulfillment of biological need. For men, their cooking must be learned through years of training and these skills then greatly surpass that of mere biology. Given the time period in which chefs were establishing themselves as an occupation, the emphasis on the public cooking of chefs versus the private cooking of women combined with the focus on the role of professional training relative to biological drive, tips the scales in favor of men. Men's learned, professional style of cooking allows for personal and professional style to be developed and is presented as superior to the cooking of women who aim merely to provide sustenance for their families.

If this reduction of women's cooking to mere biology seems antiquated, consider a more recent example from a 2005 article in the journal, *Gastronomica*. In the article, food writer and psychologist Scott Haas writes about what it means to be a chef today. He explains that, in some ways, being a chef is a maternal act because it provides nurturance to customers. He admits that this viewpoint puts chefs on a similar plane as mothers but goes on to state: "[B]ut unlike mothers whose babies survive on a diet of milk and then for years [on food] nearly as bland, chefs must use ingredients to help customers recall memories or find excitement. Restaurant cooking elevates early psychological experiences of nurturance" (2005, 42). If Haas has not yet proven that the work of (men) chefs is superior to the simple foods prepared by a mother, he goes on to write: "Yet mothers don't choose, per se, to communicate with their children through food—that's a function of biology" (42). Therefore, because men chefs choose to be nurturers and to provide food, their efforts and dedication should be lauded as they are defying biology and elevating feeding from a physiological activity to a cultural art form.

NOUVELLE CUISINE AND THE EMPOWERMENT OF CHEFS

With the movement away from noble houses to restaurants, French cuisine continued to flourish. Chefs worked primarily in restaurants and were responsible for executing what had come to be seen as traditional French cooking. There were few women cooking in fine dining restaurants and ethnic restaurants were considered unqualified to be considered high-status cuisine. In the 1960s major changes occurred in French haute cuisine. During this time period, a new cooking style dubbed "nouvelle cuisine" emerged that challenged traditional ways of cooking and being a chef. The traditional, codified French cuisine instituted by Escoffier was seen as reigning in the creativity of chefs who wanted to try new approaches to cooking. Rao et al. (2003) explained how this shift toward nouvelle cuisine radically changed French cooking through transgression, or using old techniques with new ingredients or new techniques with old ingredients in ways that broke the established rules of French haute cuisine. In addition, chefs began importing exotic foreign traditions and melding them with French cuisine. The overall result of this change in cooking style was lighter, less overcooked fare that included a focus on presentation and inventiveness. Menus became shorter, as did the length of average mealtimes.

Perhaps one of the most important outcomes of the turn toward nouvelle cuisine was the transformation of the role of the chef. Under traditional French cuisine this would not have been possible—chefs were expected to be knowledgeable of traditional dishes and their preparations and to be able to execute them flawlessly. This focus allowed less room for individual creativity to thrive. The trend in nouvelle cuisine, which included transgressing the rules of formal French cooking, provided more power to chefs. They were able to transform this new freedom into more economic and creative control of their restaurants, which allowed chefs to develop their own personal style of cooking and to design their signature dishes for which they became known (Rao et al. 2003).

These changes were influenced by growing tensions between what was considered classical French cuisine and new trends in other fields such as literature and film (Rao et al. 2003). Celebrated French chefs such as Paul Bucose, Michel Guerard, and the Troisgros brothers were inspired by this period of experimentation in other creative fields and sought to inculcate this sense of inspiration into gastronomy as well. Nouvelle cuisine and the attention it generated helped glamorize professional cooking and gave tremendous recognition to chefs as creators (Leschziner 2007). As chefs earned accolades for their own style of cooking rather than that of traditional French cuisine, it helped establish chefs as a creative occupation rather than manual labor (Rao et al. 2003).

For the first time in the modern age, chefs were being recognized for their creations. Paul Bocuse, for example, was even featured on a 1975 cover of *Newsweek* as part of a story about changes to the French culinary world. The placement of a chef on the cover of a major American news magazine may seem commonplace today but the attention given Bocuse was unheard of at this time. Rao and colleagues (2003) point out that this transformation in haute cuisine would have been impossible without the support of numerous cultural tastemakers. Without the power of these prominent agents in the gastronomic field, such as the influential Michelin Guide that awarded some of their coveted stars to the restaurants of nouvelle cuisine chefs, food journalists, and even the French state, nouvelle cuisine would have been unable to alter professional cooking so thoroughly. Soon young American chefs were moving to France in order to learn from those seen as leaders in nouvelle cuisine.

AMERICAN COOKING AND THE ROLE OF WOMEN

Women had been excluded from many areas of culinary life during the establishment of the French gastronomic field. Publishing houses, cooking competitions, and culinary schools all largely ignored the labor of women and cast women's culinary efforts as inferior to the professional cooking of men. While women had some role in culinary culture, it was limited. For example, women did publish some recipe books, which were designed to be much simpler than true cookery writing produced by men. There has long been a division between the public/restaurant sphere of men and the private/cookbook sphere of women: "The restaurant was once a place for men, a place where men ate, held court, cooked, boasted, and swaggered, and wooed women. The recipe book was traditionally feminine: the kitchen was the place where women cooked, supervised, gave orders, made brownies, to steady and domesticate men" (Gopnik 2011, 11).

There was little difference regarding the role of women in early American professional cooking. This was due in part because of the heavy French influence in many elite American restaurants, which barred women from employment. These attitudes also extended to culinary education. There were several women-run cooking schools in the United States, some of which started as early as the 1880s. However, these organizations were mainly meant to train women how to run their own homes or to work as cooks for wealthy households (Cooper 1997). Ironically, the most prestigious American cooking school, the CIA, was founded in 1946 by two women: Frances Roth and Katherine Angell. Despite being headed by women, the purpose of the CIA was to train men who were returning back to the United States after World War II under the new GI bill. Women were not enrolled in the CIA full-time until 1970 and, in 1972, only 5 percent of the student body was women (Cooper 1997).

AMERICAN CUISINE: CHALLENGING FRENCH DOMINANCE

In their study of self-described "foodies," Josée Johnston and Shyon Baumann (2010) cite Lawrence Levine's (1988) work on how cultural hierarchies are created, particularly the concept of sacralization, which refers to the tendency of North American culture to valorize the Old World culture and values, as well as to more highly value the work of cultural professionals over amateurs. They argue the gastronomic field is no different. Prior to the last few decades, our notion of what constituted a great chef or great cuisine was borrowed exclusively from the French (Hyman 2008). French cuisine, for much of the last two centuries was seen as the only true "universal" cuisine that was codified with specific rules and techniques that, once learned, could then be adapted by each unique chef (Ferguson 2004). Within the United States, most of the early fine dining restaurants operated in cultural centers like New York City and were staffed with French chefs. These early restaurants, such as Le Pavillon in New York, were decidedly French and unabashedly classist. Formal clothing was required, menus were written in French, and seating was hierarchical with desired customers given prime spots in the dining room and other seated in "Siberia" (Pearlman 2013). Such measures further solidified French restaurants as a class marker that was much sought after by the American upper class.

The continued dominance of French cuisine in the American gastronomic field was one reason why women failed to enter into and succeed as professional chefs. According to Patric Kuh, "Having a woman in the kitchen had always been a clear demarcation of styles in both French and Italian food" (2001, 63). In France, cooking was a masculine, elite skill set whereas in Italy small, family-run restaurants relied on the cooking of women to uphold a sense of regionalism. Kuh notes that, eventually, the more simplistic version of cooking that characterized Italian cuisine came to hold sway in American cuisine, but for many years, the French style of cooking and French culinary knowledge (including ideas about who should be a chef) continued to govern American cooking.

Johnston and Baumann (2010) and Alison Pearlman (2013) argue that the United States has undergone a de-sacralization within the gastronomic field. After years of French culinary dominance, the economic and cultural boom following World War II firmly oriented the country on the here and now (Kuh 2001). This movement began with the hiring of American chef James Beard to head the kitchen of the well-known Four Seasons restaurant in 1959. Beard, who was extremely influential in shaping American cuisine, made the controversial choice to include American food items on the menu at the Four Seasons. This decision opposed the French-only emphasis of many fine dining restaurants at the time. Beard, who grew up in rural Oregon, placed tremendous emphasis on food that related to personal history and believed that describing food as "homey" was a high compliment (Kuh 2001). Beard also had the ability to communicate to a broad range of people. His cookbooks helped bridge the gap between the chef-written, technical cookery writing of this time and the women-oriented, how-to manuals of cookbooks. He also became one of the first American chefs to voyage into non-cooking arenas, such as endorsement deals with food companies (Kamp 2006).

At the same time that Beard was elevating American cuisine in elite restaurants, Julia Child was making French food accessible to the American home cook with her cookbook *Mastering the Art of French Cooking* and her accompanying television cooking show *The French Chef*. Child's cookbook, written with Simone Beck and Louisette Bertholle and published in 1961, was a tremendous departure from earlier works on French food. In fact, prior to its publication, some were concerned that the book would not be well received by American audiences. Before Child's work, most books on French cuisine came from men chefs who relied upon their professional legitimacy to simplify French cuisine for nonprofessional audiences or from women writers taking a friendly, casual approach that was more guidebook to France than detailed guide to cooking French food (Kuh 2001). *Mastering the Art of French Cooking* turned out to be a clear audience favorite due much in part to Child's ability to straddle the line between educational and conversational tone and its ability to appeal to the growing middle-class American audiences who were interested in learning to replicate French cooking but who were working, as Child remarks in the introduction, as a "servantless American cook." This gift went on to be displayed on her television show *The French Chef*, a name that Child only agreed to because it was short enough to fit in the *Boston Globe* television listings (Kamp 2006).

The efforts of Beard and Child on opposing ends of the home/haute cooking spectrum actually had the cumulative effect of challenging the French hegemony in American cooking. Beard was illustrating the creativity an American culinary focus could provide while Child was democratizing cuisine by sharing her culinary knowledge with a wide audience. Child could also be viewed as reintroducing feminization threat to professional chefs. If home cooks could replicate traditional French cooking, this eroded some of the status of French cooking (Johnston and Baumann 2010). The masculinity of professional cooking could be placed in jeopardy if French chefs could no longer demonstrate why their food was superior to that which could be prepared at home.

Other changes also helped challenge the paradigm of French haute cuisine within the United States. Kuh (2001) points out that one of the causes

of the fall of French cuisine in America was the large number of medio-
cre (or worse) French restaurants that proliferated during these decades.
Although there were several restaurants in the United States that mas-
terfully illustrated the taste and technique of French cuisine, there were
many more so-called French restaurants that were pale imitations of these
remarkable establishments.

As French food was losing its luster, increased globalization opened new
markets and exposure to cooking styles and ingredients from all over the
world. These changes produced new opportunities for American chefs. No
longer did they have to copy the French, but they were freer to approach
food from a variety of different traditions and, in some cases, even create
these traditions themselves. Increased immigration also meant an expanded
audience for foods from around the globe and new chefs who could rely
upon the cuisine from their countries of origin to establish different ways
of cooking.

There were also more media outlets being created to popularize these
new American forms of cooking. During the 1960s, Craig Claiborne of the
New York Times introduced the concept of the restaurant review and his
pronouncements helped promote the status of numerous American restaurants and encourage interest in American cooking. A growing class of
Americans were paying attention to his appraisals and making special trips
to well-reviewed restaurants. Others were hosting dinner parties where they
tried to replicate a dish they read about in *Gourmet* magazine or watched
Julia Child prepare on *The French Chef.*

Chefs also began to look in their own backyard for inspiration
(sometimes literally), as a group of idealistic young people illustrated in
California in the early 1970s. With no formal culinary training, Alice Waters
and her colleagues at the Berkeley, California, restaurant, Chez Panisse,
helped create a French-inspired approach to food that emphasized the use
of seasonal, local ingredients. A group of middle-class young people who
were either college graduates or recent college dropouts had chosen to
pursue life in the kitchen, which was unusual for this traditional blue-collar
job. While spurred by their love of the French way of eating, the founders of
Chez Panisse ultimately developed a uniquely American approach to food.
The positive media and customer reviews awarded Chez Panisse helped
reduce the French dominance of the gastronomic field (Johnston and
Baumann 2010).

Some of the innovations introduced by Waters and colleagues are still incorporated by many restaurants today, including the focus on local ingredients. Whereas traditional French cuisine would sometimes name a dish after a famous person or chef, the French-inspired fare at Chez Panisse was often named after the ingredient used in the dish (Kuh 2001). This focus on ingredients and the lengthy descriptions explaining each dish on the menu was at the forefront of what would be called California cuisine, and this approach would come to characterize today's New American cuisine. Gradually, the use of French to describe dishes was replaced by English on the menus, and more focus was given to the source of the ingredients, with menu descriptions often incorporating the names of the farms from which the ingredients were obtained (Kuh 2001). Such changes were a radical departure from the French style of placing the chef and his expertise at the center of a restaurant. Instead, farmers and ingredients were given credit for the success of a dish and minimal transformation of ingredients was seen as a major source of culinary inspiration. The change in restaurant atmosphere also further distanced American food from the French. At Chez Panisse, simple, elegant food was served in a homey, more relaxed atmosphere, proving that excellent food could be produced and enjoyed in a venue far from the stuffy French norm (McNamee 2007).

FROM SERVANT TO CELEBRITY: CHANGES TO THE STATUS OF PROFESSIONAL CHEFS

For years, American chefs had been formally classified as domestic workers—a labor category that also included housekeepers and nannies. Just as in the days of the French nobility, chefs were again associated with low-skilled, low-paid, and often feminized labor. It took the efforts of several activists, including Hungarian-born Chicago chef Louis Szathmary (who held a Ph.D. in psychology from the University of Budapest), to have chefs reclassified as "Professional, Technical, and Management Occupations" by the U.S. Department of Labor in 1977 (Kamp 2006). This change was one of the first signs that the status chefs had been pursuing for centuries could finally be within reach.

Several reasons can be given for the rising status of professional chefs in recent decades. For one, Americans are devoting less time to meal preparation. Adults are spending, on average, just a little over thirty minutes a day on food preparation, including cleanup (Hamrick et al. 2011). Of course, part of this relates to new technological advances (e.g., microwaves) and the availability of new processed foods that are "heat and eat," but it can also relate to a lack of knowledge about the act of cooking. Food studies professor Krishendu Ray argues that, when few people know how to cook, the act of cooking takes on special significance (Ruhlman 2007). The same activities that might have seemed mundane just a generation or two ago (such as deboning a chicken or making bread from scratch) become part of a rarified skill set. More people now rely upon restaurants to keep themselves and their families fed either due to a lack of time to cook or knowledge about how to cook. Because much of this food is prepared at fast food restaurants, the skillful and artistic cooking of chefs takes on even more cultural cachet (Fantasia 2010). Combine this with the ability of food to evoke pleasurable memories of home and family, and we can see why cooking and the chefs responsible for it are considered especially fascinating today (Haas 2013).

Others suggest the new turn toward American cooking helped shape responses to chefs. After the sheen of nouvelle cuisine wore off and restaurants like Chez Panisse were able to highlight the veritable bounty of American produce, leaders in the gastronomic field were looking for new heroes. They found them among many new chefs in the 1980s. For example, Wolfgang Puck, who is known as the first superstar chef of the media age of cooking, is ironically, a Belgian who was trained to cook in France, and found success in the United States by reinventing and elevating the pizza (Miles 1993). Beyond his uncanny ability to combine culinary styles, Puck's career was aided by his ability to engage the public. He currently owns twenty fine dining restaurants in the United States alone. Puck has lent his name to several food products, appeared on numerous cooking shows, and made other appearances in scripted television and film. He is so identified with the development of California as a culinary scene that he was featured in the state's recent "Life in California" tourism commercials alongside such Hollywood stars as Arnold Schwarzenegger and Jack Nicholson.

This fascination with cooking, even by those who do not cook, was further fueled by a growing food media. The Food Network was launched in 1993 and now reaches 100 million American homes. The rise of the Food Network helped make its cooking show hosts celebrities, providing more attention to those who cook for a living. Other networks have taken notice of this increased interest in chefs. Overall, the amount of food programming tripled between

2005 and 2010, including the addition of food programming on networks, such as NBC and BRAVO, which traditionally had not been associated with food (Pearlman 2013). Interest in the lives of chefs also made bestsellers out of chef memoirs, such as Anthony Bourdain's *Kitchen Confidential* (2000), which detailed the "culinary underbelly" in America's restaurants. These memoirs showed readers the hidden side of restaurant kitchens, which helped heighten their allure as a dangerous or sexy space. Gwen Hyman describes how these accounts of professional kitchens paint these spaces as "the last bastion of cowboy culture" and how "The kitchen became, in the popular imagination, a realm not of exhaustion and exploitation but of energy and power" (2008, 44). Other glimpses into the gastronomic field became available with the increase in the food-related content on the Internet. Food blogs and websites allowed diners to obsessively track the openings and closings of restaurants, photograph and share pictures of meals eaten in trendy restaurants, and openly dissect and even critique restaurants in ways that had previously only been done by professional food writers and critics (Johnston and Baumann 2010).

Many chefs became actively involved in finding ways to capitalize on the newfound interest in their jobs. Instead of hiding in the kitchen, modern American chefs began hiring public relations firms and lending their names to culinary product lines. Fantasia (2010) describes this as chefs selling their symbolic capital as experts in the field of cooking and states that this marked a new level of permeability between haute cuisine and commercial cooking. This symbolic capital has been leveraged in a number of ways as an elite few of today's chefs are now seen not only as experts on food preparation, but also as experts on other food-related issues ranging from food sustainability to childhood obesity (Johnston and Baumann 2010; Rousseau 2012).

These changes have helped greatly increase the professional status of chefs. Hyman posits that one of the reasons American popular culture has started to feature chefs is that the rise of the celebrity chef serves as its own distinct version of the Horatio Alger story. She notes that this path to the American Dream looked much different than the mailroom clerk to CEO route that was normally described: "Cooking was the work of the hand that was also the work of the mind: the job fused artisanal prowess, creativity, discipline, and professionalism. It required no advanced degree or business suits, was the antithesis of nine to five. At the same time, it held out, for those who succeeded, the promise not only of financial reward but also the patina of class—a shiny aura of authority and refinement predicated, perhaps ironically, on the very Frenchness of the new American chefs' predecessors and mentors" (2008, 44).

All of this cultural attention toward professional chefs helped drive increases in culinary school attendance and lured new entrants into the occupation. In his book, *The Reach of a Chef* (2007), Michael Ruhlman documents the changing demographics of culinary school entrants. For the first time a large contingent of culinary school students are from the middle class, and, instead of seeing cooking as a career path with few options, young men and women are choosing to learn to cook professionally over attending college or university.

Another shift included large numbers of career changers applying to culinary school after years spent in other industries. Many of these people joining the chef ranks were lured to the job by the promise of working in an exciting, creative work environment (Bilderback 2007; Hyman 2008). These career changers included a more varied group in terms of gender, age, and race-ethnicity than had typically been found in many professional kitchens. One benefit to this new group's interest in professional cooking was that these career changers helped cement the idea of chefs as professionals and not as menial laborers. As more people with college educations chose to go back to culinary school, the reputation of professional cooking as the purview of the "whacked out degenerates," which Anthony Bourdain so fondly recalls in his memoir, began to shift.

This change did not occur without some tension. In fact, Michael Ruhlman noted with some nostalgia: "Part of the appeal of working in a kitchen had always been its draw as refuge for outcasts and misfits and, undeniably, immigrants needing to enter the weave of the city. Also, a kitchen was a place that worked when the rest of the world was relaxing, by nature set apart from mainstream society. . . . [Due to changes] the professional kitchen was going mainstream. It was getting respectable, and the CIA insisted on bringing standards of white-collar professionalism to every one of its thirty-nine teaching kitchens" (2007, 39). At the same time that Ruhlman appears to lament the passage of the good old days of professional cooking, he acknowledges that changes to culinary schools and professional cooking environments have been an important part of shifting the view of chefs from being, as CIA president Tim Ryan described it, "fry cooks and hash slingers" (53) and toward the concept of well-trained, creative professionals.

NEWFOUND STATUS, SAME OLD (GENDER) THING?

According to food writer David Kamp, we are in the midst of a new revolution in American cooking as "Our culinary elites—the chefs, cookbook authors, cooking-school instructors, purveyors and food writers who lead the way—are suffused with feelings of boundless possibility, having liberated themselves from the old strictures and prejudices that hemmed in their predecessors. It's okay for the traditions of peasant cookers to inform those of haute cuisine, and for haute flourishes to inform regular-guy food" (2006, xi). This turning away from tradition appears to offer new opportunities for American chefs to reinvent what is considered great food and allows for new culinary perspectives and techniques to flourish. Alison Pearlman (2013) points out in her book, *Smart Casual: The Transformation of Gourmet Restaurant Style in America*, that we're seeing a growing democratization of cuisine. For example, Pearlman notes that *Food & Wine* chose Roy Choi as one of its Best New Chefs in 2010. Choi, who is known for his gourmet food truck cuisine, was used as an example of how taste and creativity had become the benchmark for judging the talents of a chef. With this new focus on democratization and meritocracy, it could be expected that more gender inclusivity could follow. However, this revolution has not translated into greater gender equality in professional cooking. Recent numbers suggest that relatively few women are head or executive chefs. Only 20 percent of women held these positions in 2013 according to the U.S. Bureau of Labor Statistics. This number may be even lower if we consider how many women chefs are actually the owner or co-owners of their restaurants. This lack of change could be seen as particularly surprising considering the gains made by women in other traditionally male-dominated fields such as veterinary medicine (Irvine and Vermilya 2010), accounting (Dellinger 2004), and pharmacy (Tanner and Cockerill 1996).

Looking at the current culinary landscape, it can seem ironic that women are not more recognized as leaders. Some of the most popular cooking trends of the last decade have strong linkages to women's cooking. Alice Waters, who we discussed earlier, is credited with helping create California cuisine with its emphasis on showcasing local, sustainably produced ingredients through its preparation and presentation. Yet, the recent turn toward more local, ingredients-based cooking is often presented as a new approach by daring young men chefs. Nose-to-tail cooking, which includes using all parts of an animal so that nothing is wasted, has become popular in many fine dining restaurants. Items such as offal (internal organs and entrails), bone marrow, and even the skin of animals have been becoming more prevalent on fine dining menus, and this style of cooking is often presented as a macho act by men chefs who aren't afraid to use what some may label "gross" ingredients in their food. But this type of cooking is nothing new as mothers and grandmothers have been relying on offal and other animal parts as a way of stretching their food further for centuries. It could also be argued that even molecular gastronomy, a cooking style that emphasizes the transformation of the physical and chemical properties of food through a scientific approach to cooking, has some feminine aspects to it. Women's food has long been discounted because it is deemed too simple, but as Adam Gopnik reminds us, "all movements in cooking believe themselves to be movements toward greater simplicity" (2011, 57) and that even the current trend in molecular gastronomy has been proposed to be the ultimate in cooking simply by breaking down ingredients to the atomic level.

Men chefs and food media have resisted the linkages of these new cooking styles to femininity. Instead, these forms of cooking have been recast to emphasize masculine traits. Men chefs are featured in food magazines crouching in fields or traveling to exotic locales to find the best ingredients. Nose-to-tail cooking is framed as something "extreme" and "gross" and media coverage of men chefs who perform this type of cooking show them brandishing large knives, covered in blood, and butchering whole animals. Molecular gastronomy is presented as a scientific way of cooking with men chefs taking on the role of "mad scientist." In these examples, men workers reaffirm their legitimacy by emphasizing their differences from other workers through their special knowledge and skills (Vallas 2001). As most home cooks do not have the space to break down a full-grown pig or the funds to buy a sous vide machine for their home, the ultimate message is that these men are professionals and to not try this at home.

When examining the numbers of women who hold top chef positions, Hyman attributes these trends to an "American gender ambivalence towards cooking." She explains, "If meaningful labor over the stoves had previously been limited, in the cultural imagination, to foppish Frenchmen and, on another register, mothers, the work of making cooking new was also the work of making it manly. This was essential to the transformation of cooking into a viable career path in line with the American dream: serious work of the hand must, in our cultural imagination, necessarily be disassociated with the home, with the feminine, with perceived amateurism" (2008, 44). Just as American cooking had to establish itself as separate from the French, men American chefs also still have to promote their food as something different from and greater than the simple cooking of women. Signe Rousseau (2012) points out in her research on the rise of food media and modern celebrity chefs that the very trends responsible for raising the profiles of chefs (increased globalization, challenges to traditional boundaries of class and occupation) can also lead to an upsurge in insecurity (Who exactly is a chef?) and increased competitiveness over the title. While not as overt as in the earlier days of professional chefs, men chefs still face a sense of precarious masculinity. As the standing of professional chefs rises and there is more cultural attention to food, there are also fears that there may be a diffusion of this newfound status. Chefs already have to guard against the untrained TV cooking show hosts, such as the Rachael Rays and Sandra Lees of the gastronomic field, by constantly reminding the public of the professional boundaries of who really is a chef. Because many of these television hosts are women, this reinforces the need to separate the cooking of women from that of men chefs.

The fact that women continue to lag behind men in the chef occupation suggests that, although some of the older techniques of exclusion, such as barring women from entry into culinary schools or cooking competitions, are no more, there remain other elements within the field that serve as major barriers for women in professional cooking environments, such as discrimination in hiring and promotion and sexual harassment (Cooper 1997). One positive change, however, is that more people are aware of and question the gender divide in professional cooking. We are not the only ones asking, "Where are all the women in professional kitchens?" In addition to countless food-related blogs and websites, both the *New York Times* and *Time* magazine have recently examined the issue. Women chefs are also asking this question and participating in conferences, forming new culinary organizations for women, and even staging flash mobs at food festivals in order to draw attention to issues of gender representation in the gastronomic field.

As chefs have become more of a focal point in popular culture, women's underrepresentation now seems more glaring. Many of the answers given for why more women have not become chefs range from issues of work conditions (women are not strong enough, women are unwilling to work long hours) to gender discrimination. Women chefs are encouraged (often by other women chefs) to lean in at work and to not think about issues of gender because hard work alone will get them noticed and rewarded. But this advice may not always be possible for women chefs due to the history of the profession, structure of work arrangements, and workplace cultures in professional kitchens. We want to emphasize that women's underrepresentation as chefs cannot be reduced to one factor. As figure I.1 illustrates, it is a combination of historical patterns of exclusion and disparagement, the orientations of critics and other influential food writers tasked with determining who constitutes a great chef, and current workplace cultures and trends within specific restaurant worlds. Only through examining how these conditions work together can we better understand women's position within the gastronomic field.

2 · FROM GOOD TO GREAT

Food Media and Becoming an Elite Chef

After years of hard work, Chef Amanda Cohen opened her restaurant, Dirt Candy, in New York City in 2008. Her new venture soon became a success with numerous media appearances to follow. Cohen has often been asked about the place of women in the culinary world, and, during an interview with Villagevoice.com, she spoke about what may be holding women back as chefs. She singled out women's lack of representation in food media, particularly the lack of women included on industry lists of "most influential" or "most powerful" chefs (which Cohen attributed to "lazy" journalism). Such omissions send powerful messages to young women who desire to work as chefs as, according to Cohen, "If you are a woman, and you don't see yourself in those positions of power, how do you know you're ever going to get there?"

Cohen's comments were in response to the November 18, 2013, issue of *Time* magazine that featured a picture of chefs David Chang (U.S.), Rene Redzepi (Denmark), and Alex Atala (Brazil) on the cover, smiling for the camera and decked out in their chefs' whites. Across their chests was a headline anointing the three men "The Gods of Food" and promising the reader the opportunity to "Meet the People Who Influence What (and How) You Eat." Soon after the issue debuted, there was considerable attention given to the fact that no women chefs were featured in the issue. Although two women pastry chefs were mentioned briefly, the issue reinforced the idea that, although there were plenty of gods of food, goddesses were nowhere to be found.

Hillary Dixler of the website Eater.com interviewed Howard Chua-Eoan, the section editor for that issue of *Time*. Throughout the interview Chua-Eoan compliments numerous women chefs and says that women were never consciously excluded. When Dixler asks him about whether the media has a role in shaping women's representation within the field, Chua-Eoan responds that he sees the media's job as reporting what chefs are saying. He goes on to state that, if women chefs were interviewed and talked about gender issues in high-status cuisine, the magazine would print it. However, he doesn't explain how women can talk about gender issues when media outlets like *Time* magazine do not include them. Chua-Eoan seems to be blaming women from their own exclusion without recognizing the power media has to shape who is given status and deemed worthy of being heard. Throughout the interview, he is adamant: "But this story, this package is about influence. It's not about the social and gender roles in the world of haute cuisine."

Influence within the gastronomic field cannot be decoupled from the social and gender roles of haute cuisine. Expectations and assumptions about men and women's cooking and chef careers have very real consequences. It is not just the quantity of media exposure that is important but also the quality of these depictions of men and women chefs. The manner in which men and women chefs are represented by food media can have a major impact on their progression through their careers, particularly in the movement from being just a chef to becoming renowned as a great chef. In this chapter, we examine the role of media attention and accolades in earning professional status. Food writers and critics have different ways of assigning titles of greatness to chefs that play a role in women chefs' ability to earn high levels of prestige in their occupation. These different cultural distinctions also reinforce gendered discourses about men and women's cooking.

THE POWER OF FOOD MEDIA

As Pierre Bourdieu (1993) notes, to understand a field we must not look only at producers and their audience, but also the role of cultural tastemakers who influence the field. Historically, food writing has played a significant role in defining high and low cuisine and performing boundary work regarding the occupation (Trubek 2000). Early food writers were men and they used their influence and status as experts to differentiate the professional/rational cooking of men in restaurants from the emotional/expressive cooking of women performed in the home (Jones and Taylor 2001; Trubek 2000).

Today food writers and critics play an influential role in the gastronomic field. Their approval can confer status to a chef and make or break his or her restaurant and career. When food writers and critics feature a restaurant, cultural leaders begin to visit, and eventually this popularity trickles down to less cosmopolitan customers (e.g., day trippers from the suburbs) and even to tourists (Kamp 2006). Such growth in popularity, while criticized by foodies and other early adopters, can lead to substantial success for the chef and/or restaurant owners.

Research on the work of critics emphasizes the role they play in constructing and upholding boundaries of taste within a particular field. Because cultural production is a social process, objects that are classified as art can only be categorized as such when there is a collective belief that the object deserves such a designation (Bourdieu 1993). These judgments denote the merits of a particular cultural item and help establish and maintain a cultural hierarchy. By imposing "hierarchies of value and taste" in order to form "exclusionary canons," critics help establish legitimacy (Lizardo and Skiles 2008, 496). Signe Rousseau notes how, "As the world opens up to a sea of competition from professionals and amateurs alike, chefs distinguish themselves from the crowd by becoming innovators or artists, and by producing creations rather than mere recipes" (2012, 23). Yet, it is through the judgment of food writers and critics that these creations are legitimated.

We are not suggesting that food critics and writers are intentionally evaluating men and women chefs differently. Many would argue that the gender of the chef who prepares their food is never taken into account when they make their evaluations. However, both chefs and critics are influenced their *habitus* (Bourdieu 1993). Bourdieu describes one's habitus as a set of dispositions, which generates practices and perceptions. A habitus serves as a veil, invisible even to the wearer, which impacts how one moves about the world, what preferences one has, and how one interacts with others. Actors within the gastronomic field are socialized into having a similar habitus. They share the same sense about what type of cooking is worthy to be called haute cuisine and what the markers of a great chef are. The writer's role of gatekeeper can ensure legitimacy of the cultural artist, therefore, helping to ensure that the particular field continues to be viewed as valid (Bourdieu 1993). This legitimacy both benefits the chef—whose blue-collar production work can now be described as a white-collar, artistic career—and the critic who is tasked to evaluating the chef's work and who is seen as one of the few people possessing the habitus to do so.

GENDERED IMPACT OF CRITICS' EVALUATIONS

Critiques of cultural objects whether they are of paintings, symphonies, or food do not occur in a vacuum (Bielby, Moloney, and Ngo 2005; Gans 1999; Hughey 2010; Lounsbury and Glynn 2001). Social expectations about who is or should be considered a great chef can be influenced by social beliefs regarding gender, race, culture, and other social locations. Just as critics and other writers can legitimate some chefs, those who do not fit particular models of success can find their efforts de-legitimated. For example, many elite chefs are instructed in the French cooking tradition, often training and staging at the same restaurants. This helps them develop valuable human, social, and cultural capital that is recognized by food writers and critics. Because they are different, newcomers, such as women trying to succeed as professional chefs, face difficulty fitting in and meeting the definition of great chefs.

Food critics are no different than employers or colleagues who assess workers' talents, success, and skills in gendered ways. Across occupations, men and women workers are evaluated differently, even when they have the same levels of human capital (Acker 1990; Britton 2003; Castilla 2008; Schilt 2006; 2010). People learn through gender socialization and other processes that men and women are different and that masculine characteristics are valued more than feminine traits. Co-workers, supervisors, and others who evaluate worker skills appraise men and women differently because of institutionalized gender stereotypes. These gender biases, as mechanisms of gender schemas, can be intentional or unintentional (Correll and Benard 2006; Gorman 2005; Ridgeway 2007). Although women are more likely to be proponents of gender equality in some workplace contexts (Cohen and

Huffman 2007), both men and women are biased in favor of men workers (Benard and Correll 2010; Cohen and Huffman 2003).

While critics' reviews or comments may not be meant to present men's cooking as superior to women's, cultural schemas about gender, leadership, and power can result in differential evaluations of performance that often advantage men. Food writing may not be as unbiased as it appears because those doing the evaluating are both part of a gastronomic field that has long been male-dominated and part of a larger society in which the work of women is often devalued. For women chefs in an industry that is becoming more and more focused on media, expectations regarding gender (and gendered behavior) can lead to evaluations of their cooking/career that do not fit within the established (male) paradigm of greatness.

WHO IS A GREAT CHEF?: EVALUATIONS AND DESCRIPTIONS OF CHEFS

We analyzed 2,206 restaurant reviews and chef profiles (2004–2009) from the *New York Times, San Francisco Chronicle, Gourmet,* and *Food & Wine.* The appendix provides more detail about our methodology. Table 2.1 includes the numbers of articles that came from each source and a breakdown of how many featured men and women chefs. Clearly, men chefs were included in a larger number of articles. In fact, women chefs are only the focus of slightly more than 10 percent of the articles. When this number is combined with the number of articles that feature men and women chefs together, women are still only mentioned in around 22 percent of the reviews and profiles. In cases where men and women chefs were mentioned in the same article, this was usually in either "roundup" articles in which several chefs and restaurants are mentioned in one piece of writing or referred to a restaurant review where the executive chef (typically male) and pastry chef (typically female) were both named and discussed.

We examined the way the chefs, their restaurants, and their overall cooking style were discussed. We were particularly interested in identifying what differentiated a good chef from a great one and if there tended to be any gender differences in how chefs were evaluated or described in the articles. Not only are men and women chefs written about in very different ways, but these ways reinforce the home versus haute divisions in professional cooking as men chefs are described as creators who master the kitchen,

TABLE 2.1   Media Sources and Gender of Chefs Reviewed or Profiled
(2004–2009)

	Number of men chefs reviewed or profiled	Number of women chefs reviewed or profiled	Number of both men and women chefs reviewed or profiled	Total
New York Times	1,200	120	119	1,439
San Francisco Chronicle	346	86	20	452
Gourmet	88	12	44	144
Food & Wine	93	12	66	171
Total	1,727	230	249	2,206

innovate cuisine, and build empires while women chefs are depicted as being food producers who re-create traditional or homey dishes and are not highly invested in their careers unless guided by a man.

ORIENTATION TOWARD FOOD: GREAT CHEFS VERSUS GREAT DISHES

The overarching theme in both reviews and profiles of men chefs is the reinforcement of men chefs as professionals. They are specially trained, technically proficient, and masterful leaders. Men chefs do not just cook food but use these talents to create dining experiences that require high levels of dedication and control. These elite men chefs have incredibly high standards and go to great lengths in order to fully develop and execute their culinary vision.

The specialized training of chefs is commonly referenced and many reviews and profiles make a note of whether or not a chef attended an elite culinary school or worked at a particularly well-regarded restaurant. For example, several articles included notes about men chefs who had trained under the renowned Spanish chef Ferran Adrià, whose restaurant El Bulli helped establish molecular gastronomy as a major culinary paradigm. Working with Adrià was mentioned as a way of establishing a culinary pedigree and indicating knowledge of molecular gastronomy techniques. Such pedigrees are important because they confer valued human, social, and cultural capital and can help chefs gain employment when they finish their time at a particular restaurant.

Both food writers and critics commented on the training and craftsmanship that were evident in men chef's cooking. Chef David Bazirgan is described as having undergone a long training process that resulted in his "master[ing] the often complicated play of textures that distinguish his dishes" (*San Francisco Chronicle*, August 27, 2004). The highest status was reserved for chefs who had conquered the complex training required for formal French cuisine. Once these skills were learned, however, their high level of training was evident in even the simplest dishes prepared. A *Food & Wine* article pointed out that, when eating the food of Justin Quek, it was impossible not to notice his "classical French training" (January 2008). Another article discusses two sister restaurants from New York chef-owner Geoffrey Zakarian and the importance of good technique:

> But both are first-rate experiences, united and distinguished by their classically French inclinations and by unusually expert cooking. Mr. Zakarian and his executive chef, Doug Psaltis, are talented craftsmen teasing the best results out of very fine ingredients. They don't wow you with their inventiveness, but they do wow you with their execution. ("A Consistency That Works on Two Levels," *New York Times*, April 5, 2006)

While there is a tinge of criticism in the comments about Zakarian's cooking lacking inventiveness, there is no doubt that the chefs are both technically proficient. Other articles highlight the confidence that comes through the cooking of a well-trained chef and how this can lead to more experimental cooking.

> Mr. Humm's French-grounded cooking, which bridges the classically saucy decadence of the past and the progressive derring-do of a new generation, drew notice from the get go. ("A Daring Rise to the Top," *New York Times*, August 11, 2009)

> Hubert Keller is a master. He's worked for some of the top French chefs and is thoroughly grounded in French technique, but he's not afraid to experiment with flavor combinations—halibut paired with rhubarb coulis, corn and truffles, for example, or prawns with fennel, orange and red wine licorice sauce.

("Acclaimed Fleur de Lys Loses a Little Magic," *San Francisco Chronicle,* October 16, 2007)

Such commentary highlights the special skills learned in professional cooking. The words used to describe the work of men emphasize their roles as chefs and not as cooks. They bring something new to their cooking beyond anything that could be gleaned from a home cook or even a less-skilled professional cook. An example of this was found in a review of a dish created by Napa Valley chef Peter Halikas:

> Five tofu rounds, replicating scallops, framed a mound of creamy mashed potatoes topped with tender braised leeks. Crisp on the outside and silky within, the tofu was good enough to convert even the most diehard carnivore, and a sublime leek sauce proved again how Halikas elevates even the most basic ingredients. ("City Cuisine Meets Country Dining at Napa's New N.V. Restaurant and Lounge," *San Francisco Chronicle,* February 26, 2006)

Halikas and other chefs of his caliber are able to transform even basic ingredients—another marker of their professional standards. The technique and training that they employ are part of what elevates not only their individual cooking, but professional cooking as an occupation. The ability to recognize this training and discern its importance to the finished product also helps validate the work of food critics. Compare these accolades to this review of Caffe DiVino:

> The penne porcini ($13) is among the best I've had, with slivers of the mushroom melting into an earthy cream sauce, punched up with white wine and herbs. The rigatoni alla contadina ($11), with shreds of chicken and diced eggplant, wasn't as exciting. It was fine but uninspired, a dish that could easily be made at home. ("Stress Is on Food at Laid-Back Caffe DiVino," *San Francisco Chronicle,* April 1, 2005)

Similar critiques are leveled at another chef: "Overall, Massi Boldrini's food is rustic and homey, in the style of a decent home cook—but often not soaring above that level" ("Riva Cucina Wades into Restaurant Business," *San Francisco Chronicle,* July 18, 2007). According to these critics, the failure of these dishes lay with their uninspired and easy design. An entrée that could be re-created at home without any special knowledge or training was reason enough to label the dish as lacking. In Gary Alan Fine's ethnography of restaurant kitchens, he found that chefs often used specific rhetoric to emphasize their professionalism. He explained, "The problem chefs face is that everyone has cooked, while few have performed surgery or reupholstered furniture" (1996b, 98), meaning that, unless chefs highlight how their cooking is unique from that of the everyday, many would not appreciate their professional efforts. Because everyday cooking is associated with unpaid labor done by women, this emphasis on technical skills and artistry is another way of addressing feminization threat. Food writers and critics are important in the process of legitimizing chefs and separating high-status cuisine from home cooking, and, therefore, defining professional cooking as "men's work." The simple description of "a dish that could easily be made at home" isn't even elaborated on—it is assumed that the reader understands that such simple dishes are not up to professional par. Such condemnations help to uphold the home-versus-haute dichotomy of professional cooking by casting home cooking as the inferior.

Truly great chefs were not just amazing technicians. Elite chefs must also be intensely creative and they are often described in artistic terms such as composing dishes, designing menus, and orchestrating dinner services. Numerous articles celebrated the mental and creative work of men chefs. For example, a meal served by chef Laurent Gras of Chicago's L20 restaurant is described "a fully articulated aesthetic vision that elevates the restaurant experience to something transcendent" ("Should Fine Dining Die?" *Food & Wine*, April 2009). Other writers described the visionary, masterful approach to food possessed by great chefs:

In the ensuing years, inspired by pioneers of nouvelle cuisine such as the great chef Paul Bocuse, who were liberating French cuisine from heavy sauces and tired techniques, Juan Mari pursued his vision for *la nueva cocina vasca*, "the new Basque cuisine," employing the best *materias primas*—basic ingredients— along with extraordinarily inventive methods to dismantle and recast classic Basque dishes. ("Secrets of the Basque Vanguard," *Food & Wine*, August 2007)

On the right side, the quail breast is arranged over beet greens, soft polenta and a red wine truffle sauce. Each tableau is fully realized; together they create a "wow" experience. . . . The five main courses follow the same format, utilizing sea bream, duck breast, pork, Kobe beef, and lamb. Each preparation is like a main course, served in smaller quantities; the work that goes into these dishes is mind-boggling. ("Michael Mina Enters Four-Star Galaxy," *San Francisco Chronicle*, March 12, 2008)

These examples showcase the importance of the creative, thinking chef who innovates their cuisine. Each of these dishes are not simply food on a plate, instead they are proof of a chef's talent and commitment to a vision. Juan Mari is given credit for re-creating an entire cuisine, while Michael Mina's dishes go beyond mere plates of food to be fully realized tableaus. Similarly, Daniel Patterson is described as a "talented chef who has a studious, intellectual approach to combining ingredients. . . . The flavors are bold but refined, a hallmark of his distinctive style" ("At Daniel Patterson's Coi, a Complex Interplay of Flavors," *San Francisco Chronicle*, July 9, 2006).

Patterson is not the only man chef singled out for having an intellectual approach to food, and other men chefs were described as producing "amusing," "fanciful," "intriguing," and "witty" dishes. Culinary masters like Grant Achatz of Chicago's Alinea creates "provocative" and "ingenious" food that is extremely "innovative." Focusing on the mental work required to be a successful chef promotes the occupation to the rank of white-collar, creative professionals rather than blue-collar production work and further separates the food from that prepared by home cooks.

Great chefs are also expected to be strong leaders within their kitchens and to be aware of every detail of their restaurant. In an article in the *New York Times* detailing the opening of a new restaurant by chef Gray Kunz, the writer is amazed at the multitasking of the chef:

Even during the practice cooking leading up to the opening, Mr. Kunz has been a demanding master. He is the first one there in the morning, patrolling the kitchen restlessly. He prods lamb sizzling on the plancha, insists that the shallots be sliced just so, checks just exactly how much jasmine sauce his chefs have spooned onto the cured yellowtail, and quietly admonishes a young pastry cook who has dipped a silver spoon into raspberry coulis. "Never use tableware in the kitchen," he instructs. The last to leave at night, he makes sure the garbage receptacles are tucked away. Throughout the construction he managed to keep the kitchen area impeccable. ("Gray Kunz: Out of the Fire, Into the Frying Pan," *New York Times*, September 1, 2004)

New York chef Daniel Boulud, whose numerous restaurants are all highly regarded by those in the gastronomic field, is also described as extremely meticulous:

> Daniel Boulud can't stand to see a detail out of place. As pans slam around him during dinner service in the Upper East Side restaurant that bears his first name, he will pause to request that a spoon be polished. How best to marry braised endive to seared beef can absorb him as utterly as the lilies in the dining room that haven't opened on schedule. ("A Top Chef's Kitchen Is Far Too Hot, Some Workers Say," *New York Times*, January 17, 2007)

Such an eye for detail is part and parcel of having a personal "vision" or a "distinctive style" that men chefs bring to their food. Great chefs not only have this vision but go to great lengths to articulate it no matter the financial risks or inconveniences to customers involved. Instead, men chefs receive praise for dominating every aspect of the dining experience at their establishments. This domination places a chef in total control over the content and quality of his food and is referred to as a sign of the purity of one's vision and their dedication to their craft. This was also illustrated in an article about chef Rudy Mihal's work at Odyssey:

> Mihal is a one-man show, creating a French- and Italian-inspired menu of four appetizers, two pizzas, and four main courses. Dessert depends on his time and mood. On one night, there was only a cheese plate, which is always available, offering three selections for $7, five for $11, and seven for $15. Another night, he prepared an apple galette ($9), a rectangular piece of ethereal puff pastry framing meticulously cut apples that had maintained their crunch; the entire dessert rested in a cloud of chantilly cream. . . . Odyssey is small enough that it can accommodate Mihal's particular vision, allowing him to cook pretty much what he wants. He's a fine chef, so even outside the urban mainstream he's found a willing audience. . . . The restaurant is in a modest space, marked only with a small sign over the door. From the parking lot, it looks more like a suburban sports bar than an upper-crust restaurant. . . . Clearly, Mihal puts substance before flash. He has created a very personal place, one that should resonate with anyone who believes, as I do, that a restaurant should reflect the personality and dreams of the person behind the stove. ("Big Food Ambitions in a Modest Space at Odyssey," *San Francisco Chronicle*, January 6, 2008)

Chef Mihal could be described as being an unsuccessful chef—his restaurant is small, unassuming. He does a majority of the work himself, something many elite chefs would never attempt, but here these arrangements are described as a kind of purity of vision and the results of choosing more professional freedom than accolades. Part of this may be related to the changing status of chefs. As chefs are becoming celebrities, there has been a bit of a backlash with several chefs purposefully eschewing the trappings of fame in order to be artists who produce for other artists (Ruhlman 2007).

Other chefs are also applauded for taking a more challenging path. Both chef Anselmo Bello and chef Michael Huynh are singled out for praise due to their uncompromising menu choices: Bello refuses to put French fries on his menu ("Mexican-French Relations Fare Well in a Kitchen," *New York Times*, May 19, 2004) and Huynh does not "coddle" diners by preparing the overwhelmingly sweet or fiery hot dishes customers might expect from more Americanized Asian cooking ("A Familiar Formula, Until You Take a Bite," *New York Times*, January 3, 2007). An interview with chefs Grant Achatz and Heston Blumenthal—two chefs renowned for their additions to molecular gastronomy—informs the reader that their respective cookbooks are definitely not aimed at the traditional home cook ("The Gourmet Q + A: Grant Achatz and Heston Blumenthal," *Gourmet*, March 24, 2008). In fact, Blumenthal says that his book "makes no concessions whatsoever" to the reader attempting to replicate his dishes at home and he has provided recipes exactly as they are used in his restaurant. Rather than describing this attitude as elitist or as a potentially poor business decision (because of the limited market for their books), the writer provides such information as a way of proving their commitment to quality and unwillingness to compromise their visions.

Sometimes uncompromising stances were critiqued, such as in this review in the *New York Times* (November 21, 2007) cheekily titled, "Artist at Work—Taste If You Dare." In the review, Chef Sam Mason's food does not so much come under fire as much as the attitude he presents in the promotional materials sent out about his new restaurant:

> His words appear alongside a photograph of him looking pensive, above both an enormous copy of his signature and a sketch that depicts the piece-by-piece construction of one of Tailor's avant-garde dishes. They say, "I know I'm not gonna change the way people think about food, but that doesn't mean I'm gonna let them change the way I think about it." So there you have it. Mr. Mason's personal

vision trumps your pleasure. His conviction matters more than your response. This, I suppose, is the very definition of artistic integrity. But it's not the prescription for a great restaurant.

Men chefs' obsession with perfection and controlling every aspect of the dining experience also helps reinforce the notion of chef as expert. Their training, creativity, and passion all are used to suggest that chefs know better than their customers and that their professional opinions are important. Even in the mocking review of Tailor, the reviewer suggests that such posturing would be acceptable if the food presented lived up to Mason's hype-filled promotion. Above all, men chefs are shown to be professionals whose knowledge and vision are worthy of respect and accolades.

In contrast, articles describing the cooking of women chefs tend to focus on the object being produced—the food. Little attention is given to the process of creating a winning restaurant dish or the technical skill needed for its execution. Women are rarely discussed as having a vision that they then portray in their food. Their motivations are simpler and about creating dishes with a pleasing taste.

Likewise, the accolades given to women do not appear to extend to the dish (that is, the creativity and technique behind conceptualizing a particular menu item) but are limited to only the actual *dish* (the plate of food that was put before the writer). In examining the adjectives used to describe the cooking of women chefs, there appeared to be more focus on the production aspect of cooking with words such as "elegant," "precise," "simple," and "tidy" being used by writers. This language refers more to a finished product and the physical properties of the dish than the actual mental work that goes into creating a menu. Also, there were more descriptions of the physical sensations brought about by eating the women's food than in discussion of men chef's dishes. Words like "light," "silky," and "chewy" were used to describe the taste of women's food. This could be attributed in part to the fact that many of the women chefs featured were pastry chefs and that discussion of desserts is more likely to include adjectives about the taste of the food rather than its creative development. The overall difference in describing women's food highlights not the technique used to create a dish, but the sensation the diner receives upon eating. In these media accounts, the focus moves from the creator to the audience.

Other words used to describe women's cooking related to the professionalism of their cooking. Reviews announce that the pastas at Barbara

Lynch's restaurant, Sportello, are "expertly prepared" ("First Taste: Sportello," *Gourmet*, January 26, 2009) and that the food produced by chef Vanessa Dang ("and her crew") is "expertly executed" ("Cuisines Commingle at Vanessa's," *San Francisco Chronicle*, November 15, 2006).

Several women are complimented for their sure hand used in cooking a dish. In an article about the opening of a local restaurant by chef Patricia Windisch, the author informs readers that, "She's a seasoned, well-respected pro" ("Tiburon's Three Degrees Has Great Potential but Falls Far Short of the Mark," *San Francisco Chronicle*, October 8, 2006). Another example comes from a review of a Fort Worth restaurant:

> Chefs love to toss around terms like "regional cuisine" and "comfort food," but too often, the results are more fancy than friendly. Molly McCook—chef and co-owner of Ellerbe Fine Foods in Fort Worth—has bridged the gap. In the bright, sunny rooms of a prettily revamped '20s service station, the Shreveport native is turning out rootsy Southern dishes with a professional sheen. Her meltingly tender braised pork shank, for instance, is as easy to like (and to understand) as a Sunday pot roast, but a glaze of stone-ground-mustard and East Texas–based Johnnie Fair syrup gives it a touch of class. ("Restaurants Now: Ellerbe Fine Foods," *Gourmet*, October 2, 2009)

Although McCook earns raves for her food that tempers its "rootsy" nature with a "professional sheen," why do these articles contain reminders about the professional nature of women's cooking? It may be that men's historic dominance in the occupation means that they automatically are viewed as professionals and experts in restaurant kitchens. Women, as newcomers whose work has historically been devalued, have to prove their deserving-ness of their title as professionals. Because women are so heavily associated with home cooking rather than haute cooking, food writers and critics must take special pains to remind readers of their skills and that they have earned their place in the field.

Another difference relates to the limits of women's competency in the kitchen. Whereas a man chef's knowledge or expertise may extend to an entire cuisine or cooking style, the domain of women's cooking is more limited. For example, a *Food & Wine* article about the culinary scene in Valencia remarks that, in much of Spain, "cooking remains mostly a macho activity;" however, south of Valencia there is a province with many talented women chefs who are described as "rice divas" ("Spain's Next Food Mecca,"

Food & Wine, February 2007). While men may be referred to as "masters of Basque cuisine" these accomplished women chefs are reduced to mastering only one food. Another example of this comes from an article on chef Jody Williams of the New York restaurant Gusto:

> [She prepared] *spiedini alla romana*, a deluxe grilled cheese stuffed with mozzarella and pungent anchovy, then soaked in egg and fried. One reason it's so good is that Williams is an amazing fryer. Her specialty is deep-fried artichokes: They're small, tender, and crisp, to be consumed leaves and all. ("Where to Go Next: New York," *Food & Wine*, March 2006)

Although Williams helms a successful restaurant that has numerous loyal patrons—including the well-known food writer Mimi Sheraton—her talents as a chef are primarily couched in terms of one skill: frying.

Throughout the media, women chefs are not being shown as commanding leaders of their kitchen. Whether in the case we previously mentioned, in which the writer makes sure the credit goes to Vanessa Dang "and her crew" or the profile of chef Celeste Price-Bottini in which the author writes, "What struck me about Price-Bottini was the extent of her responsibilities. At 27, she oversees a couple of dozen employees" ("Cook's Night Out: Celeste Price-Bottini," *San Francisco Chronicle*, October 10, 2004). Within the description of women as leaders there is less of the all-commanding presence used to discuss men chefs. Women also are described as being more pleasing to their guests and not about insisting on controlling the entirety of the dining experience. Words like "nourishing" suggest a motherly, caring orientation toward customers, such as when Michelle Bernstein is praised for providing a "hometown sense of hospitality" to her Miami patrons ("Miami's Hottest Latin Party," *Food & Wine*, June 2006). Another review describes a conversation with a waiter at chef Keiko Takahashi's restaurant, El Paseo:

> "I'm sorry, ma'am," he said quietly, "but the chef is not satisfied with the quality of the sea bass that you ordered tonight. Would it be all right with you if she replaced it with a red snapper instead?" ("El Paseo Pampers Patrons with Inspired Cuisine," *San Francisco Chronicle*, May 23, 2007)

A man chef under such conditions might refuse outright to even cook the sea bass dish because the fish is not up to his standards, but here Takahashi makes sure that such a substitution would not displease the customer.

Unlike men chefs, women chefs place the diner's experience above their own vision or ego. Sometimes this can lead to critiques, such as in a review of Cindy Pawlcyn's restaurant Go Fish:

> The menu also offers a selection of fish cooked "your way"—a mix-and-match selection of fish, cooking methods and sauces. . . . While I like a restaurant that accommodates customers' needs, I fear that the Fish Your Way goes too far in taking responsibility from the chef and putting it in the diner's lap. . . . If I really had things "my way," the kitchen would simplify the menu so all the dishes would be fully realized. Having it "their way" would happily become "my way." ("There Are Many Fish in the Sea, and Most of Them End Up at Go Fish," *San Francisco Chronicle*, March 25, 2007)

Pawlcyn's attempt to please diners actually ends up being a major critique of her restaurant. The military origins of the chef profession places the chef as the "chief" in the kitchen and ceding so much power to the diners is actually a sign of a chef who is lacking. The writer suggests, as a chef, it is your job to guide and lead your customers. In contrast, home cooks are primarily motivated by a need or desire to nourish and please others (DeVault 1994). By placing customers first, Pawlcyn has compromised any personal vision of her restaurant, which invalidates her as a great chef.

ORIENTATION TOWARD TRADITION: RULE BREAKERS VERSUS RULE FOLLOWERS

In detailing just what makes certain chefs great, a common refrain within the articles was that the men were iconoclasts who broke rules as a means of revolutionizing their food. If talented enough, these men could end up transforming not only their style of cooking, but also influencing a countless number of chefs who came after them. In descriptions of these men, their lives were discussed in near mythic forms. The articles would take a similar pattern: introduce well-respected men, applaud their food, and link their current cooking orientation back to the influence of a mother, grandmother, or an early professional mentor. However, articles written about truly great chefs tended to recount a turning point in the chef's life when he broke with this tradition, and this was seen as key in their movement from a good to great chef. Take this example from a profile of Chicago chef Grant Achatz:

Grant Achatz, the 32-year-old chef at Chicago's Alinea, has a hyper-experimental cooking style that's put him in the vanguard of American cuisine, and earned him a slot as an F&W Best New Chef 2002. At Alinea, which he opened last year, Achatz creates exquisite, impossible dishes like a futuristic heirloom-tomato salad—a burst of sweet tomato foam trapped in a balloon of mozzarella somehow inflated like Super Elastic Bubble Plastic. Which is why it's surprising to find this groundbreaking, risk-taking chef at Alinea on a recent Sunday afternoon making meat loaf. . . . Achatz began washing dishes at his parents' restaurant when he was eight years old (he had to stand on a milk crate to reach the sink), then quickly worked his way up to preparing breakfast, lunch, and dinner as a line cook. By the time he was 12, it was obvious he had serious talent, says his dad, Grant Achatz, Sr. "He was doing a better job on the line than guys I could hire off the road. He was fast and he never got flustered. A lot can happen in a chaotic kitchen, and his strong suit was expediting—almost like you'd see on *Iron Chef*." . . . Some of Achatz's ideas come from dishes his mom used to make at home. Riffing on her spectacular pies, Achatz uses his mom's crust technique—making dough with just flour, salt, shortening, and water and kneading it quickly with very cold hands—then adds a buttery filling of fresh pears and a top crust slathered with a milky glaze. And after a recent craving for his mom's beef chili—always the highlight of childhood Halloween get-togethers with his cousins—Achatz couldn't resist re-creating the dish, with a few tweaks, of course. "My mom makes the chili using green peppers with the skins still on—something I would normally never use as a cook," he says. "But then I eat it and I'm like, 'Ah, I remember.' It's nice to have that flavor memory. My version of her chili recipe calls for chipotle chiles and fresh herbs, for a more pronounced herbaceous quality, which I think is nice in relation to the tomatoes and beef. But her basic technique of sweating down the first set of ingredients is the key to building the flavor." . . . "Working in a town of 3,500 when I was a kid, I knew people didn't want things like prune ketchup with their meat loaf. But that experience is probably what led me to a style of cooking that's a little more creative and emotional," he says. "As a kid, I was always like, 'Can we do this? Can we do that?'" He laughs. "And now, I can do that." ("Comfort Food from a Rebel Chef," *Food & Wine*, December 2006)

An article featuring Spanish chef Nicolás Jimenez similarly ties his cuisine to his mother's influence:

> Though Túbal's 33-year-old chef, Nicolás Jimenez, had worked at the Michelin three-starred Arzak in San Sebastián, he's just as influenced by his energetic mother, Atxen, who runs the front of the house. "Spanish diners are getting bored with *avanguardia*," Atxen said with a conspiratorial wink, as if to explain why she and Nicolás ignore avant-garde techniques and devote their attention to updating vernacular favorites. . . . At Túbal, Jimenez transforms the classic—and usually tragically overcooked—vegetable stew called menestra de verduras into an iridescent-green still life of artichokes, green beans, and spinach. Each vegetable is precisely blanched before being finished with a sauce made with olive oil and cured ham. ("Vegetables: What Spain's Most Creative Chefs Are Obsessed with Now," *Food & Wine*, May 2008)

Although both Achatz and Jimenez recognize their mother's influence and still use some of their recipes and techniques while cooking, the articles strongly suggest that, to reach their true potential, men chefs have to break away from tradition. Achatz, who felt hemmed in by the unadventurous palates of his parents' customers is now able to freely create what he wants. Achatz acknowledges the differences between his professional cooking, which would never allow green peppers to be used with the skins still on, and his mother's recipe. Jimenez, through his training, is able to transform a classic dish that home cooks often tragically overcook. These comments suggest how, in the hands of their chef sons, cooking is elevated to much higher status.

Numerous profiles of men chefs include similar stories. These early food memories may serve as a source of inspiration and a starting point, but men chefs are described as mastering and then exceeding these humble beginnings. Vicki Swinbank's (2002) historical research into gender and cooking found this as a common trend. Women's cooking is considered basic and an expression of nature by providing for their young. Men's cooking, on the other hand, is described as a technical, reasoned form of culture. Men chefs discuss being inspired by the food their mothers or grandmothers cooked; however, this food is not acceptable without being transformed by the man chef into a more refined dish. This home cooking (particularly the kind associated with maternal foodwork) must be mediated by the more trained palates of men chefs to have value.

Sometimes the rebellion against a mother's cooking is even more pronounced. For example, superstar New York chef Marcus Samuelsson is described in a profile as using his African stepmother's cooking as a reference point but, ultimately, he "doesn't give a damn about tradition" ("The Gourmet Q & A: Marcus Samuelsson," *Gourmet*, February 8, 2008). A story on Spanish chefs similarly details chef Raul Aleixandre's family origins to his cooking:

> Although Aleixandre's mother, Mari, is one of Valencia's great traditional cooks, he takes a perverse pleasure in defying her rules. Once he served me an inverted paella, with the socarrat (the crunchy layer of rice that sticks to the pan) presented on top as a tissue-thin hat. ("Spain's Next Food Mecca," *Food & Wine*, February 2007)

Other chefs rebelled by challenging the traditional cooking styles in which they had been trained. The recent movement toward more scientific cooking through molecular gastronomy can be used as an example of this. A profile of Ferran Adrià, whose cooking at his Spanish restaurant El Bulli has led to his description as the best chef in the world, talks about his movement away from tradition:

> One key was his recognition that in the creative world traditions are made to be broken. Mr. Adrià's idea, as he describes it, was simply to "do new things with old concepts." So, seeing chicken curry as a concept and determining to do something that hadn't been done before, he developed a dish, now famous, in which the sauce is solid and the chicken liquid. ("Adrià May Be Relaxing, but His Obsessions Are Still Abuzz," *New York Times*, September 13, 2006)

A story about a cooking event featuring New York molecular gastronomy chef, Wylie Dufresne, similarly describes his playing with traditional cooking styles:

> In the question-and-answer session, one person asked why Mr. Dufresne went to the trouble of making a foie gras terrine, a process that takes half a day of chilling, when the next step was melting it into a liquid. "We were trying to be true and honest to that aspect of French cooking," Mr. Dufresne replied. He paused before adding, "And do something kind of crazy with it." ("Food 2.0: Chefs as Chemists," *New York Times*, November 6, 2007)

As chefs challenge traditional cooking styles, those who are seen as being both inventive and able to produce good food become lauded and these accolades result in a kind of snowball effect. As their innovations became accepted by influential food writers and critics, this rebel would come to be described as an innovator, pioneer, or even genius and would win awards and increased publicity. After receiving this label, they are able to move positions within the gastronomic field and much of what they do becomes part of the new standard for food and cooking, which soon becomes emulated by other chefs (Bourdieu 1993). Being labeled a great chef becomes a form of self-fulfilling prophecy. From this point on, any decision or change receives media attention with food writers suggesting these actions are proof of the greatness of these chefs. This finding was most clear in international coverage of the recent trend toward a return to more ingredient-based cooking (which, ironically, has been associated with more women chefs in the United States). Soon, men chefs who were back to simple and local cuisine were seen as the new risk takers; however, there were still emphasis on the masculinity of the food produced. For example, in a profile of Victor Arguinzoniz:

> Extebarri [Arguinzoniz's restaurant] is Spain's new zeitgeist restaurant, reflecting the country's recent paradigm shift from sci-fi gastronomy to *cocina de producto*, or ingredient-driven cuisine. . . . [Quoting a Catalan newspaper]: "Imagine, he's gone back to the cave: meat and fire!" . . . Though he doesn't even own a kitchen thermometer, Arguinzoniz might be the most technique-obsessed chef on earth. ("Victor Arguinzoniz: The Grilling Genius of Spain," *Food & Wine*, June 2008)

Arguinzoniz is celebrated for focusing his cooking on local ingredients. Yet, his use of the more masculine cooking style of grilling food is highlighted in the article. Even grilling has connotations with simplicity and home cooks, but the article makes mention of special equipment Arguinzoniz designed that separates his dishes from home cooking and proves his rebel status. This focus on technology and skill allows Arguinzoniz to draw from simple cooking styles without falling prey to feminization threat.

For these men chefs, once they earn the title of great chef, their choices are described, not as individual peccadilloes, but as evidence of commitment to a food ideology that should be commended. Even if they reach too far when trying out new types of cooking styles, their failures are spun in a positive way, as in an article on Andoni Luis Aduriz, a former apprentice of Ferran Adrià at El Bulli ("36 Hours in San Sebastián," *New York Times*, November 18, 2007). The writer who ate Aduriz's eleven-course tasting menu complimented him for "dissecting flavors with mathematical precision," but later admitted that, "some dishes worked better on paper." However, ultimately, the writer remarks, "if gastronomy is about adventure, Mugaritz [Aduriz's restaurant] offers a thrilling and eye-opening ride." Such comments suggest that, even if men chefs do occasionally fail at producing palatable food, the fact that they are trying to cook outside of conventions still helps affirm their greatness.

In contrast, women chefs were rarely described as breaking the rules of traditional cooking. When women did prepare a dish, for example, using unusual ingredients, their actions are described as "unique" or "whimsical" but not as challenging any major culinary paradigm. Instead women chefs are praised for straightforward flavors and presentations and showing restraint in their cooking such as in the examples below:

Pastry chef Lauren Mitterer works in the same tradition as Karen Barker, the much-heralded dessert maven of Magnolia Grill, up in Durham, North Carolina. She succeeds at direct flavors. Straightforward presentations. She doesn't try dodge-and-feint moves. ("Downing Butter Beans and Buttermilk in Charleston," *Gourmet*, October 17, 2007)

When it comes to desserts, Manso shows restraint. Of the three offered, her Cuban flan ($6), made from a family recipe, is the best, unusually—and pleasantly—dense, with delicious caramel sauce. The flourless chocolate cake ($7) wasn't quite chocolate-y enough, and left me longing for a truffle. However, a house-made coconut sorbet ($5), with an intense coconut flavor, couldn't have been better. Despite Manso's broad culinary palate, she uses a light hand to execute some exquisite combinations. She knows her ingredients and how they work together, with mostly very good results. What could be a confusing experience isn't. The flavors never assault—the layered tastes intrigue and delight without overpowering. ("Chef-restaurateur Infuses San Rafael with Tropical Flavors," *San Francisco Chronicle*, January 7, 2005)

These examples suggest that women chefs receive more positive feedback for playing it safe rather than trying to transform a cuisine or style of cooking. Take for example some of the media coverage of chef Amanda Freitag from her time cooking at the Harrison restaurant:

> But it's a restaurant that stays true to the conservative, honorable niche it's carved out, which is that of a contemporary American bistro where you won't have trouble spotting something appealing on the menu, and won't be puzzled when it arrives. . . . Like the Red Cat, which is technically its older sibling but feels like its younger one, the Harrison doesn't promise or deliver out-and-out excitement. But it safeguards against disappointment as well as just about any other Manhattan restaurant. Faint praise? Nah. Just modulated. And, I should add, genuine. ("A Not-So-Old Stand-by," *New York Times*, May 28, 2008)

The review is mostly positive but it suggests that Freitag's cooking is unthreatening and easily accessible. This offers the benefit that her food will not be disappointing to diners, nor will it be challenging, which is a sign of a great chef. While the writer assures the reader they are not offering faint praise of Freitag's cooking, it is still not the kind of praise that offers a glowing recommendation that can help propel a chef's career within the gastronomic field.

Even though Freitag's accolades may seem lukewarm, an accessible approach to cooking does have some advantages. The restaurant business is notoriously difficult to master with many restaurants not surviving the competitive atmosphere for more than a few years. The industry may be even more difficult for women chefs, who can struggle to find investors when they attempt to open their own restaurants (Druckman 2012). However, even when describing successful restaurants there is a tendency to discuss women's cooking as staid and less exciting than their men counterparts. A *San Francisco Chronicle* article entitled "Iconic Restaurants Thriving at 30" (March 5, 2009) describes three San Francisco restaurants that have continued their popularity for thirty years or more. Each are headed by a woman chef and one of the many reasons given for their success is how each "have kept their focus over the decades, never trying to be hot or trendy" and that they "never fell into the trap of 'gratuitous creativity.'" The article quotes another local chef that, after eating at one of these restaurants, said, "you'll walk out of there happy." While it is also acknowledged that each of these chefs "advocated fresh, local, seasonal food long before it was trendy," these women chefs were not singled out as creating new culinary trends.

The message of the article is that these restaurants are not groundbreaking, instead the food is comfortable, satisfying but not challenging or invigorating. Overall there is the sense that this food is not special in the way that men's food can be, and while there is certainly nothing wrong with leaving customers happy, in the larger gastronomic field, this alone is not going to lead to the label of great chef and the professional accolades and rewards this can provide.

Instead, women earn more praise when they cook food that is a good example of an already-accepted culinary tradition. Chef Jody Williams was admired for serving "classic, classic, classic Italian food" ("Where to Go Next: New York," *Food & Wine*, March 2006) and Alicia Montalvo is described as a pastry chef who "interprets popular Italian-inspired" sweets ("Neighborly Local on Rincon Hill," *San Francisco Chronicle*, March 30, 2008). The *San Francisco Chronicle* comments on Amelia Ramirez's cooking of Salvadoran food:

> Ramirez's *sopa de res*, or beef soup ($6.99), is a satisfying rendition of the Salvadoran standard. This peasant dish is a richly flavored and generous portion of beef shank, a wedge of cabbage, carrots, zucchini, celery, and tomatoes in a simple broth infused with lemon and cilantro. ("Latin Flavors Star at Deliciously Kitschy Amelia's," *San Francisco Chronicle*, September 16, 2005)

In none of these examples are women praised for transforming a dish or challenging a traditional cooking paradigm. In these cases, women chefs win accolades, not by redefining culinary traditions, but by upholding them. Ramirez does not challenge what diners think about Salvadoran cuisine, but she provides a good rendition of a common dish. At best, women tweak already accepted dishes to make them subtly different as in the case of San Francisco chef Jamie Lauren and New York chef Amanda Freitag:

> The chef [Jamie Lauren] dresses up the traditional cream of celery root soup ($8) with a crisscross of beet puree and mustard oil, and her take on the classic French frisée salad ($10) includes the super smoky Benton's bacon, whole pencil-size lengths of poached baby leeks and a caviar-topped duck egg with a runny center. ("New Chef Elevates Absinthe, "*San Francisco Chronicle*, August 8, 2007)

When broken, the yolk flows over the greens and adds a rich flavor and texture to the blend. She [Chef Amanda Freitag] is a talented cook, and some of what I had at Sette was terrific, a credit to her way of taking familiar dishes and administering subtle tweaks, tiny inventions (maybe baby revisions would be the most apt phrase). ("Baby Steps on a Road of Good Intentions," *New York Times*, October 5, 2005)

Neither chef radically changes each dish. Instead, note the feminine verb of "dressing up" an already well-known dish. Freitag is described as a talented cook, not chef, and offers only "baby revisions" to her food. Similarly, chef Lisa Eyherabide at the restaurant Gitane is described as innovative not because she changes the flavors of the traditional Moroccan pastry called *bastilla* but because she slightly modifies pastry's form, making it fully enclosed like a turnover and "much easier to eat" ("Gitane a Feast for the Senses," *San Francisco Chronicle*, January 18, 2009).

These descriptions of women chefs and their cooking raise several questions. Are women chefs described as being less inventive or risk taking simply because they are more risk averse and prefer to stay in safer culinary boundaries? This is a reasonable question; however, we again refer back to the power of the home-versus-haute dichotomy between men/professional and women/amateur. Is this food really less challenging or is it merely perceived this way by critics and food writers who (like the rest of society) have been socialized to see men's food as professional and innovative and women's food as amateur and homey? And we cannot neglect the women chefs themselves and how their cooking has been shaped by these perceptions and their interpretations of how they believe they should cook. The background of cultural producers can build expectations about how people think they should create and it can be difficult to find success if someone goes against these expectations (Bourdieu 1993). If women chefs see themselves getting more positive reviews from their culinary instructors, supervising chefs, and the press for cooking in a certain style, this reinforces gendered culinary boundaries. Chefs often alter their aesthetics based upon perceptions of what the audience wants (Fine 1992). When women believe customers and food writers and critics want them to cook homey, nourishing food, this may influence the food they create. Such expectations can even become institutionalized as chefs that are perceived as cooking more provocative food may gain access to stages and jobs within professional kitchens that cook this way. These chefs cement their reputations as provocateurs, while learning more cutting-edge cooking styles that they will take on and even expand upon at their next job.

In several articles there was the comparison of women chef's cooking to home-cooking. Turkish chef and co-owner of Dükkan in Istanbul, Defne Koryurek, is described as a chef who "keeps the menu close to the basic home cooking she was raised on." A *Food & Wine* profile describes her as possibly "the world's most glamorous butcher shop owner" and traces her efforts to bring authentic Turkish food to fine dining restaurants ("Istanbul's Newest Tastemaker," *Food & Wine*, May 2008). The writer compliments how "Defne's food was delicate and refined, but at heart, it was good Turkish home cooking." Other women chefs also receive praise when they cook in the style of a mom or prepare food people remember from their childhoods. Chef Dawn Bruckner is praised for having a "more homey aesthetic" than her more sophisticated men peers ("Farm-to-Table Cuisine in a Homey Package," *New York Times*, December 4, 2009). The wine-braised beef prepared by chef Pamela Busch at Cav earns compliments because it "brought back memories of a homey dish I had at an after-harvest meal at a family wheat farm in Kansas" ("An Accomplished Kitchen to Match the Sublime Wine List at Cav," *San Francisco Chronicle*, May 20, 2007). Pastry chef Nancy Olson is mentioned in a *Food & Wine* article that details her youth in North Dakota where her church created a dessert cookbook ("Baking from the Heartland," *Food & Wine*, November 2007). Even though Olson now works at the highly regarded Gramercy Tavern in New York City, the link to home cooking remains as she is described as "tweak[ing] those homespun favorites to perfection." Her kuchen, the article claims, "easily rivals the myriad kuchens in the book." While Olson's efforts are described as equal to the homey desserts of her childhood, unlike men chefs, there is no discussion of her need to surpass these dishes.

The problem with continually comparing women's professional cooking with home cooking is that it subtly devalues the training and skill required to produce women's professional food. Just as women's cooking in the home is often taken for granted, comparing professional cooking to that done in the home makes such food seem unworthy of attention. By sticking to tradition, women chefs may ensure that diners leave their restaurant pleased or that they do not alienate potential customers, but it also prevents them from receiving the kind of recognition that leads to boosts in one's career and new opportunities that can be presented to elite chefs.

Only one woman chef, Alice Waters, was described as being a pioneer. Waters, who helped found the Berkeley, California, restaurant Chez Panisse in the early 1970s, helped transform American cooking with the development of California cuisine. This type of cooking focuses on the concept that food should be minimally transformed and chefs should obtain the freshest and highest quality local ingredients and prepare them in ways to highlight their natural properties. In the California cuisine style, the ingredients are the star and it is the chef's job to find the best way to showcase them. While Waters is described as an innovative chef, there are also jabs at her legacy. For example, there has been a long debate over just who should be given the lion's share of credit for developing the cuisine at Chez Panisse—Alice Waters or Jeremiah Tower or other early chefs at the restaurant (McNamee 2007). Instead, Waters is just as likely to be described as the restaurant's "guiding spirit" rather than its chef. And it is true that Waters is no longer working behind the stove at Chez Panisse but spends much of her time writing and advocating for food system reform. Now, much of what is written about Waters focuses on her current advocacy work to establish the first White House garden and promoting healthy changes to the federal school lunch program. When there are references to chefs who have trained at Chez Panisse, there is little discussion of their work with Waters and more attention given to how well their cooking embodies the lessons of the restaurant and not its founder.

ORIENTATION TOWARD CAREER: EMPIRE BUILDERS VERSUS AVOIDING ATTENTION

A major focus of food writing on men chefs was the men's workaholic or obsessive attention to cooking that allowed them to build their careers, earn accolades, and create culinary empires. Star chef Fabio Trabocchi is profiled in an article that described how "his rise as a chef is due as much to hard work as to enormous talent" ("A Star Chef's Italian Christmas," *Food & Wine*, December 2008). Some men chefs are applauded for cooking ten hours a day, and others are praised for the time spent making specific, time-intensive dishes, such as in this article on Portland, Maine, chef Rob Evans:

> But like anyone repeatedly indulged, diners have become spoiled, taking for granted just how much painstaking labor—and time—goes into a meal. We took a stopwatch into the kitchen at Hugo's restaurant in Portland, Me., where a single entree—rabbit with tripe ravioli, spring-dug parsnips, and fava beans—is seven days in the making (and more than six hours of hands-on cooking). Make no mistake: Speed is essential in a professional kitchen. Hugo's chef, Rob Evans, can take apart three rabbit carcasses in less than an hour, teasing out the tiny rib chops, thinning the flanks and placing the hind legs in salt for confit with remarkable confidence and delicacy. Even so, his food takes forever to prepare. Evans, who spent time at the French Laundry, in Napa Valley, and the Inn at Little Washington, in Virginia, before returning to New England, doesn't cut corners; if anything, he invents extra corners along the way. He molds the filling for his tripe ravioli into little spheres, a half-sphere at a time, "because it looks awesome," he says happily. He peels the membranes from the fava beans before blanching them, so that the final bean looks bright and fresh. Even the sauce, a mere tablespoon of which will be drizzled on the plate, requires two-and-a-half days of coddling as it reduces on the stove.
>
> You'd have to visit a hunter-gatherer society to find anyone else who devotes this much time to the pursuit of dinner. If only diners spent as much time savoring it. The total time to eat the dish? Eleven minutes and 28 seconds. ("173 Hours 24 minutes 6 Seconds Until Dinner," *New York Times*, May 1, 2005)

Evans's insistence on such precise and time-consuming cooking is given as proof of his dedication to his craft and the quality of his food. The writer implores spoiled diners to pay more attention to the hard work and talent that goes into professional cooking.

Such descriptions of hard working and obsessive men chefs were common. Chef Scott Tycer is mentioned as a "self-described control freak" by a *Gourmet* writer ("First Taste Textile," December 5, 2008). Danish chef Claus Meyer's interest in promoting Nordic cuisine is called his "mission in life" in the pages of *Food & Wine* ("Manifesto for a New Nordic Cuisine," May 2007). The magazine also discusses how Eric Ripert is "completely obsessed with fish" and says of himself and his underchefs, "Twenty-four-seven we think, cook, eat, and create around fish" ("Go To List: New York City," May 2009). The well-known chef Charlie Trotter is similarly described:

> Most would agree that it was Charlie Trotter who broke the chokehold that steakhouses and crusty French establishments had held on the city since the 1800's. His eponymous dining room remains the Chicago restaurant against which all others are compared. His reputation as an obsessive perfectionist explains why his food is so good, and why you can't swing a lobster in a high-end Chicago kitchen without beaning a former Trotter sous-chef. ("Gastrohub," *New York Times*, September 25, 2005)

The comments about Trotter link his "obsessive perfectionist" attitude to his success as a chef and the reason why so many of those who cook under him go on to have well-established careers. These are just some of the rewards awaiting those who completely commit to their work. Another reward is media attention, which can be a powerful way of attracting investors and customers to one's restaurant. Once men chefs reached a certain level of industry attention, they were shown reverence by food writers, whose articles would mention their status as a "culinary god." For example, Michel Bras is described as a "deity" and "arguably France's most revered chef" ("Dinner with a Deity: Master Chef Michel Bras," *Food & Wine*, February 2009). The terms, "legendary," "monkish," "hallucinant," and "purity" are interspersed in an article on a dinner party where he cooks. Throughout the article, Bras and similar chefs are shown as being completely dedicated to their craft. Much like Joan Acker's (1990) research on the ideal worker, the portrait of the obsessive man that devotes all his time and attention to a career is also apparent in the description of chefs. This complete dedication to one's craft and career is celebrated among men chefs and the rewards for this devotion are being named an "icon" or one of the "greatest" chefs in the world.

Another reward is being able to expand beyond a single restaurant to multiple restaurants, as well as other opportunities such as cookbook publishing, television appearances, and endorsement and consulting deals which can easily double or triple a chef's yearly income. The creation of a culinary empire is often described as the obvious next step for obsessive men chefs' careers. For example, New York chef Jim Botsacos has earned praise for his Greek restaurant, Molyvos, and recently opened an Italian restaurant named Abboccato. Botsacos splits his time between the two restaurants and when asked why he took on the new challenge, he replied:

> "It gives me growth potential for earnings," Mr. Botsacos said of his two-toques situation, "and growth potential for creativity." Mr. Botsacos has a family, and a mortgage on an Upper West Side apartment, and as a partner in Abboccato he will reap a share of the profits. ("A Chef Who Wears Two Toques," *New York Times*, May 1, 2005)

An article on chef Marc Vetri also described the push behind opening multiple restaurants:

> There's a lot the restaurants Osteria and Vetri don't have in common. There's one very lucky thing they do. Both are helmed by Marc Vetri, whose enormous talents have brought him a widespread, fervent regard he has never really exploited. And with the opening of Osteria in February, he has taken a huge step. He has bucked his obsessive, controlling nature and accepted what is apparently nearly every acclaimed contemporary chef's fate: to multitask across multiple stages. . . . He apparently spends half of every night at Vetri, half at Osteria, because he can't just let either of them be. That would be hazardous. That would also be some other chef. ("A Chef to the Few Heeds the Call of the Many," *New York Times*, May 23, 2007)

In both cases, the two chefs are described positively for continuing to cook at both of their restaurants. This is not always possible for some chefs whose empires can span continents and whose television appearances and other ventures continually call for their presence outside the kitchen. For every superstar chef like Daniel Boulud, who is praised for retaining quality at his six distinct restaurants across the United States, there are numerous chefs called out for neglecting the restaurants that helped launch their empires. These conditions help highlight an important predicament for men chefs who grow their empires: the same customers and food writers and reviewers that helped build their reputation can be extremely critical of chefs whose outside ventures lead to less than stellar food at their restaurants. Without the chef on hand to maintain quality, new restaurants and other projects can quickly turn south, and the criticism lobbed at these chefs can be harsh and result in a loss of important social capital (Stringfellow et al. 2013). Tom Colicchio, the chef probably better known now as one of the judges on the television cooking competition *Top Chef*, recalled receiving a "wake-up call" when one of his new restaurants received tepid reviews ("3 Chefs Depart, 2 with Full Plates," *New York Times*, August 23, 2006). Colicchio went on to admit he needed to "pay more attention to what I'm doing there" in order to maintain the quality of his restaurants, although the writer pointedly noted that Colicchio was preparing to open his eighth restaurant.

Perhaps the most damning critique of the rise of culinary empires came in a 2006 piece in the *New York Times* in which head food critic, Frank Bruni, blamed the rise of elite restaurant brands for causing the New York dining scene to lose some of its unique culinary flavor. He writes:

> And make no mistake: Mr. [Alan] Yau and Mr. [Gordon] Ramsay are brands. So is Thomas Keller, the chef at the French Laundry in the Napa Valley. His Manhattan restaurant, Per Se, which opened in 2004, has a different name, but it's in many senses just the French Laundry in a citified rather than countrified frock. And when he initially expanded beyond Napa, he hit Vegas first, opening the restaurant Bouchon. . . . Their restaurants, too, are brands—more rarefied and less ubiquitous versions of the Olive Garden and the Outback Steakhouse, to mention the profane among the sacred. And that's precisely why they can penetrate and dominate the New York market, where smaller, less proven establishments and operators are discouraged by the markedly increased costs of opening a new restaurant. ("Making It There Before They Make It Here," *New York Times*, September 6, 2006)

While Bruni acknowledges that comparing one of Thomas Keller's restaurants to an Olive Garden may be controversial, his point is that what these two very different restaurants have in common is that they are both built off a distinct brand. Just as someone going into an Olive Garden anywhere in the country knows what kind of food and dining experience to expect, those who visit one of Keller's outposts know his culinary vision and orientation will guide their meal. Bruni goes on to detail how several high-end restaurateurs engage in "culinary cloning"—serving the same dishes in restaurants with the same décor as their original establishments. Not only does this rob New York of less culinary creativity, it can be hard for lesser known chefs to compete. Because these empire chefs are known quantities, they can attract investors and open large, flashy restaurants leaving fewer openings for up-and-comers.

There is a fine line among elite chefs: in order to truly be considered the top of one's profession, chefs are encouraged to open multiple restaurants and explore other venues such as television shows or celebrity product lines and endorsements. But, if any part of one's empire is seen as less than stellar, the chef risks being stripped of their title of a great chef (Fantasia 2010; Stringfellow et al. 2013). One such elite chef who faced this dilemma was Alain Ducasse, who fired the executive chef at one of his restaurants when the establishment was downgraded to three stars from four. An article in the *New York Times* about the split ended with Ducasse promising to spend more time in his New York restaurant ("As Restaurant Falls to Three Stars, Ducasse Drops Chef," July 7, 2010). Men chefs must carefully weigh the potential costs and benefits and cleverly strategize in order to give the impression they can be in more than one place at a time.

Even when men chefs were lauded for their status as a cooking master with a worldwide culinary empire, they were also praised when they showed they were regular guys. In a profile of chef Laurent Bras, he is applauded for his sense of humor despite his shyness. An article on chef Joël Robuchon makes mention that he wears a black chef's coat like the rest of his underchefs even though he could insist on wearing a special jacket symbolizing that he has won a prestigious cooking competition ("Robuchon Headlines in Las Vegas," *Food & Wine*, February 2006). Two articles were particularly effusive in their praise of down-to-earth chefs:

Chef Paul Kahan has been showered with the sort of adulation normally reserved for dead poets and southern football coaches. Named an F&W best new chef 1999 for his work at Chicago's *Blackbird*, Kahan has been described as a genius more times than is healthy for anyone who's still alive. Indeed, at this point in his career, people would probably make reservations to watch him butter toast. So on first meeting Kahan, 43, one might expect some arrogance or, at the least, affectation. Instead, he's all bed-head and Midwestern bonhomie. Arrestingly unpretentious, Kahan is the sort of guy who regularly goes ice fishing and refers to himself and his partners as "knuckleheads." It's as if the coolest guy on the company softball team also happens to be a star tenor at the Met. ("Great Beer from Around the World Meets Its Food Match," *Food & Wine*, June 2006)

[The food at Mia Dona represents] . . . a portrait of a rising young chef with more practicality than vanity, even though the acclaim that's rushed his way over the last few years has given him ample reason to preen. Meet Michael Psilakis, renegade and realist. On the heels of his James Beard Award nomination, his Esquire-magazine coronation and other affirmations, you might expect him to reach for a fussier level of accomplishment, polishing his crown. You might expect a new restaurant from him to feel like a throne. ("Pampering and Beer in Pitchers," *New York Times*, April 2, 2008)

Many chefs work for years with little to no acknowledgment and to be awarded a major honor from national outlets is an exciting event. Media attention, beyond just improving the bottom line through increased diners, can propel a chef's standing within this incredibly competitive industry. Both chefs have won numerous awards (Kahan was a *Food & Wine* "Best New Chef" while Psilakis was named *Esquire* magazine's "Chef of the Year"). Such honors, the articles suggest, are sign of the talent, creativity, and hard work of the chefs and reason enough for them to act "arrogant" or to "preen." Instead, Kahan's and Psilakis' more low-key attitudes about their awards and praise earned for their cooking are testaments to their "coolness."

Another factor that adds to the regular guys portrayal of the chefs is that each has chosen to make his next restaurant a more casual place. This is part of a new trend in which elite chefs choose to open bistros or similar restaurants instead of high-end establishments. Several reasons for this change were given. Younger chefs, like the highly regarded New York chef David Chang, may choose this route because they want more control over their restaurants and don't want to feel that they have to cook in a certain style to fit the fine dining concept. At the other end of the career spectrum, some writers suggest that older chefs may turn to a more casual style because this would be less physically demanding and a way of slowing down at the end of their careers. The most popular reason given was that the men chefs want a new challenge or to cook in a way that they find fun. Paul Kahan, who was discussed earlier, is opening a more casual restaurant. His decision, the writer emphasizes, is not borne out of a desire to make money but a chance "to do what he wants, and what he wants is to open the sort of place where he'd want to eat on his nights off" ("Great Beer from Around the World Meets Its Food Match," Food & Wine, June 2006).

In somewhat extreme cases of trying to be "regular guys," two chefs renounced both the cuisine that made their careers and the numerous awards that came with it. Chef Lance Fegen boldly states "I don't want any more awards" to a writer from *Food & Wine* ("Where to Go Next: Texas," November 2006). Instead, he wants to cook in a way that he finds challenging. Another example came from chef Alain Senderens:

> "I don't want to compete anymore," Mr. Senderens said last spring. "I am 65 years old, and I want to have some fun." Whereupon he closed Lucas Carton, gave up the three Michelin stars he had held for 28 years and said he would develop a new restaurant, with "three-star cuisine but not at three-star prices." He said he would refuse to accept any Michelin stars. Earlier this year, Alain Senderens announced that he would close Lucas Carton, his venerable three-star restaurant, and reopen it as a bistro. "When I thought about what the stars represented," Senderens said, "I realized they were really just supporting my ego, and that was stupid." ("A Sober 3-Star Parisian Remade," *New York Times*, March 1, 2006)

Unfortunately for Senderens and the numerous chefs who would happily take his Michelin stars, the Michelin Guide still awarded his new bistro two stars. These chefs are perfect examples of what Bourdieu (1993) viewed as artists who create for other artists. They no longer want the praise or to follow the rules of the gastronomic field. Instead, they would rather opt out and leave the pressure behind. Just like how "pure" artists shouldn't try and earn praise from critics or other consecrating organizations, they also shouldn't appear motivated by money. In most of the coverage of a man chef choosing to open a more casual restaurant, great pains are taken by the writer to assure readers that such changes are not guided by money, but by a desire of the chef to hold control, scale down at the end of a career, cook in a more personally rewarding fashion, or make their cooking more accessible to a diverse audience. Within these stories are subtle contradictions. While a man chef who owns a culinary empire is described as being a good businessman, business cannot be at the forefront of his decision-making. To make food more about money than artistic expression risks critiques of one's motives and dedication to the craft of professional cooking. Chefs, as artists, are not supposed to be motivated by money. Applying a quote of Bourdieu (1993) to today's chefs: "Chefs can get old, but they can't get fat."

In this instance, to get fat means to become more oriented toward making money than honing and reinventing one's craft, and these articles warned chefs against succumbing to the temptation to cash in on their reputations.

Another way restaurant reviews and chef profiles reinforced the idea of respected men chefs as just regular guys was through descriptions of their families. A writer for the *San Francisco Chronicle* describes meeting chef Ken Frank a decade earlier and found him to be prickly and egotistical. Recent changes to Frank's life, including moving to Napa Valley, getting married, and having his son work in his kitchen has "smoothed out the edges" of the chef's personality ("Cooks Night Out: Ken Frank," March 27, 2005). Other men chefs were described as undergoing a change once they became fathers. Suddenly, they were more patient and less obsessive, but this did not mean they lost any of their skills or dedication to their work. These articles also mention men chefs spending time with family, which is shown as a sign of character and the ability to balance one's home life and career effectively. The profiles included cute examples of men chefs whose children visited them at their restaurant or wrote about cooking for their families on their days off. These articles helped establish that, even though these men were culinary gods at their restaurants, they were just regular dads at home.

In contrast, women chefs were rarely discussed in terms of obsession and building empires. Some are described as falling into the cooking profession, while others actively tried to avoid attention for their work. This is a far cry from the driven, career-focused man chef. However, even when women do own multiple restaurants and have branched out into other parts of the gastronomic field, they are not described as empire builders. They are motivated more by pleasing people and spending time with family. If women are described as moving up the next step in their career, it is due to their guidance by an influential man.

Unlike profiles of men chefs obsessed with their careers from an early age, several examples of women chefs depicted them as stumbling into their career. A profile of pastry chef Melissa Chou described how:

. . . when she and her boyfriend decided to move back to San Francisco, it seemed to make sense to enroll in the six-month pastry program at Tante Marie Cooking School. For one, it was a way to put off the higher degree she knew she would need to pursue in art. . . . Next thing she knew she was the pastry chef at Aziza. ("Rising Star Chefs 2009: Melissa Chou," *San Francisco Chronicle*, March 15, 2009)

Another story on chef Paula Frazier describes the "happy accident" when she bought her restaurant from its previous owner ("A Southern Hand Delivers an Italian Feast," *New York Times*, August 12, 2007). The restaurant served Italian food, which was Frazier's specialty, so she decided to leave the menu "pretty much intact." In profiles of men chefs, much attention is given to the hours worked per week and the years devoted to be a culinary master. They are dedicated to understanding the ins and outs of a particular cooking style and then developing their own approach. For women like Chou and Frazier, their efforts are reduced and their accomplishments presented as more a matter of luck than hard work. This fits with the narrative presented by other writers in which women chefs are motivated by a need to help and serve others in their careers rather than present a culinary vision.

The focus on the customer and pleasing others echoed throughout the profiles of women in the culinary industry. Women, it seemed, were not singled out because their cuisine reinvented professional cooking (which is a first step to building an empire). Instead, women were praised for being ambassadors that made food accessible to others or providing mentoring to others. An example of this comes from a story on chef Hermance Carro:

> Last year, French television producers documenting the opening of a restaurant staffed by a dozen untrained twentysomethings came to chef Hermance Carro. Could their show, based on British chef Jamie Oliver's project *Fifteen*, feature Carro's about-to-open Le Relais d'Oléa as the testing ground? She said yes: "But it wasn't to be on TV. I wanted to help young people find something they love to do." The restaurant and the show, *Madame le Chef*, premiered in April, and today Carro is a celebrity who also happens to run a lovely bistro, with three of the TV *stagiaires* as helpers. ("Where to Go Next: Provence," *Food & Wine*, July 2006)

Unlike Oliver, who transformed his cooking into a television empire, Carro had lower ambitions. She was guided by a desire to help young people find their passion and, at the time of this story, rather than gearing up for a television empire, Carro runs a lovely bistro. Other profiles of women chefs specifically referenced how uncomfortable the women were with media attention. Karen Small, a Cleveland-based chef, claimed she is "happy to remain under the radar" ("Food Across America: Cleveland, OH," *Food & Wine*, November 2007). Another woman chef asked a newspaper not to print the name of her restaurant fearing that the small establishment would be unable to handle the onslaught of new customers. Rather than seeing media coverage as an opportunity, these women were threatened by the attention.

Our critique of how women's career motives are depicted in food media is not meant to suggest that all men chefs desire empires and all women chefs just want to make people happy with their food. Writers are trying to convey complicated feelings in a way that can be understandable to an audience. But insisting that women are motivated differently than men regarding success has been used for many years to deny women power at work (Kanter 1977). Women who cook professionally in order to show that they care or to make others happy can find their efforts devalued. Just as maternal food work done in the home is often overlooked and labeled as "caring" and not as "work," women's professional cooking can also be seen as being of a lower status and not of the same value as men's cooking (England and Folbre 1999).

We were struck by how rarely women—even those who owned numerous restaurants—were still not discussed as empire builders like their male counterparts. Several articles about women restaurant owners only casually mentioned their success within the gastronomic field. For example, Suzanne Goin in Los Angeles was praised—not for owning multiple restaurants and writing a well-received cookbook—but for being able to create such welcoming spaces for customers. When describing Traci Des Jardins's career after earning a *Food & Wine* Best New Chef award, more attention is given to her work on food sustainability than the fact that she owns three restaurants.

Other articles suggest that women should be careful about opening multiple restaurants. The *San Francisco Chronicle* article about the women-headed restaurants still going strong after thirty years quoted a local caterer who gave the following as one reason for their success: "The three remarkable women who head these restaurants are not interested in attaining celebrity status and building empires. They are exactly where they want to be, she says—at the stoves of their kitchens." Later, one of the women chefs says, "Our goals haven't changed—we want to make people happy" ("Iconic Restaurants Thriving at 30," *San Francisco Chronicle*, March 5, 2009).

These three women are described as successful at their current venture—helming one restaurant and making people happy with their food. This alone is quite an accomplishment as one in four restaurants close or change owners within the first year, and this figure rises to 60 percent within three years (Parsa et al. 2005). While the commentator was emphatic that these women were "exactly where they wanted to be," it raises questions about the longevity of their careers. Cooking is a physically strenuous job and part of developing a culinary empire is that one can move into management rather than production roles. Such comments also could dissuade other women chefs from attempting to branch out. In a story on chef Meg Grace in the *New York Times*, the writer details Grace's efforts to open a bar with some partners in the trendy East Village neighborhood. Their goal was to expand the bar's food offerings and eventually become a full restaurant:

> For more than six months Ms. Grace was a kitchen staff of one, more or less. As she put together her once-a-week prix-fixe menus, which presented season-conscious comfort food that bore the stamp of her years in New Orleans, she did the ordering, the prep work—all of that. On Thursdays she'd get a helper to plate the food and clean up, though Ms. Grace did as much of the dishwashing herself. . . . And it's here that Ms. Grace, 36, has taken a leap forward in her career, which is clearly one to watch, because of her ego-restrained way of preparing familiar, even lowbrow fare with such exacting standards and such sagely chosen grace notes that it takes on an unfamiliar luster. ("A Chef Walks into a Bar," *New York Times*, August 19, 2009)

However, after complementing her on a dish, the critic warns Grace (and readers) about the risk involved, asking, "Now that she's doing a full menu to a full (and frenzied) house, are there a few more missteps?" This question is rarely asked of men chefs who are expected to expand out their empire and continuously challenge themselves. Men may be critiqued for stretching themselves too thin but it is usually only after they open a new venture and it is clear that their oversight is lacking.

These articles reduce the professional nature of women chefs' careers. This is further noted in the numerous articles that describe women chefs as needing guidance from men in order to reach their full potential. This guidance can be aimed at women's cooking, such as in a 2007 story from

Food & Wine about a pizza created by Nancy Silverton for a restaurant she has opened with star chef Mario Batali:

> I especially love Pizzeria Mozza's most decadent selection—the Bianca. It's covered with creamy mozzarella (Silverton is L.A.'s mozzarella queen), pungent Fontina, and the truffle-infused, aged-cow's-milk sottocenere, as well as a few well-placed crispy fried sage leaves. The dish was Silverton's idea ("I love the look of a white pizza"), but she consulted with Batali on the components. ("Best Restaurant Dishes of 2007," *Food & Wine*, December 2007)

Batali is also mentioned in an article about the cooking career of Lidia Bastianich, a New York chef who is known for her restaurant, Felidia, and who has hosted several cooking series on PBS for over sixteen years. Bastianich has opened other restaurants with Batali and her son, the restaurateur Joe Bastianich. A writer from the *New York Times* called her cooking "between regal and rustic," and explained how Batali's partnership in the restaurant received the most attention. The article mentions how "Ms. Bastianich leaves most of the cooking these days to her longtime executive chef, Fortunato Nicotra" but goes on to note:

> [When designing and opening del Posto] Ms. Bastianich did more than stand there for hours on end, whisking zabaglione and courting carpal tunnel syndrome. She contributed recipes, ideas, and a crucial refinement, evident in some of the roasts, risottos, and flourishes. ("Comfort, Between Regal and Rustic," *New York Times*, August 20, 2006)

This article notes the assumption that, because Batali is such a superstar chef, he would be awarded credit for their collaboration. Bastianich has built much of her public persona around the concept of the caring Italian nonna on her TV shows, so the idea that she is also an extremely successful restaurant owner is contradictory to this image and, therefore, the writer must remind readers of her contributions.

Perhaps the most telling example of women depicted as needing men's guidance to succeed came in a profile of Miami chef Michelle Bernstein from *Food & Wine* ("Miami's Hottest Latin Party," June 2006). In it, Bernstein is described as in the process of "becoming a superstar;" however, when asked about her restaurant, Michy, Bernstein explains, "It's not really a concept. . . . It's kind of just a restaurant." This is given as proof that she needs guidance from a man restaurateur to live up to her promise. Jeffrey Chodorow, who selected Bernstein to be a concept chef for his chain of Social restaurants, is said to have seen in Bernstein "a talented chef with a perfectly marketable package" that includes her status as an attractive woman who is an ex-ballerina. When discussing future collaborations with Bernstein, Chodorow is quoted as saying, "We're going to give her tremendous exposure." In contrast, a description of Chodorow's collaborations with chef Todd English describes their working together as a partnership, suggesting more of an equal footing that the Pygmalion-esque transformation he seems to suggest Bernstein needs.

Women's career aspirations were shown to be more modest and focused on the availability of time for family or even integrating family into the restaurant by working alongside a spouse. A *Gourmet* profile of pastry chef Megan Garrelts describes her waiting tables "while cradling her two-week-old daughter in the crook of her arm" ("A Snooty Response," June 17, 2007). There were also several examples of women chefs who altered their career ambitions in order to fit in work and motherhood. Women chefs moved out of restaurant kitchens and into catering or cookbook authoring. Mary Ellen Diaz actually left the world of restaurants behind to work at a Chicago soup kitchen:

> I had a great restaurant career, but I felt like I had to make a choice about whether or not to stay. I wanted to be home at night reading books to my little girl instead of slaving away in the kitchen. So it actually started with me wanting to have time for my family while I was figuring out what to do. ("Soul-Soothing Soups," *Food & Wine*, November 2006)

Chef Allison Vines-Rushing ("A Pair of Rising Stars Opts Out of Manhattan," *New York Times*, May 11, 2005) and Chef M. J. Adams ("Meat Rules," *Gourmet*, July 2008) also based career decisions on family needs. In both cases, the women decided to leave larger cities to move closer to their families (Vines-Rushing to Louisiana and Adams to South Dakota). Vines-Rushing cited a desire to be closer to family once she had children, and she also said her decision made business sense as she was doubtful how long southern-inspired cuisine would be able to support a restaurant in New York. These portrayals of work and family are quite different for men and women chefs. Men are made more human when it is shown how they balance family life into their work, but women are shown to alter their careers to fit in family. In contrast to family providing a sense of balance for ambitious, overworked men chefs, the women chose to alter their career paths in order to better meet family needs.

NO "GREAT" WOMEN CHEFS?

Our examination of food media suggests that men and women chefs are evaluated differently along a number of axes. Great chefs appear to be men who have multiple restaurants, whether they actually cook in them or not. They are avant garde iconoclasts who create food movements, such as molecular gastronomy. Women chefs who are good, but not great, stay out of the media spotlight, avoid being interested in celebrity, and try to teach and help others. Overall, women chefs receive much less attention than their men counterparts.

When journalist Charlotte Druckman (2010) approached the women editors-in-chief of *Gourmet* and *Food & Wine* about the discrepancy in how the media covered men and women chefs, the editors expressed concern that any systematic effort to provide more equal coverage to women would be seen as sexist because it would insinuate that women were unable to compete with men professionally on a level playing field. This response is similar to that of the editors of *Time* magazine's "Gods of Food" issue who proposed the circular argument that, as long as women chefs weren't being included in the media, the media shouldn't force women's inclusion into food coverage. Such responses fail to acknowledge the institutional power critics and other journalists have in shaping and reinforcing ideas about how artists are evaluated (Baumann 2002; Bielby et al. 2005; Bourdieu 1993; Townley, Beech, and McKinlay 2009). The playing field for women chefs is already stacked against them because of industry norms that are biased toward stereotypically masculine work behaviors, such as challenging authority and single-minded devotion to one's career and cultural ideas about what types of cooking are valued (Druckman 2010). The chef profiles and restaurant reviews we analyzed reinforce the traditional home/haute and women/men dichotomy in professional cooking. Men's efforts were described as groundbreaking expressions of individual talent and vision and, therefore, evidence of their fit with the term "great chef." In contrast, the creative, technical, and business acumen of women chefs are called into question as their food is compared to less valued home cooking and their career outcomes are linked to their ability to be recognized by powerful men in the industry.

Of course, it could be that men and women chefs are depicted differently because they are different. One could argue that men and women have radically dissimilar cooking styles and career aspirations because of gender socialization and differing choices and desires. However, an experiment conducted by journalists to try and guess the gender of a chef after a blind taste test of food have shown that 1) it is difficult to deduce the gender of who prepares a dish and 2) the chefs, knowledgeable of the stereotypes of men and women's cooking, confound the experiments by purposefully cooking dishes that go against these gender norms (Druckman 2010). In contrast, numerous studies offer convincing evidence that people evaluate men and women differently, even when they have the same skills (Castilla 2008; Correll and Benard 2006; Roth 2006). If asked, critics might say that they are evaluating merit fairly and equally. We did not interview food critics themselves because evaluators often do not know that they are in fact relying on gender bias to evaluate merit. But the continued celebration of great men chefs comes less from natural differences in how men and women chefs express themselves than by culturally constructed ideas about how men and women should cook and what kind of cooking is valued. For women, subjective industry standards of greatness appears skewed in favor of men, and such standards may serve as a mechanism that perpetuates gender segregation and discrimination within the gastronomic field, as well as other creative industries.

3 · FITTING IN AND STANDING OUT

Entering the Professional Restaurant Kitchen

At the time of her interview, Tabitha was thirty-four years old and working as a pastry chef at a fine dining restaurant, although she had experience working as a sous chef on the hot side of the kitchen as well. Tabitha had graciously offered to meet Deborah at her workplace before her shift started to talk about her job, and the interview took place in the large, formal dining room of the restaurant. A tall, broad-shouldered woman of mixed racial ancestry, Tabitha sported several burn scars on her hands and arms from her work. She was an entertaining interviewee, and her answers were often punctuated with boisterous laughter even when she was discussing serious topics, such as what it was like to be, as she referred to it, a "double minority" in the kitchen as a woman who also identified as African American.

Recalling different points of her career, Tabitha described several times she felt her gender and race impacted how she was treated at work. Sometimes the stories involved small concerns, like coworkers who tried to accommodate Tabitha by playing rap music during prep time (Tabitha admitted she'd prefer listening to Black Flag). Other times she candidly described larger issues that could have direct impact on her career, such as when the head chef-owner wouldn't send Tabitha out into the dining room to interact with customers who wanted to meet the pastry chef responsible for their desserts. Tabitha felt this was related to the fact that she didn't look like a typical chef who is often "a big white guy in a coat." Even when her words implied that these issues bothered her, Tabitha's demeanor suggested she was the type of person who did her best to not let personal or professional slights get the best of her. The one exception to this positive attitude came about three-fourths of the way through her interview. As Tabitha and Deborah were discussing her work, the door to the restaurant opened and the head chef-owner walked in. He looked curiously at Deborah and seemed to wonder why a stranger was sitting in his dining room with a tape recorder out on one of the tables. At this point, Tabitha called out her hellos and explained that Deborah was there to interview her about what it was like to be a woman chef. "Ooooh," the head chef-owner responded laughing, "Avoid them at all costs. Remember the magic words: Not bad for a chick [laughs]!"

Tabitha returned his laughter and replied that, when it came to his cooking, the kitchen staff says, "Not bad for an old dude." The laughter and banter continued as the head chef-owner continued on to the kitchen, but as soon as the door to the kitchen closed behind him, Tabitha's expression became serious. She turned and said through gritted teeth: "*That* is the type of shit I was telling you about."

The chef-owner's comments and Tabitha's radical shift from jovial, contented worker to frustrated, put-upon employee is an excellent example of the ways women chefs are commonly called upon to respond to gender stereotypes at work. Tabitha's reactions, both the joking comebacks lobbed at her boss and the annoyed response she shared with Deborah, demonstrate how women chefs are often aware of the numerous roles they are called upon to enact in the kitchen. Women chefs face discrimination, mistreatment, hazing, and sexual harassment at work (Cooper 1997; Fine 1987; Fine 1996b). This treatment serves as constant reminders of women's token and outsider status within specific restaurant worlds and the gastronomic field as a whole. It also reinforces notions that men and women are different and bolsters hegemonic masculinity in workplaces (Bird 1996). Women who work in male-dominated occupations report that they must toughen up and show men that they can "hang" with the guys, as one of our respondents called it. Similar to women in firefighting (Yoder and Aniakudo 1997), construction trades (Denissen 2010a), and coal mining (Tallichet 2000), women chefs report that they must endure various tests of their strength and mettle to fit in, gain respect, and move up the hierarchy at work. These additional demands increase the physical, mental, and emotional labor expected of women employees and can become another stumbling block to women hoping to succeed as a chef.

A likely reason that men sexually harass, test, and discriminate toward women is to keep them out and protect their occupation from feminization threat. Actually, men chefs' concerns about their occupation feminizing are not unfounded. The higher the percentage of women in an occupation, the lower the pay (Cohen and Huffman 2003; Mandel 2013; Reskin and Roos 1990; Tomaskovic-Devey 1993). In fact, we see decreases in pay in occupations that were at one time male-dominated and became female-dominated. For example, elementary school teaching was a male-dominated occupation until the early 1900s. In the twentieth century, it became female-dominated as more men entered manufacturing work and left these jobs. Teaching then became associated with femininity and women's "true calling." Over time, the pay started to decrease. According to Paula England, a major explanation for this gendered pattern in pay is the devaluation of femininity. These jobs are compensated at such low levels because they are viewed as "women's work" and unimportant. These conditions have become entrenched and she notes, "[T]here has been little cultural or institutional change in the devaluation of traditionally female activities and jobs, and as a result, women have had more incentive than men to move into gender-nontraditional activities and positions" (2010, 150). Carework is particularly devalued (England and Folbre 1999), so men chefs have had to work to distinguish professional cooking from cooking done in the home to delineate the boundaries between masculine work and feminine work. Because men have controlled the majority of professional kitchens, over time, these environments have developed workplace cultures that are hypermasculine. Fitting in to these workplaces can be difficult for women who want to work as chefs.

How do women chefs deal with issues of gender stereotypes and mistreatment at work? Because they are a numerical minority, women chefs generally find themselves surrounded by men in the workforce. We find that women chefs not only have to prove they can physically and emotionally handle the stresses of the job, they also have to assure their men coworkers that they will not try to change the insular and hypermasculine environment at work. When professional kitchens are faced with feminization threat as a woman begins working within male-dominated spaces, the women are expected to neutralize the threat and sustain the precarious masculinity of men working in the kitchen.

Before continuing, we want to address some potential issues with our interviews. Our sampling procedure and number of participants (33) doesn't allow us to speak for every woman chef. When conducting qualitative research there is always the question of sampling bias and whether or not participants have self-selected due to having extreme opinions. In other words, were the thirty-three women we interviewed outliers within the chef occupation? Were they so willing to participate in our study because they had axes to grind or were a group of complainers looking for an audience? We actually found that the overwhelming majority of our participants were reluctant to criticize their jobs, fellow employees and supervisors, and the larger gastronomic field. The women chefs we interviewed had complicated feelings about their roles in the kitchen. While all of the women we spoke with could recall negative experiences, many argued that these conditions ultimately made them stronger and better able to work in professional kitchens. Other women said that gender no longer mattered as a chef and used the concept of gender neutrality to question why we were even doing this study but, in the next breath, they shared stories about times when they were discriminated against or mistreated in highly gendered ways. Universal among the chefs was a love of food and cooking that came through despite everything else. Part of our goal in this chapter is to explore these complex positions. In doing so, we do not want to define these women's experiences for them, but we try to untangle some of the contradictory meanings our participants have assigned to events in their work lives and explore the ways in which these conditions help explain women's continued underrepresentation as professional chefs.

HOT, CROWDED, AND DIRTY

So what are professional cooking environments like? First of all, as the women chefs pointed out, they are nothing like the sparkling, relaxed atmospheres that are shown on the Food Network. Time and time again our participants informed us that being a chef is not a glamorous job. Many chefs work in restaurants, which are divided into "front of the house" jobs like hostesses and wait staff and "back of the house" jobs as chefs, cooks, and dishwashers. Kitchens are hot, loud, messy, crowded, and often even dangerous places to work. Generally, kitchens are divided into "hot" and "cold" sides. The hot side of the kitchen is where entrees are cooked on large cooktops or baked in ovens. The cold side is where the bakery and dessert stations are located.

Rose, a culinary instructor, described: "The kitchen is a weird mix of people. We're not normal. We're very artistic. We follow our own beats. We work weird shifts. We have weird days off." All of this, the women argued, combined to create a work environment that not only was different from many white-collar professional jobs, but that this difference was what drew such unique people to the occupation. Much of white-collar work has been transformed via a corporate influence that diminishes individual freedom of expression in the workplace and replaces it with strict, bureaucratic rules about everything from lunch breaks to defining professional attire. As a result, the "raunchiness" of some kitchens can prove to be a reprieve where social misfits can bloom.

These misfits work together for incredibly long hours. It was not unusual for our participants to work ten-to-fourteen-hour days, six days a week, spending much of this time constantly on their feet. Fine dining restaurants may only be open at night, so chefs who worked on the hot side of these kitchens would come to work around noon and get off work from midnight to 2:00 A.M. Pastry chefs tended to have different schedules and would come in early in the morning (5:00 to 6:00 A.M.) to begin baking bread and preparing desserts for that night's diners. While some of the pastry chefs we interviewed were able to leave by 3:00 or 4:00 in the afternoon, sometimes they would return to the restaurant during dinner service to help with plating and serving desserts.

The physical conditions of many restaurant kitchens can be trying (Sinclair 2006). On the hot side of the kitchen, temperatures can easily reach 100 degrees. Chefs often have to lift and carry heavy items, like industrial-sized stockpots filled with hundreds of pounds of bones used for making stock. They work with sharp knives around open flames and are expected to move quickly around the kitchen, which can be cramped and crowded due to the number of people all trying to navigate the kitchen at the same time. This becomes even more critical during the peak dinner hours when chefs are "slammed" with orders. Working quickly with precision is a must. Slips and falls are common and many of the women we interviewed had visible scars on their hands and arms where they had been burned or cut themselves on the job. It is also important to note that being a chef is not a high-earning career. Unlike the multimillionaire chefs who are presented on television, in the real world, chefs often work for not that much money. According to the U.S. Bureau of Labor Statistics, in 2012, the annual earnings of a chef or head cook were only $42,480.

Working in a professional kitchen is filled with contradictions. In order to have a successful service, kitchen crews (as well as the front-of-the-house staff like waiters and waitresses) have to work together. Cooperation is crucial and just one person having an off night can ruin dinner service for everyone. Because of this, tempers can run high and kitchen workers can often be filled with adrenaline each night. Chelsea, a culinary instructor, describes these pressures:

> You're all about getting it done as perfect and as fast as you possibly can. . . . You're constantly coming in trying to race the clock, get your station set up, and then boom, you're in service. It is intense. Waiters are coming in and asking for things. Nobody's happy. Nothing is right. There's fire. There's knives. Everything's going very quickly and moving around. Your mind is going a million miles a minute. So somebody screws that up, then you are going to start whaling on them (laughs). You know what I mean? It's very important that that group be in a good dynamic. If they're not, then the whole thing just kind of falls apart. Everything you've all worked for that night is demolished because one person . . . so it's this teamwork kind of thing.

Not only do chefs have to learn how to work together as a team, they have to learn to do so quickly. Sharon, a culinary instructor, described how it was common for new employees to be trained via a trial by fire. She laughed as she explained that, "Training is not 'Come see this. This is how we do it.' It's 'We're going to have you work the line tonight.' You're excited because you get to work the line, but then you go, 'Oh my God, it's Friday night.' You have to jump in with both hands, both feet, and just do."

Teamwork is crucial to complete each night's dinner service, but restaurant kitchens can be extremely competitive places to work with many cooks all vying to move up to more prestigious cooking stations or even to the position of sous chef. It is not unusual for cooks to try and undermine each other by blaming their fellow chefs for improperly preparing food or for coming up with an idea for a dish that was not successful. Sometimes these spats can become physical and three of our participants discussed how it was easy for women to be "pushed around" in the kitchen as chefs jostle for position at the busy stoves. If women were not able to claim their space, they would be unable to complete their tasks, which would reflect poorly on them.

While the women we interviewed tended to agree that the days of the "old school" chef who screamed at staff and routinely threw fits (and food) in the kitchen were ending, many of them had worked or trained under a chef like this at some point. Some women even suggested this behavior was important to the well-being of the staff. They argued that the negative treatment they experienced was ultimately for the best as it helped make them stronger and better able to handle the stresses of professional cooking. This was the case for Karen, a pastry chef who had spent a few years working in Germany. Karen, as well as some of our other participants, commented that European chefs tended to be more old school in terms of discipline and how they taught and mentored younger chefs. They were also said to have more disapproving views of women chefs. Karen recalled getting yelled at by her supervising chefs and being hurled with insults that she was "stupid" and an "idiot." She didn't necessarily believe she would have been treated any differently if she were a man, but her point was that women who were "wallflowers" or sensitive would be unable to make it as a chef. Those insults, although hurtful at the time, helped Karen develop a thick skin that she believed help contribute to her current success. She explained:

> I've had to work very hard to achieve the level that I have. Now, although I don't believe in those practices . . . this is going to sound very sadomasochistic, I do think that it has helped me have a better appreciation. If you've had it hard, you know what good is. . . . There are a lot of different occasions that will come up in your career where you're pushed and you've got this incredible weight on you and you have to see what you're made of. Those bad experiences, those hard chefs that you worked for, they're putting you under the gun for a reason. They want to see what you're made of. Are you going to pull it out and do the job that you're meant to do or are you going to break down? If

you break down, then you're really not supposed to be there in the first place. It's kind of a learning tool. It's kind of tough love.

Karen's comments indicate a certain level of ambivalence about her training experience. Initially, she says that she doesn't believe in those kinds of kitchen practices (the yelling, the insults), but she reluctantly admits she received some benefit from her time under these chefs, which she says makes her sound "sadomasochistic." Karen wasn't the only woman chef to have mixed feelings about some of her early cooking experiences. Jane, a culinary instructor, believed that having high standards and working for exacting chefs was a benefit, not only to herself, but to the entire profession. She described how there were fewer of the stereotypical aggressive men chefs than there used to be, but she suggested that this could actually be a bad thing. She believed that having high standards is what gave professional cooking its value and that, "In order to do anything that's really demanding, you have to have discipline."

A FOOT IN THE DOOR

Being a chef is a demanding career that typically requires years of hard work and training before any hope of advancement. For chefs who wish to maximize their career outcomes, they must move between different restaurant worlds within the gastronomic field to accumulate as much human, social, and cultural capital as possible. Individual restaurant worlds have varying levels of status and offer different types and amounts of these forms of capital. Because of this, training and early jobs were crucial in order to accrue capital and become a successful chef. Chefs are encouraged to get the best training possible, either in culinary school or through on-the-job training, and then to leverage this experience to move on to better jobs. If women chefs are discriminated against in the early years of their work and training as a chef, this could have long lasting repercussions for the overall trajectory of their careers.

Gender discrimination in culinary school and in hiring was reported by several of the women chefs. For example, when Anna was eighteen years old and exploring careers, she recalled visiting the French Culinary Academy and being rebuffed by office staff who told her they accepted only men students. While Anna's case of being barred from classes due to her gender was extreme, other women felt more subtle differences while in culinary school. Camille, who generally had very positive things to say about her early training and job experiences, felt that the chef instructors at her school took the men students more seriously than the women in the classes. Although she said the difference wasn't "flagrant," she went to say that women students "knew right off the bat you weren't gonna get the same attention" and that there was the attitude that "The men were going to go on to be *great* [said in deep, dramatic voice] and the girls were kind of biding their time [until marriage]."

Cathy also felt similarly that men and women students were treated differently while in her culinary program. Cathy had spent several years working in the hospitality industry before going back to school to become a chef and believed the combination of her gender and age proved to be a disadvantage in culinary school. Culinary school stresses hands-on learning of the skills needed in professional cooking. Cathy recalled how many of the most important in-class learning tasks, such as how to make a perfectly clear consommé, were always given to the men students. She was never called upon to help demonstrate skills in the classroom and Cathy attributed this to the feeling that "I shouldn't take up that time" because she was not expected to have as impressive of a career as the men students. Eventually, Cathy would go on to complain about this discrimination to the school's president. In an ironic twist, Cathy admitted during her interview that, as a chef-owner of a restaurant, she is sometimes skeptical about hiring women chefs because she fears they received similar treatment in culinary school and, therefore, they could lack the skills needed to work in a restaurant kitchen.

Both Camille and Cathy had attended culinary school at least ten years previously and were working as established chefs at the time of their interviews. There appeared to be less gender discrimination reported by our younger participants, although this didn't mean that there wasn't some gender-based treatment. Dana, a twenty-four-year old executive chef, was still enrolled in culinary school at the time of her interview. She discussed working in teams at school and how there was one instructor who would mark women students' work lower than their men counterparts even when they had the same answers. Dana didn't feel his behavior was fair, but, at the same time, she felt that grades were not as important as work experience for chefs so she was not bothered by the instructor's actions.

If work experience is most important for a chef, what happens where there are problems on the job market for women chefs? According to Vanina Leschziner (2007), one's work history as a chef is vital because knowing that someone worked for a well-known chef gives a view of the amount of human, social, and cultural capital they have accumulated, which can be easier to judge than cooking skills. However, Katharina Balazs's (2002) study of 3-star Michelin chefs in France found that one's résumé was less important than one's approach and personality. In both of these cases, women can be disadvantaged. They may not fit in as women within certain macho male-dominated kitchens, which would exclude them from developing the types of capital needed to move ahead in the field.

Donna Bobbitt-Zeher (2011), in her study of sex discrimination cases in Ohio, found that some men managers didn't hire women because they assumed women would be unable to fit in to certain workplaces. Research on women chefs similarly indicated that women were sometimes judged as being unable to work in all-men work teams specifically because of their gender (Fine 1987). Two of our participants, Melissa and Lyndsay, were denied jobs in kitchens because the chef "didn't like to work with women." Some of the other women claimed they also knew men chefs who refused to hire women. Melissa was finally able to gain a stage position under the chef who originally turned her down after three pastry chefs quit and a man chef at the restaurant vouched for her. When asked why she thought the chef had originally responded in that way, she attributed his attitude to his being from a racial-ethnic group that has more of a machismo culture.

Four of our participants also said that gender inequality in earnings was another issue faced by women chefs. They detailed men chefs being given higher wages and larger raises than their women counterparts. There were also problems with promotions, as women were sometimes turned down for higher positions. In one case, Jill recalled losing a promotion to a man chef who worked at another restaurant owned by her bosses, even though she and one of her men colleagues would technically have been the underchefs in line for the new position. The reason given was that he had a family and needed the higher salary to provide for them. Jill described this situation as "enraging" and these events seem particularly ironic given that two other women we interviewed had been passed over for promotions due to the fact that they had families and it was assumed they would not be as committed to their careers.

PROVING STRENGTH

A large barrier to employment opportunities seemed to be stereotypes about the physical and emotional limitations of women that were used to deny them chef positions or promotions. Rosabeth Moss Kanter's (1977) research into women's tokenism at work suggests that, when women make up a small percentage of a workplace, this exposes them to even more scrutiny. According to our participants, a common complaint about women chefs was that they lacked the physical stamina to work as a professional chef. Being a chef can mean lifting and carrying heavy things. Tabitha, the pastry chef we mentioned at the beginning of this chapter, for example, had recently had to help carry in a 200-pound pig that was specially ordered for her restaurant.

In Cynthia Fuchs Epstein's (1989) review of how men create gender boundaries in the workplace, she notes that men can emphasize the physical nature of their work as a way of discouraging women's entry to these occupations. Among chefs, when physical tasks were required, men coworkers were always there to see if the women could handle things. Camille, an executive pastry chef pointed out:

> I also think there's a lot of physical side to the kitchen that maybe isn't obvious unless you're in it. You've got a bag of flour [that] weighs fifty pounds. And you need to be able to move that from one place to another (laughs). Asking a boy to do that for you would *not* be a good idea. 'Cause you're definitely going to get put in a category (laughs) of "You Can't *Really* Do Your Job" because you're not physically strong enough.

During our interviews, everything from women's periods to pregnancy was mentioned as a reason why women were seen as less physically capable than men chefs. However, several women pointed out that this heavy lifting could also be difficult for smaller men as well. Elisa even likened women chefs to women who worked in the construction industry, and suggested that, while maybe a larger percentage of men could handle the demands of a physical job like construction or being a chef, that didn't mean there wasn't a sizeable proportion of women who could also work in these fields. Marisel, a chef-owner whose French sous chef didn't like working with women, dismissed concerns about women's physical limitations. She believed in working smarter rather than harder and described how this could be accomplished by either gender:

> I mean, there are some things that are heavy, but they're heavy for everybody, not only because I'm a woman. I mean, some of the guys are silly and they hurt themselves trying to show off. So, when trying to lift a heavy stock pot, I'm smart enough to know that I'm not going to fill it up first and then put it on the stove. I'm going to put it on the stove and fill it up with water.

Even more ubiquitous than doubts about women's ability to physically handle the demands of working in a kitchen were concerns that women would lack the emotional strength needed to be a chef. Being a chef can be a high-pressure, intense job, and there were plenty of people who doubted women would be able to handle the emotional stress of the positions. Our participants were aware of these criticisms and took great pains to prove them wrong. The number one rule we heard mentioned from the women chefs: there is no cry-ing on the line. Things can get stressful and chefs can yell and curse when a dish is improperly prepared or it takes a long time to finish. When this happens, the important thing is to keep cooking and not to break down emotionally.

Several of the participants shared this rule with women they taught as culinary instructors or those that worked beneath them. Jane, a culinary instructor, advised her women students, "Don't cry in the kitchen. It's nor-mal to cry. I cry all the time. But go to the bathroom. Don't let anybody see you cry and then come back in." Rose advised women she worked with to go into the large walk-in refrigerator to literally cool off, cry, and even punch the walls if needed. Melissa even joked that sometimes it is fine to cry—as long as you keep working your station.

An example of just how strongly women chefs felt about crying came out in the interview with Alexandra, an events planner, who described some of the difficulties working as a woman in an upscale hotel:

> When I was a sous chef there, one girl cried on the line and I took her aside and just yelled at her. "You crying on that line just set me back five years. Not once did I ever cry on the line, no matter how much the guys were trying to get me to cry. Not once when I cut myself [did I cry]. I held it until service was over to get first aid. Not once did I cry whenever I got burned. I did not leave the line to get first aid treatment until we were done with service. So you

crying on the line because the chef said you made the dressing wrong set me back five years."

Crying in the kitchen was so demonized by our participants because it spoke to a particular type of gendered weakness. When women were referred to as emotional it meant crying and not being able to take criticism well or handle the intense pressures of working a busy dinner service. It was believed that crying would lead to a complete "breakdown" on the part of a woman chef, who would then be unable to continue to fulfill her job in the kitchen. Crying disrupted service and left the entire kitchen scrambling. If a woman cried while working in a kitchen, it was seen as proof that all women—not just the woman chef who committed the sin of crying—were too emotional to work as a chef (see Furia 2010). According to Kanter's tokenism framework (1977; see also Wingfield 2013), numerical minorities must often consider their behaviors carefully because majorities (in this case, men chefs) will overgeneralize any faults or mistakes to all numeri-cal tokens (women chefs). Gary Alan Fine's (1987) ethnographic study of restaurant kitchens echoes this pattern as he found that women chefs were seen as representing all women within the gastronomic field. As tokens, their work and comportment was highly visible.

The participants had internalized these messages to the point that cry-ing or showing "womanly" emotions was seen as a major failure. Natasha, a chef de cuisine, had described a tumultuous relationship with her previous restaurant's owners and admitted the situation brought her to tears several times during her years working for them. She described how: "They would definitely make me feel very much like a woman. Like very emotional. They really brought out the worst in me."

For a woman chef like Natasha, fitting the emotional, hysterical woman stereotype was the "worst" in her. In fear of confirming these stereotypes, the women chefs felt pressure to hide their emotions at work. Chelsea, a chef instructor, described this process as "learning how to hide the girliness." She laughed when she remembered the only time she ever cried at work:

I really don't cry unless I am so frustrated . . . it's not really emotional it's more about frustration. "I can't go this way, I can't go that way. I can't get anything done. Everything is closing in on me and I'm just going to lose it." So I will never forget doing that [crying at work] (laughs). I went around and hid in this closet that we had and I was sitting down. I thought, "Oh my God. I'm going to cry. No one can see me do this." I went and was hiding. Then our purchasing guy opens the door and sees me. That scared him even more. Like, "Oh my God! She has emotions!" (laughs).

Chelsea's comments highlight the power of the stereotype of the weak, emotional woman chef. Even years later and when she worked at a different job, she still made sure to emphasize that she was crying out of frustration and not because of any type of "emotional" response (even though frustration is an emotion). Until this point, Chelsea had made it a point to be tough and professional at work. The purchasing manager at Chelsea's restaurant was so shocked at finding her in an emotional state that he just closed the door and backed away.

Throughout these stories, there is the underlying current that women chefs are required to manage their emotions at all times. Expressions of frustration, anger, and disappointment, particularly when displayed through the gendered act of crying, were used as a sign of women's lack of professionalism and inability to handle the requirements of being a chef. Even chefs who stressed that *they* would never cry at work, accepted the stereotype that other women were overly emotional. Kate, a restaurant owner and former chef, described her thoughts on this during her interview.

I do think women can bring an emotional aspect to things, which is really healthy sometimes, but, if it's not done professionally, which I think a lot of times it's not, then it's not something I want to take the time to deal with, and I don't think it's productive and I don't like it.

When asked to elaborate on what she meant about professionalism and emotions, Kate explained:

Women tend to take things more personally and they're more apt to show it that they're taking it more personally whereas men would never do that. So, maybe that's what it is: Maybe it's the sensitivity in women that they allow themselves to show it while they work.

Ironically, men were not held to such high standards. Chelsea explained that men chefs "can get away with a lot" and "act like little boys." During a dinner service "they can talk smack and do that kind of stuff all day and they get away with it. It's funny how women don't get away with typical female stuff." Chelsea's comments and the experiences of our participants suggest that, throughout the history of the gastronomic field, masculine ways of interacting and expressing emotion have become accepted and normalized. In the kitchen, men could get angry, yell, and curse to vent their frustration without being questioned about their level of professionalism. Rosabeth Kanter (1977) argues that it is much easier to stereotype tokens than numerical majorities. If one particular man chef was known to be a "hothead," his reputation as having a temper did not extend beyond the individual. That is, no one made the assumption that, because one man chef lost his temper, all man chefs were angry and temperamental. But for women, just one isolated incident of a woman chef crying at work spoke to the lack of emotional strength of all women in the kitchen.

These experiences suggest that it is not so much the emotionality that is viewed negatively but the display of emotion in stereotypically feminine ways. Chelsea and other chefs recalled times when they saw men chefs cry, which was usually described as understandable. However, women were never supposed to cry at work. Men chefs who cry might be permitted to do so, much like the hypermasculine professional football player who can cry when his team loses, with no perceived threat to his masculine status. As tokens, crying is perceived to indicate weakness instead of passion or dedication to the craft of professional cooking.

GUESS WHO'S MAKING SALADS?

Stereotypes about women chefs were used to deny women jobs or sort women into less desirable positions in the kitchen. When asked about times when they were treated differently than men chefs, one of the most common examples provided by our participants involved the types of jobs women chefs were assigned. Within the kitchen hierarchy, there are several stations in the kitchen where various chefs de partie, or line chefs, work under the supervision of the sous chef and, ultimately, the executive chef. One of these stations is known as the garde manger, or pantry station, and it is where salads and other cold appetizers are prepared. The pantry station, because it is where salad ingredients are prepared, is a cooler part of the kitchen and was described as "less intense" than the other stations on the hot side of the kitchen. Working the pantry station is one of the lower positions in the kitchen hierarchy (Leschziner 2007). In describing the status of being a garde manger, the women agreed "It's not very glamorous to say you're the pantry cook" and it's "one step above the dishwasher."

Numerous times in our interviews, women chefs referred to "getting put on salads," often in a derogatory way. According to Erin, a chef de cuisine:

> It has happened to me several times when I've gone to interview for a job in the past I was offered the pantry position which, basically, it's an insult that all women can do is make salads. The pantry is cold appetizers and salads. And it is very insulting to be offered that position. They just assume that the women don't want to work hard. They can't handle the hot line and they don't want to get hot and sweaty. And the pantry is sometimes a hard position but a lot of men assume that that is where the women should go.

Our participants emphasized it wasn't that being assigned as pantry cook was beneath them, it was that the garde manger station is where men chefs tended to put women in the kitchen. Erin, who called the pantry position an "insult," was offended not by the job itself, but by the men chef's assumption that this was where she belonged without even looking at her résumé. Erin and several other participants had worked in very well-known establishments; yet, when they changed jobs they were immediately bumped down to pantry again. Tabitha had experienced this pattern as well. Even though she would eventually move up to become the sous chef or head pastry chef, at every job she had held as a chef in the last fifteen years, she was started in the pantry station. It had become such a frustrating recurring joke to Tabitha and her husband, that she recalled coming home and announcing sarcastically, "*Guess who's making the salads?!*" the day she had been hired for her current job.

Sometimes this gender segregation by station was blatant. When Lisa applied for an internship as part of her culinary school training, she was directed to the salad station by a manager who said, "Well, we start all the girls in the appetizer section." Other times it was more subtle. For example, Melissa, a pastry chef, explained that all new cooks get started on the pantry station—men and women. But later in her interview, she described a contradiction: "I think that maybe everybody starts on pantry. . . . But if you walk into a kitchen, and there's a woman in there, more than likely she's working the salads." Camille, who worked as an executive pastry chef, shared kitchen space with the pantry chef at her restaurant. She had noticed that, while both men and women started on pantry unless they had a remarkable résumé, it seemed to take women longer to get moved up. According to Camille, "A lot of guys will be on salads for a week and [hits table and makes 'liftoff' motion with hand]."

Michelle, an executive chef-owner, believed assigning women the salad station—regardless of past work experience—was intentional.

> That's where they'll generally put you [the salad station]. They will put you over there and give you some fancy name and all you're really doing is making salads. [The men chefs are thinking] "Out of the way. They [women] can handle that." . . . Those are kind of the things that men do. They play their little games but they won't give you any responsibility. They will keep you in an area and you will either succeed in that area and make a transition to another one or you'll get so frustrated that you will leave.

Michelle saw the pantry station as the place men chefs assigned women to work because they doubted women would be able to handle the hot stations in the kitchen. Once in this station, if women were not able to prove themselves, they would remain in this low position or eventually leave for some other type of work. This arrangement benefitted and helped uphold all-men work teams as women had to either prove they could adapt to the kitchen or quit. If the women did the latter, men chefs could claim they had given a woman chef a chance in the kitchen, but that she (and by extension, all women chefs) had not been up to the task.

When discussing how job tasks are assigned, it is important to understand that within the same job, certain tasks are gendered. In addition to the gendered associations of salads with femininity and meat for masculinity were different cultures in these various workplaces. For chefs, working on the fast-paced, hot side of the kitchen fits within the "macho" work environment of professional kitchens. This side of the kitchen could be raucous, competitive, and largely male. The salad station, in contrast, was quieter, cooler, and less intense and this could be part of the reason why men chefs associated the less demanding position with women. Chefs who are relegated to making salads are likely to be stuck in an area of the kitchen that receives little status or few accolades. It is difficult to imagine a customer in a fine dining restaurant asking, "Who made the salad?" Not only is this a low-paying station, often with little input into the creative work of the kitchen, but there can be impeded mobility as well because a consequence of this internal job sorting is that women are less likely to be able to demonstrate their skills on the hot line.

HOLD YOUR OWN

Our last few sections indicate a major problem facing women chefs is that men often do not believe women have the physical or emotional strength necessary to work in professional kitchens. According to Tabitha, this translated into women starting in the kitchen "about two or three steps lower than everybody else." In order to receive respect, women had to prove they deserved their positions in the kitchen and "hold their own" when things got tough. At times men chefs would test their women coworkers to determine their toughness. This is a common practice for women in male-dominated jobs, such as construction worker (Denissen 2010a; Denissen and Saguy 2014), in which men would observe women carrying heavy items to see whether they pass the tests. For example, Rose recalled working under several European chefs where there was: "The constant eyes watching me to see if I was going to cry if they yelled at me. How I would react if I burned myself. How I would hold my own against the waiters. They'd be yelling at me, 'Are you going to cry and run off?'" Karen also felt the German chefs who used to hurl insults at her were testing her. She said this behavior was a way to determine if "you were going to pull it out and do the job that you're meant to do or are you going to break down?" Karen explained how, if women chefs broke down, it was a sign that "you're really not supposed to be here in the first place."

In these all-male work cultures that already tend to paint women as weak, how can women prove themselves? There were numerous ways women attempted to fit in and gain respect at work. One common practice among the women was to make sure that none of the men could question their work ethic. This meant women had to work harder and cook better than their men counterparts just to be taken seriously as a chef. Cathy, a chef-owner who had been cooking for over twenty-five years by the time of her interview, recalled how women had to work more just to receive the same respect as the men in the kitchen: "In order for me, as a woman, to be recognized by my peers in the hotel business or in the or in the restaurant business, I knew I had to be at least as good or better. . . . You cannot leave yourself open for [criticism]. . . . You have to stay above reproach. And, so, it takes more time to do that." Working harder included coming to work earlier in order to get set up and claim one's workspace in the crowded kitchen. It also consisted of staying later to make sure essential kitchen duties were done before the restaurant closed each night. Rose, a pastry instructor, echoed this sentiment. She believed women had to work "twice as hard just to gain any respect from anybody." During her early years as a chef in the 1980s women were rare in professional kitchens, and Rose felt she had to prove that she wanted and deserved a place in the kitchen. When her men coworkers would make a mistake in the kitchen, they would brush it off. If Rose made a mistake, she would offer to stay late to fix things or learn what she had done wrong. Although she felt these efforts ultimately made her a better chef, she did remember feeling pressured at the time to work extremely long hours.

> I felt like I never could say "No," to anything. If the chef asked: "Who can stay late? Can somebody work tomorrow morning?" and they asked me, I would say yes. I figured that the day I said, "No," it would be like, "Oooh. Do you have a *date*?" These types of things where the guys could say no to, but when I would try it, it was always assumed—'cause there was another girl who had done that—and they were always like, "Oh, yeah. All she cares about is going out." [I thought] "How can the guys say 'No,' and when we say 'No,' it's like 'Oh, you got a date?'"

Rose's comments also speak to the earlier point that individual women were often tasked with representing all women working in professional kitchens. Just because another woman chef was viewed as caring less about her work and more about going out, this perspective was automatically transferred to Rose, the next woman to begin working in the kitchen.

Alexandra, who currently works as an events planner at a restaurant, also discussed some of the extra time it takes for women chefs to be accepted in the kitchen. In her case, it meant spending extra hours reading and studying so that she was never caught not knowing the answer to a question her chef might pose to her. Unlike her men colleagues who could bluster through, if Alexandra found herself without an answer, this would invalidate her knowledge, and even her very presence, in the kitchen. Another chef, Natasha, similarly made sure she "did her homework" so that she was never caught unaware and so that no one could "put her down" as a chef.

Some of the ways to earn respect included directly addressing the physical and emotional stereotypes about women chefs. To prove physical toughness, women chefs would have to make sure they could handle all the physical tasks required in the kitchen—and that their men colleagues witnessed this. This was described as showing you could "hold your own" in the kitchen. Christine, a culinary instructor, even described how the men she worked with gave her the nickname of "Ant" because she was a small woman who appeared able to carry items almost as heavy as herself. Other women recalled feeling like they could never ask for help in the kitchen and even refused help with tasks out of fear it would make them appear weak. While their men coworkers could share some of these tasks, the women were aware that this could be a test and sometimes the women even injured themselves trying to prove their toughness.

In order to demonstrate emotional strength, our participants urged women chefs to never complain or "play the girl card" in the kitchen. It was common for women chefs to mentor each other, particularly in culinary school, and provide warnings about what working in a kitchen was really like, especially in terms of the different expectations of men and women. For example, Rose remembered one of her women teachers in cooking school telling her: "Remember, you've entered a male's world, so don't go pulling 'I'm a girl. I can't do this.' Or 'I'm a girl. I can't do that.' . . . So I always kept that in the back of my mind. I've felt that sometimes it wasn't fair, but it was like, 'Well, you chose to go into this profession.'" Many of the women chefs we interviewed felt similarly. Rarely did they attribute mistreatment to sexism or misogyny on the part of men chefs. Instead, many women interpreted this behavior to the long history of completely male kitchens. Jane, a culinary instructor, remarked "they [men chefs] felt like this is a guy's area and if you can't hang with that then you need to get out."

Women chefs also had to learn to advocate for themselves. Part of femininity includes being humble and apologizing for mistakes. Women are expected to work together for the communal good of the team, but can be penalized if they are seen as being too dominant (Rudman and Glick 2001).

For chefs, these prescriptions can be harmful as a certain amount of confidence and even bravado is necessary to get noticed and get ahead at work. Michelle explained:

> If you develop a dish and you want to sell it, don't come to them and say, "This didn't come out quite the way I wanted it to." Put it out there. Then you put it out there and be ready for the judgment. Dress it up. Do what you need to do but then be able to accept the criticism. Don't come already with, "This didn't [work]" because they're just going to eat you up.

Numerous workplaces have gender preferences for what kinds of employees and employee characteristics are hired and promoted. Often these preferences are couched in terms of "fit" (Jeanes, Knights, and Martin 2011) and this can disadvantage women workers who, as minorities, have to prove their ability to fit in within male-dominated workplaces. Women chefs had to prove they could perform, not only the duties of working in a kitchen, but that they could fit in with the male-dominated workplace culture as well. Because of the precarious masculinity experienced by men chefs, women chefs had to show that they could enter professional kitchens without disrupting the workplace atmosphere or sense of camaraderie that had developed among the men (Fine 1987). In Fine's ethnography of restaurant kitchens, he described how men chefs claimed they did not discriminate against women—as long as the woman could perfectly fit in at work and work just like the men. Our participants had internalized this view and felt that it was up to them to fit in at work because "this was a man's area" and the women chose to enter it. Therefore, it was up to the women to adapt to this new work environment and expecting the environment to adapt to them was a sign the woman did not belong as a chef.

One way to fit in was to make sure their appearance was not too overtly feminine. Camille, an executive pastry chef, jokingly said women did this because they have to prove themselves more than "some guy with a shaved head and tattoos" indicating how women visually stick out in the kitchen. By dressing more androgynously and downplaying physical differences, women could blend in more with their coworkers. They could appear to be a "chef," which meant acceptance and respect in the kitchen and not a "woman chef," which could mean much more work to earn the same level of respect.

Some of the rationale for changing one's appearance to better fit in at work came from beliefs that restaurant kitchens were sexually charged workplaces. We will discuss sexual harassment later, but part of the reason women were sometimes seen as invading kitchens was that men executive chefs saw women as a distraction in male-dominated workplaces. According to Melissa, when there was a mixed gender composition in the kitchen, the chefs assumed sexual tension would result and that there could be flirting or romantic relationships between coworkers that could distract from the work environment.

This idea that women could create distractions in a male-dominated workplace could explain why some women chefs were critiqued as being too attractive. Women in other occupations report that they have to be hyperaware of how people might interpret their appearance as an indicator for whether they fit in (or not), or will be dedicated workers (or not) (Dellinger 2002; Dellinger and Williams 1997). Alexandra, an events planner at a restaurant, recalled being told she was "too pretty to be in the kitchen," while Melissa described being handed hostess applications when she visited restaurants about chef jobs. In both cases, the women's appearance was used as a way of suggesting they did not belong in the kitchen. On the other side of the spectrum, Jane, a culinary instructor, felt that, because she had grown up around boys and identified as a tomboy, she was able to "blend in" at work, particularly because she doesn't wear a lot of jewelry or makeup. Chelsea, a culinary instructor, described how kitchen work often dictated women's appearance:

> It's not a pretty job, you know? You don't wear makeup. You don't wear jewelry. There's none of that. So you give up a lot of being feminine by what you do, by working in the kitchen. You're not the hostess (laughs). You're the ugly chef, with no makeup, and nasty nails. But people respect you. They don't respect her. They want to date her.

According to Chelsea, there were two models of femininity in restaurants—the dirty, hard-working woman chef who earns respect and the feminine, attractive hostess that the men see as a potential romantic partner. Part of earning the respect of men peers, the women suggest, is de-feminizing one's appearance in order to avoid criticism that they are too girly or feminine for the kitchen. Women chefs, therefore, have to become what Peter Levin

(2001) and Suzanne Tallichet (2000) call "social men" in both appearance and behavior to be accepted into all-men work teams.

At various times in their interviews, the women alternatively described working in a kitchen as 1) being part of the military or a sports team, 2) working as paramedics or construction workers, and 3) even as a troop of baboons. Those in the military and those who work as paramedics experience work environments characterized by extreme conditions, high pressure, and that are very goal-oriented (in the case of a chef, completing a dinner service each night). For example, in kitchens, like the military, chefs work very hard and usually for a very long time before seeing any reward or rise in status ("You don't get it until you earn it."). At the end of the long night of service, coworkers described feeling like they had been through a "battle" together. And just like among a group of primates, women had to show the more dominant members of the group they were just as tough. Because of demands of the job and its reliance on teamwork, it was important for men chefs to determine whether or not women could fit in (Fine 1996b).

Working in an all-men environment can be a large adjustment for some women and men coworkers test the women chefs to make sure they can "hang." Chelsea recalled how this transition can be difficult:

> You work with a bunch of men but you're not one of the guys. I've learned how to be in that [environment]. I've learned how to get along with men really well. I think it's about learning how to motivate them. You know what I mean? It's just like working with a bunch of women. There's a dynamic there too that you have to learn. You have to learn how to survive within that group.

Tabitha also described how women chefs could prove that they would not be disruptive to the current climate at work:

> What you have to do being a woman working in the kitchen is you have to become a guy. And you have to make them feel okay enough that they can say their comments around you. It's not like you come in there and get a certain amount of respect or people watch their language or words around you. . . . And, there's some great things about it, too, as is. It's like being a paramedic or something. It's just rough and some day you're gonna get pissed and upset and things are gonna get stressful and you're gonna tell someone to go to hell.

And, we just sort of have an acceptance level and that's just when something goes on. I think that's actually a guy thing, but it's come over [to the cooking world], so it's just kind of always like that in the kitchens where you go—that you have to be a little bit tougher. You know? You have to just put up with stuff.

When asked how women chefs can fit in with this dynamic, Tabitha replied:

Try to be offensive [laughs]. You don't bitch. You have to be tough constantly. You have to push people's buttons and then let them push yours and then fight back constantly. That's a male thing. I mean, look at the baboons. They push, then fight, fight, fight. Then "Grrrrr." [makes growling noise] "Okay, you're cool."

Women in construction (Denissen 2010b) and coal mining (Tallichet 2000) have described similar ways of negotiating fitting in. Women in these fields report that they must show their male colleagues that they are tough and able to "fight back," or else they risk never being a part of the boy's club. Ultimately, success in their work hinges on being able to fit in, and as Chelsea said, survive.

Although it may seem that women chefs have to expend a lot of effort in order to become accepted as part of a professional kitchen, there were certain benefits available to women who accomplished this feat. Not only were they able to perform their jobs, learn new cooking and leadership techniques, and sometimes even advance within the kitchen hierarchy, they also formed close bonds with their men coworkers. Amber recalled feeling protected by the men she worked with after they accepted her as one of them. Rose, who had been tested by her men colleagues by goading her about whether or not she was going to cry in the kitchen, recalled with some bemusement how the men's attitudes changed once she was accepted as part of the team:

Once I got in and proved myself, it was like I had a room full of brothers. I knew they had my back when we'd go out places. Just hanging out in the kitchen, you'd fight with the waiters all the time. Waiters and cooks always fight. I had a waiter in my face arguing something—the waiter had had a bad night and screwed up a table and was trying to blame me, and it wasn't my fault, he forgot to put a ticket in or something. And he started going off on a rampage, just no big deal, but I remember seeing two of those guys come flying off the line and right over to my defense like, "You got a problem with her?" And I'd be like, "Guys, guys, I got it. I can handle it." And they're like, "Don't you talk to her like that again! Do you understand me?" And it was just like, "Wow! I've got my brothers now and a few months ago they would have watched this go on for hours and not done a thing, but now. . . ."

After Rose proved herself to her men colleagues, the men began to protect her against external threats, such as wait staff who would try and argue with her. Her supervisor even made sure there was someone available to walk her to her car when she worked late at night. Rose appreciated these gestures, although she laughed about the contradiction of the men working together to protect her from harm after they had put her through an intense period of hazing to prove herself worthy of working in the kitchen. Despite the women's acceptance of these new "brothers" who looked after them, there can be downsides to these familial relations at work. Protection by male colleagues can manifest as paternalism. In building trades, for example, protecting women from certain aspects of their work can make women seem incompetent or weak (Denissen 2010a). Nevertheless, women we interviewed perceived these forms of protection as acceptance and evidence that they had passed the tests.

IT'S ALL SEXUAL HARASSMENT

Numerous accounts of life in professional kitchens from journalists, social researchers, and even chefs themselves, detail the high levels of sexual joking and teasing in these workplaces. Alicia Sinclair (2006) even described sexual harassment as "pervasive" and "accepted" within restaurant kitchens. Research by Fine (1987; 1996b) suggests that this behavior serves as a form of teambuilding among men chefs and, when women join the kitchen, some of this sexualized joking and teasing is a way of socializing women into the all-men work environments. Each specific restaurant has its own culture, and women chefs are expected to learn and adapt to this atmosphere. However, when does teasing or teambuilding become harassment? We wanted to know if women chefs deemed some of these behaviors sexual harassment and how it affected their ability to fit in and succeed at work.

Camille, an executive pastry chef, was one of the first women we interviewed for this project. When asked about sexual harassment at work, she let out a big laugh and said, "The kitchen is just like the schoolyard in sixth grade. It's *all* sexual harassment."

Other chefs mentioned the ubiquity of sexual references and teasing at work. Rose, a culinary school instructor, admitted she was surprised early in her career at how sexualized kitchen work could be. Reflecting back on these days, Rose attributed the conditions of these kitchens to the all-men work environments.

> I used to be actually quite shocked about how bad it was in the kitchen. And how it was almost like they thought, "Well, you entered this world" type thing. "You chose to come into this." It's like being in a guy's locker room, the way they talked, the way they acted. They didn't feel like they really had to worry about me, I chose to go there . . . and [they acted like] "You can't change the way we are." And it was an accepted way [to be]. I used to see, even guys [who] went into the kitchen who were not like that—they were clean-cut, prim and proper outside, but once they got in, they would get caught up in the talk. And the cussing. And kind of get the whole, I like to call it, trashy attitude. But when they left, they had their girlfriends and everything, and they were calmed down. But when you got them all together, all the testosterone, it was like who can outdo who. It becomes a really crude, crude environment.

Christine also described how professional kitchens were unique environments that fostered a particular type of culture. She described telling her husband, who worked as an engineer, some of the conversations she had at work that involved sexual topics. Her husband was shocked that talk like this happened at work. Upon reflection, Christine admitted it was "weird" that such things were normalized, but tried to explain why this was the case:

> It's ridiculous. People touch you. It's totally inappropriate. I don't know why we tolerate it. I guess a lot of us have been indoctrinated into it for so long. And we're so young. Everyone is so young when they start. I think that has a lot to do with it. We haven't grown up . . . and no one works hours like we do. . . . We're working all night long, all morning long, with each other all the time in really close quarters. This is going to sound crazy . . . but something about working with food, and it's so many people's passions that the lines get

blurred because your emotions are all up. Your adrenaline is pumping because you're there because you're passionate about your food. The people who are the best at what they're doing and the most passionate about it cross the line even more. It feels like we're all in it together in a way different than other places of work. Maybe it's all the testosterone from all the men (laughs) since there's only a few of us women in one place.

Both Rose and Christine make reference to the gender composition of kitchens as a reason for some of this behavior. Their comments reflect the highly sexualized workplaces when men work in homosocial work environments (Bird 1996; Britton 1990). Even men that Rose noted were "prim and proper" would turn rowdy once they entered into the kitchen. The fact that these men would revert back to their more "clean-cut" selves outside of work suggests that, when work environments are almost entirely male, this can foster a sexualized and competitive work environment fueled by, as Christine supposes, all the testosterone. These environments can be particularly hostile to women's inclusion and behaviors like sexual harassment can arise as a way of defending men's territory at work or, as Rose suggested, reminding women that kitchens were not their place and they were expected to change in order to fit in and not the other way around.

Some of the behaviors cited by the women chefs included sexual jokes, teasing, using sexualized or raunchy language, talking about sexual acts, and propositioning someone for sex (either in a serious or joking manner). However, the women didn't always label these actions as sexual harassment. In sexualized work settings, employees often draw boundary lines about what constitutes sexual harassment, what behaviors are pleasurable and "fun," and what they consider to be simply a part of their work (Erickson 2010; Giuffre and Williams 1994). Whether or not a behavior was called sexual harassment depended on the nature of the action (talking versus touching), how it made the woman involved feel, and, most importantly it seemed, the rank of the person engaging in the behavior.

Numerous times our participants would explain that they had never been sexually harassed or witnessed any sexual harassment at work. With further questioning though, the women usually clarified that, while they may have experienced a sexualized work environment, they did not classify this as harassment (see Dellinger and Williams 2002; Giuffre and Williams 1994). For example, if the behavior was restricted to talking about sex or making sexual jokes, this was considered just part of working in a kitchen. Chelsea explained how "there's a lot of talking in a kitchen that is not very appropriate" and described this as "guy talk." Similarly, Natasha said of the young men who worked with her, "They talk about just the nastiest things," then she added, "But most of it I can just laugh at. I'm unaffected. It doesn't bother me."

This type of sexual talking and joking was seen as a normal part of working in restaurant kitchens, which is a common pattern in male-dominated work settings (Bird 1996; Denissen 2010b; Tallichet 2000). For example, Patricia agreed that she wasn't bothered by her coworkers' sexualized humor and, at times, found some of their banter funny. She gave the example of a typical joke in the kitchen where the chef threatened a cook by saying, "If you don't behave, I'm going to take my dick out and hit you in the head with it" and the cook mockingly replied back, "Well, you're going to have to stand real close." Patricia admitted she found this joking a good way to relieve stress at work, but she also believed this type of humor meant walking a "fine line" in the kitchen. She continued her comments with "Now, if somebody was grabbing someone, that's what I would call crossing the line." Other women felt similarly. Joking could be tolerated and there could be an atmosphere that Chelsea described as "how far are we going to go until somebody gets offended" but crossing the line into groping or touching was seen as unacceptable.

Joan, a selling manager at an upscale grocer, provided an example of when someone stepped over this line. Over the course of her career, Joan had worked in numerous restaurant kitchens as a chef. She described leaving a job at a restaurant once because of sexual harassment. Earlier in our discussion, Joan was critical of women chefs who complained about all the innuendo in restaurant kitchens. She believed that these experiences "toughen you up and make you a stronger person because you're able to be in a man's industry." However, she believed that unwanted touching was unacceptable and once a coworker crossed the line from talking to touching her, she made a formal complaint:

I was working at a restaurant that was in New York. A new cook came on and kept making these lewd sexual [comments]. I asked him to please stop, I wasn't comfortable. . . . You know, it [sexual harassment] takes place and you have to have a tough enough skin, but you also have to realize when enough is enough and, unfortunately, some people don't understand that. There's a fine line. They can take it just a step too far. There's always the lewd, the crude comments, but when somebody touches you and you ask them not to do it again, that's when it becomes a problem. I don't mind the comments. That, to me, is a start, but the touching is what [crosses the line].

Joan was adamant that she wasn't opposed to a sexualized workplace per se. She could handle joking and teasing and believed that other chefs should be able to tolerate this as well. It was the escalation to touching that was seen as problematic, particularly after she requested that her coworker stop touching her. Eventually, Joan ended up leaving the restaurant because of the inappropriate touching from her coworker and her supervisors' lack of response to her complaints.

Other women reported experiencing inappropriate touching and, like Joan, this came early in their careers when they were in culinary school or training at a restaurant. Similar to findings of women workers in various industries (McLaughlin, Uggen, and Blackstone 2012), when there was touching and a definite power differential between coworkers, the women were more likely to define this behavior as harassment. Erin, for example, described having an older man chef who would use the excuse of checking on her work to stand very close behind her and rest his chin on her shoulder while she worked at the stove. Later, he refused to talk to Erin about a menu decision unless she sat in his lap during the conversation. Shelley recalled being grabbed by her employer when she was a young chef and, although at the time she attributed this behavior to the fact that he had an alcohol problem, looking back she now believed the situation was incredibly improper.

Just as sexualized behavior could be deemed harassment if it was done by a supervisor, our participants also labeled certain incidents as harassment if they involved coworkers who were not chefs, such as dishwashers and waiters (see Giuffre and Williams 1994). In our discussion about sexual harassment with Melissa, she began by saying "No one's ever harassed me" before going on to describe how some of the dishwashers she had worked with had made her uncomfortable. Melissa didn't consider this harassment because she was above these men in the kitchen hierarchy. Four other participants recalled having incidents with dishwashers, and they tended to describe these encounters as issues or problems rather than label them harassment.

Natasha described how some of the dishwashers or prep cooks would follow women chefs into the walk-in refrigerators and tell the women "I like your breasts." Christine also recalled being cornered in walk-ins by dishwashers. Both Karen and Lyndsay had dishwashers repeatedly make sexual advances toward them even after they had told the men to leave them alone. In these cases, the dishwashers were from Mexico and Cuba and their status as immigrants was given as a reason for their not understanding what was inappropriate at work. Melissa admitted these situations could be confusing for the men dishwashers who overheard the women chefs cracking sexual jokes with the men chefs, but who didn't realize that, because they occupied a different place in the workplace hierarchy, the same familiarity did not apply to them.

While our participants didn't always label sexual behavior at work as harassment, or couched their definitions of harassment depending on the offender's place in the kitchen hierarchy, it was agreed upon that women should take care of these situations on their own. This appeared to be partly attributed to beliefs that management would either ignore harassment or be ineffective in dealing with it. Joan and Tabitha had approached the chefs in charge of their restaurants when they experienced unwelcome advances from coworkers and restaurant owners. In each case there was little done to remedy the situation, although Tabitha joked that because of her there was a mandatory meeting about avoiding sexual harassment—which the owner of the restaurant and perpetrator of Tabitha's harassment did not have to attend. Therefore, the women believed it would be better to handle these situations themselves.

Another reason why the women believed it would be better to handle these situations on their own is because sexual harassment was viewed as normal within all-men kitchens and, therefore, this behavior was just one more example of how women had to prove they could tough it out in the kitchen. Patricia, an executive chef-owner, was one of the chefs who believed that sexual harassment was inevitable in restaurant kitchens. She thought that learning to deal with those issues was part of figuring out how to fit in to an all-men staff:

You're going to have to learn how men talk to men and interact with each other. You're going to have sexual harassment. Are you going to be part of that game? Or are you going to be the rule keeper and know when things get out of hand or when things are still in a playful mode? . . . You just have to find a way to get along.

According to the chefs, some of the sexual joking and teasing was meant to determine if women were tough enough for the kitchen. If women were sensitive and got offended by what went on in professional kitchens, this served as proof they did not belong. Rose remembered men coworkers trying to get her to react by talking about sexual dreams they had about her. When this happened, Rose had to make sure the men didn't think they were getting to her:

> [I]f you blushed, it just would not stop, it would go *all night long*. But they would do it to anybody. They would do it to gay guys, they would join in on that. You just had to hold your own. But once I proved myself to them, it would be really funny because then the guys would spend more time asking me what they did wrong to get their girlfriend mad at them. And they would need the girl's point of view.

Women chefs had to adopt different ways of addressing sexualized workplaces. Some of the chefs would ignore sexual comments or pretend they didn't hear them. Natasha, who worked with a staff of young men in their early to midtwenties, complained that the men would talk about "the nastiest stuff" but she would put on her imaginary earmuffs and try and ignore all the conversation around her.

Ignoring didn't always work, however, and sexual talk and teasing would sometimes escalate (see Denissen 2010b). At this point, most of the women would choose to be very blunt and "put them in their place." Some of the women would make remarks like, "I don't need to hear about that" or "That's inappropriate" to get across that they wanted these conversations to end. Erin, a chef de cuisine, would say to the men she worked with that "You're going too far" in response to some of their jokes. She explained, "Guys don't know when they've crossed that line and you need to remind them."

The more serious cases involved men who openly propositioned or touched some of the women. If being blunt and telling the men they were not interested or to stop touching them didn't work, the women would have to come up with stronger reactions. Alexandra, an events planner at a restaurant, recalled how she had to show a coworker that she was tough: "I've had a guy, every time he walked by me on the line, he would feel my ass. So one day when he did that, I pulled a knife and held it to his throat, 'Do it again and I will cut you.'" Other women found less physical ways of making their point known. Karen, a pastry chef, recalled two separate occasions when dishwashers would say sexual things to her. In one case, after repeatedly telling him to stop with no response, Karen ended the harassment by insulting the dishwasher's mother in his native language. She claimed he didn't speak to her for two months after the incident, but the harassment ended. In the second case, Karen knew the dishwasher was in charge of cleaning the large walk-in refrigerator in the kitchen, and she threw eggs all over the walk-in to make a large mess he would have to clean up. When the head chef asked her what happened, Karen feigned innocence but noticed that the dishwasher no longer made harassing remarks to her, so she assumed he had gotten the message she had sent with the eggs.

Women who had proven they could deal with harassment on their own were critical of women who did not make the same choices. Brenda, who had worked as a pastry chef for some large hotel chains, recalled her frustration with some of the women chefs at her job who wouldn't address some sexual behavior in the kitchen.

> This one guy he used to pull the bra ads out of the Sunday paper and tape them up along the line where the tickets would go. Just 'cause he thought they were good looking or whatever. And, there used to be a couple of girls on the line when he was doing this and I would ask them: "Why do you let Mark do this?" [They would answer] "Oh, that doesn't really bother me. He's fun [said in a high-pitched dopey voice]." [I would say] "Okay" [skeptically].

Like in many of the examples of sexual harassment we have discussed, women are ultimately tasked with policing the environment at work. For Brenda, some of her fellow women chefs lost her respect because they would not put a stop to the sexualized atmosphere at work. Men are not seen as responsible for creating a sexualized workplace—that had been accepted as normal. Instead, women are expected to put up with these conditions and, once a line is crossed, to find ways to stop this behavior. Not only are they expected to stop the harassing behavior, they are expected to do so in a way that does not cause friction within the team (Fine 1987). At the same time, women have to make sure the behavior they find problematic would be viewed as such by the entire kitchen. If not, they run the risk of being labeled "killjoys" who are too sensitive to work as chefs.

Only two of our participants had ever gone through formal channels to complain about sexual harassment in the workplace. For Joan and Tabitha, this avenue did not stop the behavior and they both eventually left these jobs for positions at other restaurants. Overall, there was a strong unspoken norm to avoid making formal complaints. Women who had turned to management were discussed in derogatory ways, such as during our interview with Monica, a sous chef. Earlier in our conversation, Monica had mentioned she had never experienced sexual harassment, although she believed it was "bound to happen" due to the eclectic mix of people who tend to work in restaurant kitchens. She said that, because of this inevitability, women needed to know how to "put their best foot forward." When asked if she knew of any cases when this wasn't enough to stop sexual harassment and management had to be involved, Monica stated that yes, that did happen, but only when women weren't "assertive" enough. Monica's comments suggest that the true blame for these events weren't the men who were acting inappropriately, but women who were not strong enough to make the behavior stop.

Much like women who have experienced sexual assault or violence, there was pressure to avoid getting the "authorities" involved. For those working in restaurants or hotels, this meant on-site management or even corporate headquarters. When outsiders became part of a sexual harassment case it was described as "*way* too many people involved and *way* too much tension between everybody in the kitchen." This could lead to events getting "blown out of proportion." Our chefs warned that things could get "ugly" for those involved, even for those who were the victim of sexual harassment. Chelsea explained: "But if you make it like a whole big case, well, you better make sure that you're squeaky clean. In the kitchen if you engage in [sexual] conversation and then you get offended because someone touches you, then you've opened yourself up to it, too." According to Chelsea, this created another fine line for women chefs to walk. If they did not partake of some of the sexual joking and teasing, they could be considered poor team players and could be criticized for not trying to be more a part of the kitchen. However, if they did act like "one of the guys" by joking and teasing and one of the men ended up taking the behavior further to touching, the women's earlier joking could be used as a sign that she had asked for the harassment.

Brenda recalled a time when she was in the role of management when dealing with a case of sexual harassment. One of the men chefs had touched the breast of a woman coworker and this made her very upset. When Brenda learned of this from the woman, she brought the issue to the head chef at the large hotel where everyone worked. The situation was eventually resolved with an apology from the man chef and, after a few months, much of the kitchen tension had been resolved. What struck Brenda was the fact that so many of the staff were shocked that Brenda had taken the matter to management. From her perspective, there was no other way to properly handle the issue as a manager, but others were surprised to have things addressed in an official way.

Several of the women noted that sexual harassment seemed to be on the decline. They attributed this to a generational shift in which older men chefs who were used to acting in a sexually aggressive way toward women staff were leaving the industry. The chefs also cited a movement toward more corporately owned restaurants. When restaurants and hotels are owned by large corporations, this means that millions of dollars could be lost if a sexual harassment suit was filed. Another reason for decreases in sexual harassment may come from the women themselves. As more women enter and advance to leadership positions within the gastronomic field, fewer all-men workplace cultures will develop. In addition, when women become leaders of professional kitchens they may find ways to reduce sexual harassment (we will discuss this further in chapter 4). Several of our participants make it known to their employees what they expect in terms of the tone and conversation that goes on in the kitchen. Michelle, an executive chef-owner, reminds the men on her staff: "This is how I work. I don't like profanity. I will not tolerate sexual jokes. I will not tolerate jokes with racial tones. I will not tolerate any jokes that are hurtful to anyone." Through setting explicit standards about what she expects from her staff, Michelle and other women executive chefs demonstrate that strong teams can be developed without a sexualized and insensitive work environment. Anna, an executive chef, also worked in a kitchen that emphasized mutual respect between coworkers. She felt that this atmosphere helped promote the idea to the chefs and the outside world that the restaurant kitchen "is a professional place and it has to remain that way." Therefore, as chefs strive to be seen as highly trained professionals, some of the more vulgar aspects of professional kitchens may be discontinued.

GENDER DOESN'T MATTER, EXCEPT WHEN IT DOES

Even though gender serves as one of the primary ways of experiencing the social world, it can be very difficult for people to parse out and describe how they feel that their gender has impacted their lives. This may be even more the case for women like our participants who work in extremely male-dominated occupations that include harsh conditions and significant physical labor. Research on women in construction (Denissen 2010a; 2010b), coal mining (Tallichet 2000), and firefighting (Yoder and Aniakudo 1997) found women often downplay any negative experiences in their work, particularly when talking with their male coworkers. Within these jobs there is a strong emphasis on being tough and not complaining about the circumstances at work. Discussing problems constitutes weakness, and would only serve to confirm men's beliefs that women do not belong in those occupations. For women, this can also translate into beliefs that one should not complain about gender discrimination and mistreatment at work. As a result, sometimes when women are asked about their gendered experiences, they claim that "gender doesn't matter" or even "I don't see gender." Researchers have dubbed this "gender neutrality" and it refers to reluctance or even refusal on the part of research participants to acknowledge the ways gender has impacted their lives. Sharon Bird and Laura Rhoton (2011) review the research on gender neutrality and discuss three dimensions of the concept: 1) casting oneself or their actions as gender neutral ("I see myself as a 'chef,' not a 'woman chef'"); 2) rejecting others' attempts to frame actions as gendered ("But I don't think it's a gender thing"); and 3) supporting the ideas that organizational structures, cultures, and practices are gender neutral ("But it's the same for everybody [man or woman]").

Throughout our interviews there were several times when the participants denied the influence of gender on their work experiences, and they did so in ways that drew upon the concept of gender neutrality. There is always a fine line between the desire to respect the opinions and perspectives of our participants—we do not want to take on the role of the omniscient researchers who know our participants' lives better than they know themselves—and recognizing specific patterns and contradictions within our data. One of the strengths of qualitative research is the ability to allow researchers to examine inconsistencies and ambivalence, and we wanted to examine some of the ways our participants adopt the concept of gender neutrality in their interviews. This can also help demonstrate that these women chefs truly were providing the most generous accounts of their work experiences and that their descriptions of incidents at work including discrimination, harassment, and other forms of mistreatment were not exaggerated or evidence that these women were merely embittered employees trying to present excuses for their own shortcomings.

Among the participants who denied the impact of gender on their careers, there were two major positions that were taken: 1) gender doesn't matter *anymore* and 2) gender doesn't matter *to me*. The first category is more abstract and refers to the overall position of women within the gastronomic field and how it has changed over the past few decades. The second category refers more to personal experiences and whether or not women chefs believed that negative experiences in their careers could be directly attributable to their being a woman. These categories were not mutually exclusive and some of our participants drew from both in responding to questions about their work experiences. There were also numerous times when the women cited gender neutrality—asserted, sometimes very strongly, that their gender absolutely did not impact their work experiences in any way—then, in almost the next breath, provided an example of an incident that appeared to the researchers to be very much a gender issue.

For some of the participants, their insistence that gender didn't matter was attributed to the fact that conditions for women in professional kitchens used to be much worse. Therefore, in comparison, gender was not an issue anymore. Jill, for example, talked about how things were now a "pretty mixed workforce" but that this wasn't the case just ten years ago. With more women working as chefs, this translated into better treatment for women in the gastronomic field. Rose, who had worked in the culinary industry for twenty-five years, had definitely seen a change. She described conditions for women now as "*way* better" and compared this to how things were when she was just starting out and she felt that she was "at equal level with the dishwasher that nobody acknowledged." Christine agreed with this sentiment and said that now women were treated "almost as equals" in the kitchen and she said it had been two or three years since she could recall having problems with people thinking less of her because she was a woman chef.

Some women also stated that gender did not matter as a professional chef because of the nature of the occupation. Amber, the owner of a meal delivery service, did not believe her gender had impacted her career. When asked if gender ever mattered in success as a professional chef, she ascribed failure not to gender, but to "trying too hard." She explained that most people "think they can cook" but really cannot. Ultimately success is not a gender issue, but one of talent. Dana also believed that cooking professionally was much more meritocratic than other careers and, because of this, gender mattered less than one's abilities in the kitchen. She explained:

> With my experience I would say that I don't see a difference [in how men and women chefs are treated]. If you work hard, your efforts are rewarded in some way. If you're lazy or you don't really get it, maybe you're not going to go as far. With food, the results speak for themselves. Are people happy? Are they coming back in? If they are, you're doing your job. You're doing a good job.

Other women with more experience in the kitchen also cited work ethic and talent as the chief determinants of success. Camille stated that "what proves your ability and ultimately your success is how well you work" and, because "anyone can work," success is not be determined by gender. Jill, a restaurant chef, also believed that success was determined by performance and that "if you can do it, then you'll be rewarded."

Another way of referring to gender neutrality during the interviews involved referencing well-known women in the gastronomic field. The accomplishments of these women were cited as examples of how being a woman did not necessarily preclude success as a chef. Women like Julia Child and Alice Waters were mentioned, as well as more contemporary chefs like Nancy Silverton who founded La Brea Bakery in Los Angeles and Monica Pope, a Houston-based chef. Even women cooking celebrities like Food Network hosts Paula Deen and Rachael Ray were given as examples of women who were able to make it within the gastronomic field. While it could be argued that these examples of successful women chefs were so visible because they served as tokens within a larger male-dominated field, these respondents used these women's success to suggest that 1) there are actually a lot of successful women chefs, and 2) any highly skilled woman can make it. This is similar to the argument that racism has disappeared because we now have an African American (actually mixed ethnic) president of the United States. Relying on Kanter's theory of tokenism, Adia Harvey Wingfield (2013) argues that highlighting visible and successful numerical minorities downplays structural and systematic inequalities, such as overall race or gender underrepresentation. For women chefs, noting that there are women chef media superstars may be a way to focus on women's strengths rather than their limitations.

Several women pointed out that gender inequality exists in every major field; thus, being a chef is no different than women trying to succeed in any other job. While Jane admitted, "You may have to work a little bit harder," she went on to add: "but I don't know of any field where you're a woman and you don't have to work a little harder." According to this perspective, because of the ubiquity of gender inequality, its impacts were actually reduced in the day-to-day experiences of the chefs.

Being a chef was compared to working in numerous other fields that had long been dominated by men in jobs such as doctors, veterinarians, and astronauts. Elisa, an executive chef-owner, reminded us that, "When you go into a new kitchen, office, everywhere, it's hard at first. You have to know the people and prove you are qualified for that job." This process of proving oneself in a new work environment is universal and, therefore, Elisa believed, "It doesn't matter whether you're female or male."

Instead of gender, individual characteristics like personality and confidence were cited as the most important factors in determining success as a chef. For example, Kate, a restaurant owner and former chef, said that she never really noticed being treated differently than her men counterparts at work. She attributed this to the atmosphere set by her head chef and the fact that she wasn't a "competitive" person who tried to compete with her men coworkers. Instead, she was a "confident" person and that this helped her at work.

Lyndsay also cited her personality as a reason why she did not experience gender mistreatment at work, but she also admitted she wasn't sure it was truly her individual personality or her status as a lesbian that impacted how she was treated the most. "I get along with everybody and I don't know if it's because I'm a lesbian or my specific personality—but I don't take a lot of crap. If there's something I don't agree with, I will say what I think. I'm also someone you can rely on in the kitchen as a team player." Earlier in her interview, Lyndsay had discussed how being a lesbian marked her as "other" in the kitchen. She generally wasn't seen as a sexual object at work (although she had been harassed by a coworker in the past), nor was she accepted as another one of the guys because she was sexually attracted to women. Her comments suggest awareness of just how difficult it can be to ascribe reasons for certain workplace experiences. In general, she enjoyed her work but didn't know if her success was attributable to her personality, willingness to be a team player, or something else.

Natasha also cited her personality as one of the reasons why she had managed to be successful as a chef and to move up the kitchen hierarchy. At one point she mentions that her personality allows her to "be one of the guys" because she hasn't ever been "the girly girl." She describes this part of herself as natural and "just how I've always been" but later she also cited the "softer side" of personality that allowed her to connect with customers and provide a public face for her restaurant that didn't reflect what many people consider a "rough and tough career." Natasha's statements challenge the idea that personality is fixed. For several of our chefs, what they refer to as their personality took on more of a type of performance. Other women discussed taking on different "personas" in male-dominated kitchens in order to fit in and be accepted. While it can be seen as a source of pride that one has an appropriate or strong personality, often the way one's personality is reflected is based upon gendered expectations about those working in restaurant kitchens.

Some of the chefs referenced an empowerment narrative and insisted women in the gastronomic field choose how they are treated. Anna claimed that women are "probably treated however they expect to be treated" and they "set the pace for whatever their experience in the culinary world is going to be." Likewise, Chelsea described how this emphasis on self-determination played out in her own career:

> There are always people that are going to harass you, make fun of you because you're a woman or whatever. But you have to keep going. I really see myself as equal to them and I always have. And that is part of you. You can't doubt that. A lot of it comes from you. I mean, you can go, "Wah, they're harassing me." But you are treated the way you want to be treated. You have to take responsibility for yourself.

Karen also shared these beliefs and claimed, "I don't believe that anyone can hold you back. The only person that can hold you back is yourself. I've only worked for the best places. Those were decisions that I made."

Comments like these can be beneficial for women in male-dominated jobs. Claims of gender neutrality can provide a sense of power in dealing with the gastronomic field. By refusing to see gender as having an impact on their lives, women no longer have to face negative feelings about discrimination or unfairness in the workplace—particularly since their gender (and how men coworkers view their gender) is not something they can control. At the same time, for women who are successful in these competitive fields, attributing success to their personality, work ethic, or belief in oneself paints these women as "survivors" and as being "worthy" of the positions they have attained. Much like in Sharon Bird and Laura Rhoton's (2011) review of gender strategies at work, women who align with the expectations of male-dominated workplaces are able to gain tolerance and even acceptance at work. Therefore, there is strong pressure to denounce the effects of gender in favor of the strengths of individual personality.

An example of this came from an interview with Sara, a culinary instructor. Over the course of her career she had worked in many different environments with varying levels of gender segregation. In one workplace, all the executive chefs and managers were men. She definitely felt things were different there, but, eventually, cited her own personality and standards as the reason for how she was treated.

> You wouldn't complain there. If you did, you would look whiney—not that anybody ever said that to you. No one ever said, "You really shouldn't complain." . . . But the impression that you get from being around men and things like that, if you were to complain, you'd seem a little weak. . . . I never felt like they gave me bad jobs or anything because I was a woman. I felt like I was respected in that manner but that's because that's what I demanded of myself. I think that people who are looking for sympathy or looking for things like that, they are the ones who typically get picked on more. I wouldn't accept that of myself and I wouldn't allow somebody else to treat me that way so I found that I was usually in a good situation with those things.

Sara's comments highlight what researchers have pointed out as the danger of gender neutrality. She says that she did not experience any discrimination at work (being given "bad" jobs), but also there was the pervasive atmosphere that, no matter what happened, you could not complain. By denying the impact of gender on the work experiences of women, this ignores larger, institutional gender inequalities and recasts career outcomes as just the result of individual will, talent, and effort. Jill's earlier insistence that "if you can do it, then you'll be rewarded" is tempered by the fact that she was passed over for a promotion despite being the next worker in line because a man chef needed the higher position and greater income to provide for his family.

Gender neutrality discourses appear to have emerged as a version of girl power rhetoric in concert with third-wave feminism (Giffort 2011). Saying that there is no gender inequality may help women in male-dominated occupations to focus on their own strengths and skills, and doing so may serve as a form of everyday empowerment. Similar discourses appear to resonate with many women workers, particularly younger women. In 2013, Facebook's chief operating officer, Sheryl Sandberg, published and sold millions of copies of *Lean In: Women, Work, and the Will to Lead*. Sandberg argues that "men still run the world" (5) but that things are much better for women today. Although she recognizes institutionalized gender inequality, Sandberg claimed that "women are hindered by barriers that exist within ourselves. We hold ourselves back . . . by lacking self-confidence, by not raising our hands, and by pulling back when we should be leaning in" (8). She compels women to self-promote and ask for they want at work instead of waiting for gender inequality to decrease.

The responses to Sandberg's book from scholars and media commentators were quite divided. Some lauded her for saying that women can make changes and empower themselves. Gender scholars were concerned that the book ignored structural inequality and ultimately, placed blame for women's unequal work experiences squarely on their shoulders. In other words, a problematic consequence of a "lean in" strategy is that solutions to gender inequality become individually-based. We believe that many of the women we interviewed were opposed to labeling their experiences as gender inequality as a strategy of empowerment, very similar to Sandberg's instructions. In this framework, women can be survivors, and this viewpoint is appealing because the underlying message is one of women's strength, not victimhood.

Too often the mindset of "I am a woman who succeeded, so you should be able to do so, too" can then turn from being an encouragement to a criticism used to silence women who speak out against gendered mistreatment in the workplace. Such feelings can also lead women to resist changes to the gastronomic field and individual restaurants, such as the creation of women chefs' organizations or policies to promote women's entrance to and promotion within the field (Bird and Rhoton 2011). For example, Elisa, a chef-owner, commented that, "If I had more chances and opportunities because I'm female, I wouldn't like that." Because the workplace culture requires women to prove their merits, women are concerned that any appearance of special treatment (even if this treatment merely serves to level the playing field) would invalidate all their hard work.

Patricia, an executive chef-owner, mentioned this reluctance for change when she was asked about women's roles in the gastronomic field and if there were any ways to make the career more open to women. Throughout her answer, Patricia goes back and forth between acknowledging the structural impediments to women's progress in the field and stating that individuals are able to dictate their own paths. She began by asserting that she didn't like programs meant to increase women's entrance to the career. She went on to describe being discouraged from enrolling in veterinary school when she was younger because many schools did not admit women. Because there were no rules (currently) banning women from enrolling in culinary school or working as a chef, Patricia felt that just having "free will," or the ability to do these things, should be enough for women. Those who really wanted to be a chef would fight against the current "like salmons going upstream" in order to make it. However, she later admits that, without special programs and laws opening veterinary schools to women, there would not be any women vets.

Some women felt that, because there were times when it felt like being a woman helped them at work, this invalidated any claims that women experienced negative treatment as chefs. Melissa, who we discussed earlier because she had initially not been hired as a pastry chef by a head chef who did not like to work with women, pointed out that the chef who eventually campaigned for her to be hired did so because he liked working with her and because she was "cute." Even though she had been passed over for the job first, she framed this as an example of a time that her gender ultimately helped her at work. Karen, another pastry chef, recalled times when she knew women had been hired by the head chef not because they were good at their job, but because they were attractive. Ellen, who worked as a culinary instructor and in sales for a pastry company, believed being a woman helped her at work because she was an anomaly to the usual group of men who worked in the industry: "It made a difference because you have a chef and he's been looking at men all day and a woman comes in and they are like, 'Sure I will give you the time of day.'" Because she was something different to look at she felt that chefs and clients actually gave her more of their time than men in the same position—an ironic effect of subtle sexism.

Accompanying this insistence that gender didn't matter, but that personality and whether or not women accepted mistreatment was the main determinant shaping women's experiences in the gastronomic field, was a belief that gender should not be brought up at work. For some of our participants, even suggesting that men and women had different work experiences was proof that women were "looking to be offended" instead of working hard and getting ahead. Lisa described women who paid attention to gender differences as work as having an attitude of "I'm female. Hear me roar." These women, she explained, would be limited by their focus on being a woman instead of being a good chef. Even Tabitha, who cited issues like women getting stuck as garde manger or being kept away from the public side of cooking, was adamant that "whining and bitching isn't helping anybody."

This reluctance to discuss gender may stem from internalizing the norms of professional kitchens. The focus on meritocracy and hard work is delegitimized if the women acknowledge that there are times when working hard and doing good work may not get women as far as men in the gastronomic field. By focusing on personality and choices, women in male-dominated fields are able to distance themselves from women who did not follow the rules of male-dominated workplaces and are able to excuse gender-based mistreatment as "one-offs" instead of systematic arrangements (Rhoton 2011). However, ignoring gender inequality at work, or reframing it to be just the problem of women who don't work hard enough at fitting in, has been found to reproduce the same workplace cultures that devalue femininity, uphold the status quo, and inhibit change (Rhoton 2011; Bird and Rhoton 2011).

There were several examples of contradictions regarding the women's view of when gender did or did not matter. When asked if there were any differences in how men and women were treated in the culinary field, Camille asserted that, "with experience and success, they're treated exactly the same." She went on to say, "I think a man and a woman both walk in for the same position with the same or similar experiences, the man might get the job first." Even when discussing her personal experiences as a chef, Camille denied the effects of gender on her career. When discussing the challenges of balancing work and family (which we will examine in chapter 5), she explained that she and Joe, the current chef at her restaurant, started out working together at the same restaurant several years ago. Joe had no children while Camille was the mother of two, but she did not attribute their disparate career trajectories to different family circumstances:

> And we're kind of the same age and he doesn't have a family. He doesn't. And, if he did, I don't think he'd have to stop (laughs) what he's doing to go take care of them [the children] very often. I'm sure he'd have a woman do that for him. You kind of get to a certain point of your career and then—I'm sure this happens in every career—the females kind of have other things going on. But the men kind of don't. In that case, Joe can kind of concentrate on this [work] more. But, I don't think that . . . I don't think I could say there's an overall male-versus-female characteristic thing that makes men seem to advance faster.

Throughout her comments, Camille acknowledges that, if Joe had children, he would be exempt from many of the childcare tasks that could interrupt a career. But, she goes on to state this happens in every career not just as a chef and that she didn't see that it was really a gendered issue despite her statement about how women are more likely to be responsible for childrearing.

Some of the women's viewpoints could possibly be traced to their positions within the gastronomic field. Research cited by Bird and Rhoton (2011) found that some women in male-dominated fields initially engaged in claims of gender neutrality only to revise their opinions later in their careers. This was attributed to the women realizing over the course of their work lives that, even if they "play the game" and adopt the ideology and behavior of male-dominated workplaces, this didn't always translate into acceptance and chances for advancement. We actually found that some of the most well-established of our participants were the most adamant in their affirmations of gender neutrality. These women were more established in their careers at the time of their interviews, which seemed to offer some form of protection from gender-based mistreatment. These opinions tended to come from chef-owners or some of the chef instructors who no longer worked in restaurant kitchens. Because these women currently did not experience these conditions, they were skeptical of claims that women chefs faced challenges in the workplace. Susan, the owner of a pastry store, said that "I don't think it's a man's world" and that women chefs had to remember "You're the driver. You're the machine." When questioned more specifically if this meant that she had never seen any gender inequality in the profession, she admitted, "Maybe if you work for somebody else. If you own your own shop, nobody can tell you what to do." Susan, in her comments, dismisses the fact that most chefs do work for someone else, particularly when just starting out in the career. Similarly, Karen, the well-known pastry chef we quoted earlier, described how she decided to only work at the "best places" and that, because of her choices, she did not feel she had experienced negative treatment as a woman chef. In both of these cases, these women had worked their way up the kitchen hierarchy. They were in positions that demanded respect and included hiring power and the ability to fire employees who were disrespectful. But these chefs did not seem to acknowledge that many women did not have these advantages at work and that it often took years to reach positions with such influence.

One reason women such as Susan and Karen were so resolute in their assertions that gender no longer mattered could be because they had the most invested in the current gastronomic field. If there were changes that radically altered the field to make it more woman friendly, this could invalidate the years of hard work they contributed prior to reaching their current positions. These women had learned and followed the rules of the game and felt that any changes to the rules could unfairly affect them (Bird and Rhoton 2011; Rhoton 2011). These views help illustrate how male-dominated workplace cultures continue to thrive even after women enter these fields. Individual women chefs come to identify with their ability to navigate these male-dominated spaces and can be reluctant to alter them for fear this could eliminate some of the gains they have made in their careers.

A PLACE IN THE KITCHEN?

Women who work in professional kitchens face a variety of barriers to becoming accepted as valued members of the kitchen team. Because the gastronomic field and most restaurant worlds have been male-dominated for such a long time, women entering these all-men spaces can be seen as invaders who have to prove that they belong. They have to demonstrate that they are both physically and mentally strong through working longer hours, refusing help, and learning to avoid any forms of feminine emotional displays.

Even more vital is for women to prove that they will not be disruptive to the masculine workplace culture that permeates many professional kitchens. Chefs are known to be an eclectic mix of individuals. Women have to make sure they are the ones adapting to the workplace and not the other way around. To do this, they often learn to manage the sexualized joking and teasing that happens in many kitchens, and they also take on the responsibility of handling cases when this behavior goes too far and crosses the line into harassment. When this happens, the women have to make sure their response ensures both an end to the unwanted behavior while still preserving the camaraderie of the kitchen (Fine 1987).

All of these efforts become part of additional labor expected of women chefs. They perform this labor under the watchful gaze of their men coworkers who appear quick to generalize any signs of weakness from *a* woman chef to represent failings in *all* women chefs. The pressure to fit in within the kitchen is strong and many women chefs adopt claims of gender neutrality to assure themselves and others that gender is not the primary force shaping their career outcomes. Although many share experiences that indicate that their gender does matter at work, for these women, denying the influence of gender is a way of reclaiming power and coping with inequality over which they may have little control. It is more empowering for them to highlight their strengths and why they have been successful instead of emphasizing the discrimination and mistreatment they have experienced. However, at the same time, these denials serve to reinforce some of the same workplace cultures that questions the worth ethic and the place of women in the field.

4 · BITCHES, GIRLY GIRLS, OR MOMS

Women's Perceptions of Gender-Appropriate Leadership Styles in Professional Kitchens

At age twenty-four, Dana was the youngest executive chef that we interviewed for our project. Dana was juggling her new position heading the kitchen at a small, bistro-style restaurant with completing her degree at a nearby culinary school. Finding the time for work and school demands wasn't Dana's major source of stress, however. During her interview with Patti, Dana described how her biggest challenge involved earning the respect of her coworkers. As Dana described her job, Patti was struck by the discrepancy between how the media so often presents chefs (for example, the yelling, cursing Scottish chef Gordon Ramsay from the television show *Hell's Kitchen*) with the reality of Dana's situation. According to Dana, many interactions with staff involved her having to walk a "fine line" between being assertive enough to be seen as a legitimate leader and avoiding criticism for being too harsh when giving directions or feedback:

... it's such a fine line. It is a double standard. A guy can say whatever he wants, well, not whatever he wants, but he can say the same thing and get a result. For me, it takes more. I can't say it the same way. I have to find another way to say it. . . . To get what I want, I have to know how to manipulate how I am. . . . One time [one of the servers] said, "It's your tone when you ask me." I said, "John [the owner] says the same things to you and you just shut your mouth and do what you're told. But when I say it, it's a problem." He said, "It's just the way you say it." I was like, "You just don't like that I'm saying it." I got really upset. "It's not fair that he can say that, a guy can say that, and you just do what you're told." He said, "You're just being mean." I said, "I'm not being mean." It's my biggest pet peeve.

It seems impossible to imagine Gordon Ramsay (or many other men chefs) spending part of his day worrying that his "tone" may hurt the feelings of his restaurant staff. Unlike the dramatized versions of men chefs' leadership styles, Dana has to spend a good deal of time managing how she presents herself as a leader at work. Dana's experience demonstrates the power of workplace culture, particularly the role of gendered norms and interactions in maintaining occupational sex segregation (Ridgeway 2011). The circumstances of various workplace cultures and the day-to-day interactions between coworkers play a significant role in disadvantaging women chefs as they attempt to move up within the gastronomic field. Part of these interactions includes the leadership styles that women chefs adopt in their careers and how their (often male) coworkers respond to having a woman in a managerial position.

For many women, management is filled with numerous obstacles based upon the perceived fit of their gender for leadership roles and how well individual women are able to conform to these roles. Like Dana, these women are forced to walk a fine line between professional competency requiring assertive, agentic behavior and gender normativity that stresses passivity and commitment to communal goals. If women err on the side of being seen as professionally competent by adopting a masculine leadership style, they risk being labeled "bitches" who are "trying to act like a man." But if they adhere too strictly to feminine gender norms while leading, they can be dismissed as "girly girls" who are unfit to even work in a professional kitchen, much less lead one.

In this chapter, we discuss the role of gendered leadership styles in professional kitchens and rely on our in-depth interviews to discuss how women chefs view the options available to them and other women in management roles. Our chapter describes women's perspectives of three different management styles available to women chefs. First, they describe a bitchy form of leadership characterized by adopting a masculine, authoritarian approach to managing. Second, the chefs interviewed describe a girly girl leadership style, which relies on a more feminine, friendly approach. Both of these options are seen as less than ideal for navigating professional life as a chef. A third alternative is to adopt the role of "mom" or "big sister" in the kitchen. Many women preferred this leadership style because it relied on qualities that, in their view, made women chefs different and better than men who lead.

These descriptions will demonstrate how women chefs naturalize styles of leadership as though they are biological. They talk about how men lead in one way and women another. While respondents describe these essentialized ways of leading, we do not argue that there is a female way to lead. Modes of leadership are coded masculine and feminine through a social, not biological, process. Men and women then adopt these modes based on their desire to effectively lead while maintaining socially appropriate gender roles.

WOMEN'S LEADERSHIP IN MALE-DOMINATED WORKPLACES AND JOBS

In male-dominated jobs, men are immediately assumed to possess leadership qualities, while women must prove they are capable leaders. Men have historically held positions of authority; thus, masculine styles of leadership have become the default (Katila and Eriksson 2013). One is not described as a "masculine leader" but just as a "leader." Over time, this default form of leadership becomes viewed as preferable to other styles that are perceived as having feminine traits. Women who attempt to move up organizational hierarchies may find their efforts hindered by tensions with colleagues when they do not fit traditional, masculine ideas of how leaders should be such as rational, respected, able to delegate, aggressive, and stoic. Women supposedly cannot lead or manage employees as well as men because they are seen as too emotional, irrational, sensitive, or lacking authority.

Women have to demonstrate they are exceptional to even be promoted to positions of leadership (Eagly and Johannesen-Schmidt 2001). When in these positions of authority, women often face gendered scrutiny of how they lead. For example, women in male-dominated jobs often report that they have to work harder to get respect from their employees and coworkers.

Most of the sociological research on women's leadership in male-dominated workplaces has been informed by Rosabeth Kanter's (1977) classic theory of tokenism. In order to explain mechanisms of the glass ceiling, Kanter conducted a study of a predominantly male corporation. She theorized that numerical minorities will always be disadvantaged in workplaces as those who try to lead never quite fit in with the numerical majority and rarely earn respect. Women in male-dominated occupations and work settings often must grapple with whether they act like men workers. Taking on masculine leadership traits is not necessarily the key to success for women as numerous studies find that women who are perceived as too dominant, aggressive, or assertive often face disadvantages in their careers (Carli 2001; Furia 2010; Rudman and Glick 2001).

Kanter's (1977) work identified how women were subjected to stereotyped informal roles that largely shaped their occupational experiences within the corporation. Kanter argues that when women are too friendly or flirtatious, they risk being viewed as the seductress, who is classified as a sex object in such a way as to obscure her other skills and talents. There is also the informal role of the mother in which men "brought her their private troubles, and she was expected to comfort them" (1977, 233). These women engaged in nurturing and caring in ways that allowed them to navigate their management roles. Kanter was concerned that the mother role—like the seductress role—ultimately hides women's competence. Finally, Kanter suggests that women who resist these stereotyped characterizations of seductress or mother become the iron maiden whose refusal to be cast according to familiar generalized representations earns her the label of being difficult, tough, brittle, and militant. Kanter notes that women attained the label if they stood up for their rights, self-promoted in any way, or "cut off sexual innuendos" (236). To some degree, our participants tend to describe leadership styles similar to the three options presented by Kanter. However, one major difference we will discuss is the women chefs' redefinition of the mom/big sister role to become a source of feminine strength available to women who lead.

WOMEN MANAGING THE KITCHEN

The movement into head or executive chef positions can be fraught with challenges for women. Women chefs were sometimes discriminated against in hiring and promotion decisions. It was common for their skills to be questioned and a long process of proving oneself was required in order to be taken seriously within the occupation. If women were promoted to head or executive chef positions, it was a sign that they had demonstrated both strong cooking abilities and leadership potential. However, it was not always smooth sailing once they reached these positions.

On top of all the other duties that fall to head chefs, women chefs found themselves having to prove themselves again as capable leaders. Before we continue, we want to acknowledge that one could argue that women and men experience identical challenges in the kitchen as leaders. In other words, perhaps the chefs we interviewed are not encountering gender inequality, but typical challenges as managers. It is true that both men and women chefs experience a brutal brigade-based kitchen atmosphere on their way up, and we do not want to imply that men always make smooth transitions up the kitchen hierarchy. However, taken in context (history of the occupation, cultural schemas that mark women's leadership as less legitimate, gender stereotypes that women in male-dominated jobs face, and critics' gendered evaluations), the women's descriptions and perceptions of their situations suggest that their experiences are unique to women as tokens in this male-dominated occupation.

The question of how much their struggles with leadership should be attributed to gender was demonstrated in our discussion with several chefs. Anna, an executive chef, suggested that all chefs—men and women—have to prove themselves and their skills at "being a leader, and being a manager, and being a good example for your staff," but other comments from our participants suggested that women chefs faced challenges to establishing authority that directly related to their gender. For example, Camille, an executive pastry chef, recalled an early job working at a resort in a Latin American country. Camille's job entailed flying in and working as a pastry chef during the tourist season. As a young woman chef in a foreign country, Camille had a hard time establishing her authority among her older, Latino staff. "At first there was a lot of 'I don't have to do what you say.' You know, 'First of all, you're a girl. Second of all, you're younger than me (laughs). You don't speak Spanish very well.' There was a lot of initial grumbly, 'I don't have to do that for you' kind of stuff."

Camille recalled that these tensions worked themselves out in time, but the added stress of proving oneself can add to the already overloaded schedules of women chefs. Although Camille's situation was complicated due to age and language differences, sometimes this opposition to women in leadership positions happened closer to home. It was not uncommon for men staff members, even those who happily worked alongside women chefs when they were peers, to suddenly refuse to take orders when this woman was promoted to management. Part of Dana's (the young executive chef we discussed in this chapter's introduction) experience was learning that men she used to joke around with and see as friends responded very differently to her once she was named executive chef.

Problems with establishing authority could even lead some women to change jobs. Lisa, a culinary instructor, recalled getting promoted within a corporate restaurant, which made some of her men coworkers resentful and "ruffled their feathers." She eventually left this job in part because of the treatment of the men on her staff.

> There were very wise-assish, side comments, like, "I realize you're my boss but I don't listen to what chicks say." Some of their comments were not sexually explicit, but very overt in "I'm not listening to you." Some would come out and say, "I'm not listening to some dumb bitch. You don't know what you're talking about." Like, "Can't you see that there are dudes in this kitchen?" These are subordinates [making these comments].

The comments directed at Lisa included gendered language and insults (referring to women as "chicks" and calling her a "bitch"). Lisa's frustration with the situation was compounded by the fact that the managers at the corporation did nothing to stop this behavior, even though it had potential to hurt the restaurant's bottom line. Other women acknowledged that, once they were in a position of authority, it was up to them to handle any conflicts with men who opposed having a woman as a superior.

Tabitha, who currently worked as an executive pastry chef, had previously had jobs on the hot side of the kitchen. She explained how difficult it could be to earn the respect of a staff of men:

> I've been a sous chef and manager before, and it's tough being a woman, to be a chef. I worked at this [large local restaurant] and I had forty guys underneath me, and they were mostly guys, they were about maybe 5 percent women. But, yeah, they don't take orders as well. Once you get past a certain level—I mean, it's all about proving yourself constantly. And, once you get past that level, they will respect you the same.

According to Tabitha, upward career mobility for a woman chef is about "constantly" proving oneself. This would continue, she said, until a woman chef reached a level where she had more control over the kitchen. Then women were able to draw a line with men chefs who would not listen to a woman supervisor:

> And, really what it boils down to is, once you get to that point [of being the boss in the kitchen], it's their job that depends on it [working for you]. It's their livelihood. So, they know that, and once you make that clear, that that's the situation, that's how it works. You know, I've had guys who are, like, sexist and stuff, and I had to fire them because there was no going around it. They were so adamant about this [not taking orders from a woman], that it was like, "You cannot work here if I'm working here. Because your disrespect is causing me not to be able to work . . . and, I'm better than you at this" [big laugh].

Ideally, women chefs should be able to manage a kitchen without having to fire employees. Part of their difficulties when moving into management positions relates to the violation of the expectation that "manager = man." Dana admits that people are sometimes surprised when they come into the restaurant and see that she's in charge because "they still don't look for the woman to be the boss." Another example came from Anna, an executive chef who generally believed that issues of establishing authority were not different between men and women chefs. However, she did recall an interaction with her meat suppliers that she attributed to her gender and physical stature:

They [my suppliers] don't me see on a regular basis. They don't see me interact with other people, so they think that because I'm soft-spoken on the phone, they can get away with whatever they want. . . . I once had a meeting with these two guys [from a meat supplier]. They were probably 300 pounds each. I was like "I have been cutting beef tenderloins for ten years. Do you really think that you guys were going to get away with this [delivering an inferior product]?" I think they were so shocked that I stood up for myself that they didn't know exactly what to do about it. . . . I was in the kitchen and I stood right underneath them. I said, "You know, if I was tall and big, you would have packed that meat and taken it away with you and you would have gotten me a refund. I am small and a woman, and you're questioning me about whether or not I know what I'm talking about." I said, "Do not question me. Pick up your meat and get me a refund."

For Anna, her staff saw her every day. That meant, over time, she had established that she was the boss and workers would listen to her and follow her orders. The meat suppliers did not have this history with Anna and made assumptions that, because she was a woman, she would be easy to manipulate and would not fight back when presented with an inferior product.

Our participants agreed that, in order to be seen as legitimate leaders, women chefs have to find a leadership style that allows them to do the necessary creative, production, and management elements of their job. This would help the kitchen to run smoothly with the ultimate result being a successful restaurant. The women we interviewed described three major leadership styles employed by themselves or other women chefs (bitches, girly girls, or mom/big sisters). Each of these styles were highly gendered and each had unique advantages and disadvantages in terms of accomplishing day-to-day tasks and overall career advancement.

I'M A BITCH . . . I MEAN, NOT REALLY: ADAPTING A MASCULINE STYLE OF LEADERSHIP

Several of our participants discussed the pressure women faced to act like "one of the guys" and adopt a leadership style marked by masculine qualities. It was common to hear that one had to be tough to make it in professional kitchens and women who had worked in the gastronomic field for a long time had become "hard" or even "leather-backed" as Ellen described it. She said that, after years working in and then leading a kitchen, it was important to develop this thick skin and not let issues with staff get to you. Much like the "iron maidens" Kanter (1977) studied, these women refused to be cast in familiar gender representations and pulled from a sense of toughness to succeed in their organizations.

In order to establish their authority participants talked about adopting a communication style that could include yelling, cursing, and making sexualized jokes. Bluntness was also described as ways of leading like men. It could also refer to a more formal, less caring attitude toward staff and customers. Because the profession grew out of the military, having a rigid, top-down management style, which is more commonly associated with men managers, was seen as the correct way to run professional kitchens. Taking on a masculine form of leadership could be beneficial to women because their behavior lined up with already established norms in the kitchen. In these scenarios, relying on the power of one's hierarchical place in the kitchen could help establish authority.

Acting in a masculine way could help women chefs downplay the sense of "otherness" that could alienate women in these work environments. When men chefs acted in this masculine way, it was accepted as natural. It is important to stress again, that these women did not necessarily state they were acting like a *man*, but said they were acting like a *chef*—indicating just how thoroughly this career has been associated with men. However, there were times when doing gender in this way was seen as going too far, which could lead to negative responses from both men and women colleagues. When women were seen as violating gendered norms of leadership through being too blunt, too aggressive, or too hierarchical, they could be labeled a bitch. Some of the different behaviors that could get a woman labeled a bitch ranged from yelling to insulting or demoralizing coworkers to even failing to say "please" and "thank you" when making a request. Chelsea, a culinary instructor, noted: "I'm like most of the women I've seen manage and have managed—they're very to the point. They're very in control. Everyone calls them a bitch (laughs) but they are in control of it. They're very decisive and to the point." Dana, an executive chef, had also experienced trouble when she was regarded as acting too masculine:

[Discussing a conflict with a staff member]: But I need for him to understand that when we're busy, we need things done, I don't sugar coat it. I don't go like,

"Oh pretty please can you get me this?" I don't have time for that. It's just, "I need this. Thank you." I don't take it personally and if they're in a hurry and want to throw it at me, I'm like, "thank you." So I told him, "You shouldn't take it personally when I'm demanding something." . . . [About a man cook]: He had a problem taking orders. He thought I was barking at him. I'm just very frank and to the point when we're busy and I don't have time to throw a "please" in there.

As we described in the previous chapter, professional kitchens are busy, rushed places. Both Chelsea and Dana point out the benefit of making quick decisions and relaying to staff if a dish is up to par or asking for an item in the heat of a busy service. This decisiveness could be seen as a positive trait among men chefs, but, as Chelsea notes, for a woman it earns the title of bitch.

A common issue raised by our participants was that the same behavior, when performed by a man, would earn them praise as a strong leader, while a woman doing the same thing was a bitch. In her role as a culinary instructor, Chelsea often had to provide direct feedback to students. If her feedback was not positive and/or delivered too directly, she would get critiques that she was being a bitch because "It [criticism] always seems tougher when it comes from a woman (laughs)."

Karen, an executive pastry chef at a hotel, spoke about how this double standard regarding the response to men and women's leadership styles didn't fit with the traditional model of kitchen work:

If you're a chef you can say whatever you want in whatever way you want because [staff are] supposed to do what they you tell them to do. Most of them don't really care about the delivery of what they're saying, not only what they're requesting but their critique of what you're doing. It's just expected and you just follow the instructions. You do what you're told. You just shut up and work. If you're a woman in a management position and you use those techniques, it's very difficult to get people to do what you're asking them to do, especially, I've found, if that person is a man. I would say that I still have difficulties with a couple of male employees of mine right now.

She points out that, traditionally, cooks have followed the hierarchy of the kitchen because the nature of the job is to "do what you're told." But, when the person who is being told is a man and a woman is doing the telling, this adherence to the established chain of command isn't always followed. In order to gain respect, Karen admits she has to "push back" even though that has gotten her labeled as "difficult to get along with":

> I also believe that had I not been the way that I've been I would have never achieved all that I've achieved. You do have to have a strong personality to lead and to manage, to be calm under pressure. That's a big part of this job. You can't do that if you're meek and you're highly sensitive and if you have a thin skin. No one's going to follow a person like that. It's a double-edged sword and I can live with that. I can live with that "she's difficult to deal with" but chances are there are other men who do the same thing but it's acceptable. . . . That I'm difficult to deal with because I push back, but if I were a man and I pushed back, then I would be assertive and I would be aggressive. I would be a go-getter. But because I'm a woman, I'm difficult to deal with.

Women like Karen grudgingly accepted the label of bitch because they felt it allowed them to accomplish a lot within the gastronomic field. Karen was a well-known pastry chef who had won numerous national and international pastry competitions while also overseeing the desserts at a highly regarded hotel. She believed that, without a strong personality and being able to push back when men questioned her authority, she would not have progressed as far in her career.

Our participants highlighted some of the interesting ways the bitch label could be both accepted and rejected by women chefs. For example, Chelsea actually openly described herself as being a bitch: "I really think women have two mechanisms . . . they either choose to be slutty or they choose to be bitchy. I mean (laughs) you're either tough or you're not." On one hand, Chelsea seemed to be accepting, if not a little proud, of being called a bitch. It was an indicator that she was tough, in charge of the kitchen, and other people knew it. She even recalled her no-nonsense way of responding to men subordinates who didn't like the way she communicated with them:

> I mean, he [another chef instructor] and I can say the same thing but I would be the mean one. I'm okay with that. I'm okay with that because again, it's not really my problem. It's like, "Okay if you want to perceive everything I say as an attack against you, then I'm sorry for you but I have a job to do. Let's just get to the point."

However, Chelsea's further comments about this label suggested a more complex experience of gendered leadership:

> I became the bitch . . . when I became management. I learned that's the only way I could be. It's not that I'm—I hate saying I'm a bitch (laughs) because I'm not. It's just that any woman who's put in that level of authority is a bitch, you know? Like here [at the culinary school where she worked], I still have that problem here with all the guy chefs. They do not want me to tell them to do things. I'm like, "Are you kidding me?" If it was a guy, you'd have no problem with it. I find that they . . . with me, they want me to hold their hands. They want me to be super nice to them, and I'm just like, "Sorry. I'm not your mother."

Chelsea's description of being a bitch contradicts her early comment about women's choices to be a bitch or not and suggests that she felt this was the only option available when she moved into the upper echelons of the kitchen. At the same time that Chelsea claimed that she chose to be a strong, tough bitch in the kitchen rather than a weak, "slutty" woman, she acknowledges that this choice is influenced by others' perceptions about how a woman in a leadership position should act. Her comments also speak to the personal conflicts that are experienced by some women in leadership positions. Although she claimed to have accepted the bitch label, she also says she "hates" having to refer to herself in that way because she is not really a bitch. She understood that the word is mostly used as a pejorative aimed at women who are not fitting traditional gender roles. Instead, her remarks speak more to her recognition that other people see women in charge as "bitchy." Women like Karen and Chelsea claim that, in the position of manager, they can be considered a bitch, but that is more a characteristic of their job role than their actual personality. Cecelia Ridgeway (2011) states that part of the negative response to women in leadership positions, particularly in male-dominated fields, stems from perceived norm violations. Because any woman in a managerial position violates the gender dichotomy of men/leader and woman/follower, these women are already perceived as overly masculine because they are in a position of power.

Several of the women expressed concern over such labels. Dana, who was referenced in the opening to this chapter, talked about how her confrontation with a coworker made her question her behavior. She recalled thinking: "Okay, I will watch my tone. Maybe I come across really bitchy." Our participants generally agreed that men chefs were not evaluated on interpersonal communication in the same way as women. Men were not tasked with watching their tone or criticized for not being "super nice" to staff. However women did have to think about these things. Women like Dana had to constantly reflect on how they "came across" to their colleagues to make sure they were seen as professionally competent without seeming harsh or bitchy.

Walking this fine line of a gendered leadership double standard requires women chefs to engage in forms of emotional labor that men do not. Emotional labor refers to "the management of feeling to create a publicly observable facial and bodily display" (Hochschild 1983, 7). In her classic book, *The Managed Heart*, Arlie Hochschild applied this concept to interactions between service employees and customers. Scholars have since applied the term to mean any falsification of emotions produced for the workplace. These studies find that emotional labor can be stressful, and it has a gendered component (Bellas 1999; Leidner 1991; Wharton 1999). Leaders in workplaces often have to produce particular emotions in order to be perceived as legitimate by their employees (Gardner, Fischer, and Hunt 2009). In order to be successful, women leaders in many jobs must routinely manage not only their staff, but also their presentation of self, in ways that men do not. Women chefs have to expend mental and emotional energy as they constantly manage interactions with employees so as not to be labeled bitches. When a male chef is in the midst of a busy dinner service and snaps at one of the cooks that he needs a dish prepared at that moment, he is merely being an assertive leader who is looking at the big picture. Women chefs in similar positions risk negative responses if they do not add in niceties to their directions to those working under them. Dana affirmed that it's hard to remember to "sugar coat" things in the heat of the moment, and she resented feeling that she would be judged by her staff if she didn't say, "Oh pretty please can you get me this?" for every request.

Dana's experiences fit with research that found women leaders who were viewed as being too direct were criticized while males were not (Carli 2001). When women were direct at work, they had to balance this presentation of self with warmth so as not to face negative sanctions. This additional work required when performing emotional labor becomes just one more task the busy women chefs also have to complete. While emotional labor may be an invisible form of work, failure to adequately manage one's emotions can yield negative work evaluations and even insubordination on the part of one's staff.

It was not just men colleagues that labeled women chefs bitchy. Women chefs could also be criticized by other women. Joan, who was currently a selling manager at an upscale grocery store, was critical of women who felt they had to be a bitch in order to lead:

> Women tend to think that, in order to be successful, you have to be a bitch. And that's not the case. I think you can earn the respect of people if they see you doing things like they do. I've always thought with the old adage my father used to say: "You get more flies with honey than you do with vinegar." And you can get people to do things for you, but you don't have to be a bitch about it. And that's where a lot of women, as they're going up, feel that they need to be a bitch.
>
> INTERVIEWER: How exactly do they act that makes them a "bitch?"
>
> Well, they tend to be a little bit more forceful and, you know . . . it's just different. They just carry themselves differently. It's like all of a sudden, they're in the position and it's like, "Okay. I'm in a position of authority. Now I get to be a certain way." But men don't have to do that. They [women] think that by being a bitch you get respect. And that's not [how to do it].

Joan's comments are interesting because they acknowledge that men do not have to act "like a bitch" to get respect. Again, this is related to gendered expectations of leadership. Men acting dominant and assertive would not be labeled bitchy because these traits are seen as acceptable, and even preferable, for men leaders. Yet, women were warned against acting too masculine or too much like the masculine stereotype of a chef. These women were seen as going overboard in their attempts to fit in with their men colleagues and as acting more like a caricature of what they thought a chef was supposed to be like instead of as a true leader in the kitchen. According to Ridgeway (2011), certain traits that are seen as undesirable for women in the workplace (dominance, abruptness, etc.) are viewed negatively because they contradict women's inferior position in society. When women take on masculine traits at work, they are criticized for going against, not just workplace norms, but larger prescriptions about how much power women should be given at work and in the outside world.

Younger chefs were particularly singled out and descriptions of their tough demeanor and rigid rules was seen as more a sign of a young leader who had not yet learned her own personal style of leadership and, instead, had to rely upon stereotypes. When asked about women who acted masculine or bitchy, Dana mentioned a woman from her culinary school classes:

> I find that there is one girl in particular who goes to school with me that goes about it the wrong way. She overcompensates for being a woman. She's overly vulgar, to the point that it alienates everyone, you know? She tries to be tough but at the same time to be respected, you have to be yourself. . . . I don't really know her that well but, from what I've observed of her, she seems afraid to be herself in groups of people. One-on-one, she's calm and she's herself. You can respect someone who is themselves. But when you overcompensate, or you're overly crass to try to relate to the guys, or overly tough, people are going to see through that and they're not going to respect you. In the end, it's all about respect. If nobody respects you, then you're never going to be a successful leader. I see her making that mistake and I want to say, "Just bring it down a little. Just be yourself. People will respect that and you'll work your way up."

Cathy, our oldest participant at sixty, described her younger self as fitting this pattern. She recalled that, as a small woman who was sometimes literally talked over by some of the men chefs she worked with, she developed a bit of a Napoleon complex and felt she had to be very strict and controlling in order to earn respect. Over time she realized that this method of leading was causing conflict in her restaurant. Through experience and trial and error she eventually developed a leadership style that she felt was a more authentic expression of her personality and she currently described herself as a collaborative leader, which she felt fostered better cohesion between the front and the back of the house.

Not all bitchy women chefs were able to self-correct as Cathy had done. Some of the more experienced chefs recalled times when they had to pull women aside and suggest that they didn't have to be a bitch in order to lead the kitchen and that there were ways to get the staff to work together that were not as harsh. Lisa, a culinary instructor, said that a previous manager had asked her once whether she knew she was a "masculine" woman. Lisa interpreted his query as meaning that she had a dominant personality, which earned her the label of being bitchy. Because of accusations that she was masculine and bitchy from supervisors and coworkers, she actually warns her female students about how to act:

> It's a tough industry. Yes, the tides are changing and there are a lot of females going into this business but it is still a male-dominated industry. I tell female students that the best defense you have as a female in this industry is not to be that bitch. Come into it confident and knowledgeable but don't be that bitch because that's what they expect of you. . . . I'm trying to steer them away from being that stereotypical male expectation of what a female is going to be in this industry. They're expecting that a woman is going to come in an absolute bitch, crabby, trying to be masculine in a feminine way. Like being that hard core, take no crap from anybody kind of woman, and you can't do that.

As Lisa emphasized, men coworkers assumed that women leaders would fit the stereotype ("that bitch") of the bitchy woman chef. She believed that her women students should not adopt this persona when leading a kitchen because doing so would prevent them from gaining the respect of their staff. Her thoughts echo research on women leaders who find that women are expected to be both competent, yet communal when they are in charge (Rudman and Glick 2001). Women chefs had to be able to do their jobs, but still put the overall needs of the kitchen ahead of their own. According to our participants, women who responded positively to this correction eventually grew into their leadership positions, while those who retained a more masculine leadership style lost the respect of some of their coworkers.

CAN YOU HELP ME?: DEMONSTRATING WEAK FEMININITY AT WORK

Just as women chefs could be critiqued if they were viewed as acting too masculine, or bitchy, they could also face negative judgments if others believed they were acting too feminine or playing up their femininity when they led. None of the women described themselves this way but several criticized other women they knew of or had observed acting like "girly girls." They were critical of girly leaders for relying on a flirtatious manner in order to get special attention or favors from their men coworkers. Chelsea, one of the chef instructors, described women who flirted or acted overly feminine as "slutty." This didn't necessarily mean she believed the women chefs were having sex with their colleagues, but that by playing up their femininity and sexuality, they were using sexual attention to get what they wanted.

Women chefs often go to great pains to manage sexually charged situations, and events that could be considered sexual harassment in many workplaces were fairly common in kitchen environments (as we discussed in the previous chapter). When some women chefs were perceived as flirting and using their sex appeal to their advantage, it galled other women who felt that the girly girls were benefitting from unprofessional behavior. Also, by flirting, these women were concerned that this could open the door to unwanted sexual situations between coworkers and dismantle some of their carefully constructed ways of reducing sexual harassment in their workplaces.

Another reason for the negative view of playing up one's femininity was that women who engaged in this behavior could get special help from their men coworkers. Chelsea believed that, while being a girly girl might be beneficial in the short term because men may be willing to help out a woman cook who was flirty, in the long run, it made it less likely that the woman would get promoted:

> They won't respect you if you're a slut. Ultimately you have to work, work, work, and show them that you can do the work. That's just a distraction if you go down that route, the route of flirting with people. It's like go in there and work your butt off, stay focused, don't listen to all of their crap, and all of their like sexual advances toward you. Because they're just testing you. Just do the job and kick ass. Then that will lead you to somewhere.

Much like Kanter's (1977) description of workplace "seductresses" who are friendly and flirtatious at work, a downside of this approach is that it classifies women workers as sex objects and obscures their other skills and talents. While this strategy could be helpful in the short term, over time, this woman would never be seen as proper chef material because of her reliance on others to do her job. Tabitha, a pastry chef, mentioned another problem with being too feminine at work. She believed even if the woman chef did get promoted due to her talent and hard work, her girly appearance and behavior would still leave people thinking: "Oh, she got a hand up. She slept with the owner." Such suggestions upset women chefs because they feared that these beliefs would be applied to all women in managerial positions and not just those who were girly.

As we discussed in chapter 3, professional kitchens require a lot of physical strength and stamina from their workers. Playing up the physical demands of kitchen work has been one way for women to be excluded from professional cooking environments. Therefore, when women either asked for or received help with some of their more physical job duties, they were criticized for what Camille, an executive pastry chef, called "acting like a girl" and playing into the idea that women couldn't handle the physical demands of the job. The best example of interacting with a girly woman chef came from Brenda, the owner of a pastry shop. During her interview, Brenda described her conversation with Cheryl, a well-known woman chef, when they were both setting up displays at a food festival:

> BRENDA: Cheryl asked, "Oh, and can you do this for me? Can you do that for me? [said in a weak, low-energy whining tone]." And, my staff we would look at each other like, "Who is this? Does she know how to work? What's going on?" But she'd use her feminine wiles to get everyone to do everything for her. . . . I just don't work like that. I'm going to get in and get dirty with them [her staff], too.
>
> INTERVIEWER: What do you mean by "using her feminine wiles"?
>
> BRENDA: Just [saying things like] "I'm so busy. I'm tired. Can you help me put this together? Can you help me bring in my equipment? [said in a weak, pathetic voice]." Instead of getting out there [and getting it herself]. I think it was the way she asked. . . . [I said] "Do you need us to help you? We'd be happy to help you. Do you need us to move this thing? [said in a loud, strong voice]. Whatever you're bringing in, we'll help you move it. We'll help you get whatever it is prepped . . ." But, yeah, she'd pull that "Oh, I'm so tired and I've had such a long day" routine, and I'm like, "And we haven't?"

Throughout her example, Brenda took care to distance herself from Cheryl (who Brenda made note to mention, was a former model), even going so far as using different voices—a high-pitched, weak voice to represent Cheryl and a booming, lower pitched voice for herself—to illustrate their differences in leadership. In telling the story, Brenda was vocally performing in a more masculine voice that emphasized her strength and ability to command respect while playing up the cartoonishly feminine, whining tone of her counterpart who had to beg for help in order to get the job done. Brenda emphasized that it wasn't so much that the woman was requesting help that bothered her, but it was her tone and the way she referred to being "tired" that emphasized her weakness. In contrast, Brenda made it clear that asking people to do things for her wasn't the way she worked and she proudly admitted that she got just as "dirty" as her staff. For Brenda, this was a symbol of a strong leader within the kitchen.

From the perspective of Brenda and other participants, women in professional kitchens should not rely on their weaknesses in order to get people to do what they want. Not only is it unfair to women who do their own work, it's an approach that presumes that women have no skills or merit and can set a dangerous precedent. When women leaders are a minority within a particular occupation, the traits and behaviors of one woman can become the default way of viewing all women in that occupation (Kanter 1977). Unlike men chefs who are seen as individuals and judged only on their own performance, too often the traits of one highly visible minority group member becomes indicative of the leadership abilities of all members of that group. Perceived weaknesses of a few girly girls—that they cannot keep up with work demands or effectively lead—can then be used to deny leadership positions to all women. Brenda's critique of Cheryl also highlights that just because women have passed the initial tests to become a part of a professional kitchen, they have to keep proving themselves when they move into leadership positions. The threat that their femininity poses may become even more potent when they reach levels of leadership; thus, women chefs have to be sure to present themselves as strong leaders, but not bitchy ones, throughout their careers.

PRETEND YOUR MOM IS GOING TO SEE IT: ACCEPTABLY FEMININE LEADERSHIP

If women chefs should not lead by being "too masculine," or "too feminine," what is their best option to be considered a legitimate leader? For several of the women chefs, a third style of management was preferable: leading like a mom or big sister. Leading like a mom was different than leading like a girly girl. In this scenario, women take on the role of an authority figure that is intrinsically feminine and they are able to exhibit what can be viewed as positive feminine traits (the ability to nurture and mentor) while distancing themselves from negative feminine traits (physically weak; being too emotional). The women felt that their young men coworkers were able to relate to women as authority figures when they played the mom and big sister roles because people's first brush with authority often comes from their mother. For example, Cathy, the chef-owner of a restaurant, explained that: "There are certain men who work well with women and there are certain men who don't work well with women. I find that men who have good relationships with their mothers work really well together in the kitchen because they probably have worked in the kitchen with her before." According to Cathy, men who were used to working in the kitchen at home with their mothers were more likely to accept women in the kitchen, as well as women with authority in the kitchen.

The chefs enacted this third style by caring about employees and their families, emphasizing nurturance and mentoring with staff, and decreasing the kitchen hierarchy by doing the same tasks as their subordinates. Adopting this third method of leadership allowed the women to take on roles that are associated with women and femininity but that were still considered legitimate sources of authority. Some of the women even argued that this way of leading not only helped them successfully manage coworkers but did so in ways they felt were better than how their men counterparts managed.

Caring about staff was important for several of our respondents. When describing their restaurants, several of the executive chefs described the restaurant as a "family" with some participants taking on the role of mom or big sister to their employees. Brenda recalled her time working as the executive pastry chef of a large hotel. She tried to foster a sense of openness with her staff and let them know they could, "Just tell me, whatever your problem is." She described the benefits to this approach:

> So, I think it was easy for them to be more open with me 'cause I was a female. I don't know if they saw me as their sister or what. But, they also knew that I would go fight for them. And I would. I always did. It was just easy. And, I honestly think that because I was nice—I wasn't a bitch to everybody—I was nice to everyone from the steward on up to everyone. I was nice to them. And, I think that makes a big difference in how they treat you.

Brenda felt that being nice to her staff made those she supervised more likely to respect her as a leader. While Brenda describes the sisterly approach to her staff as easy, other women chefs had to move beyond the mindset of the stereotypical masculine chef or the bitchy woman chef to reach a more nurturing place with their leadership. Lisa, a culinary instructor, discussed how it took some time for her to transition from being a bitch in the kitchen to taking on more of a mom role: "I think what I've done is turn the tide on myself, so I know how to come into it strong and confident and deal with [managing] on a daily basis but also allow some of my feminine traits, some of that nurturing and that ability to help and mentor. I bring more of that into it now." For Lisa, the confidence she developed in herself and her abilities allowed her to drop the persona of the "Type A" chef and, instead, she could let more feminine traits come through. Elisa, an executive chef-owner, also believed this and felt that, by highlighting their ability to nurture, it could help a business function better:

> I like to have a nice connection with my people. I like to see them as humans. They have problems. Sometimes something happens and they don't show up. I want to know what's going on. I think this is a very small place and we have to be happy. We have to connect to understand and respect each other. I don't like to see people like numbers. I don't like that. It's important to know the people and know that they're happy. If they're happy, I'm happy and it's easy. It's easy for everybody. When somebody comes in and they're in a very bad mood, "I don't want to work." We can talk and then finally they can work. That's what I like.

Elisa viewed expressing a caring attitude toward her staff as part of her job as a chef. It helped the staff both understand and respect each other. There was also the practical issue that, after taking some time to listen to and talk with an upset member of her staff, Elisa was able to help them reach an emotional place where they could return to work. Alexandra, who managed a large special events staff at a restaurant, also said she paid attention to the staff and any problems they were facing with their families. In contrast to men managers, whom she noted, "were more ready to punish" when someone missed work, Alexandra tried to empathize with her staff and "remember who it is that you're talking to and where they're coming from." This personal connection to staff led to happier kitchens and restaurants.

Natasha, a chef de cuisine, supervised a staff of young men. She said her staff let her "baby them" and "take care of them." As a result she saw herself as "a motherly figure to them." Because she was seen as a mom or big sister to her staff, she was able to lecture them (as a mother would) and point out mistakes they had made and how they should be corrected. This leadership style allowed Natasha to establish her authority and receive a positive response from her staff. For Natasha, the gender and slight age differences between her and her staff marked her as an "other." By taking on the mom role, Natasha was seen as a legitimate authority figure without having to adapt to masculine forms of kitchen leadership. For example, chefs often emphasizing working "clean," which means cleaning up one's area, or station, throughout the work shift. This prevents a station from getting too messy and makes it easier to keep track of items during busy times. Not everyone keeps up with this practice, however, and Natasha recalled reminding her staff to clean their stations. She explained, "I said, 'Please go clean up your station. If you were coming into that station, you know you'd be so mad at that other person, right?'" Much like a mother would remind a young child about the fairness of keeping shared space clean, Natasha was able to remind her staff what needed to be done in a way that did not get her labeled a bitch. She even drew on a parent-child metaphor when describing just how clean she wanted the kitchen to be and told her crew to "pretend your mother's going to see it." While providing a lecture may take more time than barking an order, at the end of the day, Natasha got her desired outcome because: "they clean their room."

Expressing a caring, maternal attitude toward their staff carried over into training activities. Several of our participants had been given training duties as part of their jobs, and some believed their gender was one of the reasons they were chosen to help train new members of the kitchen. Women were described as being more patient and invested in the success of the other person than their men counterparts. For example, Candace, a pastry chef, compared her experiences being trained by men and women: "They'll [women] will make sure you're a little more comfortable. A man will say, 'Do this' and wait and see how you juggle things. . . . In my experience, I've just felt less thrown to the wolves so to speak if it's a woman who's the head of the kitchen as opposed to a man." Erin, a chef de cuisine, expressed a similar view. She believed that men chefs could be very impatient with their students and "instead of teaching someone how to do it, they expect them to know how to do it [already]."

Lisa, who had worked in several different positions in the gastronomic field before moving to a cooking school, attributed gender differences in training approaches to fears on the part of men chefs. She claimed training was "the most intimidating aspect of food service" and that many man chefs shied away from these jobs because they were so challenging. She linked this to the fact that good trainers had to realize people learn differently and, therefore, the trainer had to be flexible and willing to try new techniques in order to help people learn. Because teaching can also highlight what the teacher does and does not know, it can be intimidating to take on such tasks and chefs who want their knowledge and expertise to go unquestioned would feel very uncomfortable in these arrangements. Women chefs, Lisa explained, did not have the egos that men chefs possessed and, therefore, were willing to admit when they didn't know something.

As part of their mentoring, women chefs would be careful about the feedback they provided to their employees. Melissa, a pastry chef, had worked under very critical chefs in the past. She believed that part of her role was to show those under her charge at work what they were doing wrong, but it wasn't "to make people feel like shit" at the end of the workday. Elisa also discussed how she used her nurturing side when addressing problems in the kitchen: "You don't have to be rude. It's the way you approach it, the way you say things. It's very important. I learned that. 'We can maybe do this. What do you think of this? We can do that.' They feel better. That's what I learned. I like that." Melissa and Elisa felt that by altering their words and tone they could point out problems with her men subordinates in ways that allowed them to feel appreciated and part of the decision-making process rather than as someone who's been given an order. This left staff feeling more listened to and less reprimanded, which was good for restaurant morale.

It could be argued that these additional job tasks could limit women to certain jobs within the kitchen, and research by Heather Hopfl (2011) suggests that, within male-dominated fields, women are allowed to be feminine, but only in ways that benefit the organization. Women who take on the feminine role of teacher are able to do so because these arrangements channel feminine characteristics into jobs that help individual restaurants. Kanter also expressed concern that taking a motherly approach at work, in which men colleagues "brought her their private troubles, and she was expected to comfort them" (1977, 233), served to obscure women's ability to be strong leaders. In male-dominated workplaces, tokens who are supportive, caring, and nurturing may be appreciated, but not necessarily viewed as authority figures.

Despite these critiques, many of these women enjoyed the training aspects of their jobs and used this experience to earn positions as chef instructors once they left professional kitchens. The women we interviewed felt that nurturing young talent and allowing new chefs to make mistakes in order to learn were important parts of their jobs. Cathy explained:

> I give my staff a lot of opportunity to mess up. And sometimes they do. But, in doing so, they learn. And I don't have to watch them the next time because they've learned that themselves. And they are the kind of people who work here and they are the kind of people who learn every day. And they always strive to do better.

Cathy went on to describe one of the "games" she plays with her cooks that ultimately helps them learn how to cook consistent food:

> I have cooks that pride themselves on the number of steaks that they put out that are the right temperature consecutively so they get up to the ninetieth or the one hundredth and then a steak comes back and they didn't cook it to the right temperature and they fall all the way back to number one again. Those are little games that we all play. But, they learn by doing it.

Women chefs also discussed how they felt responsible for setting a positive example for those working with—not beneath—them. "Motherly" chefs were less likely to enforce a strict hierarchy at work, unlike the traditional brigade system in professional kitchens. The chefs discussed working more in a consensus model than a formal hierarchy where the chef has the last word. This attitude even applied to the variety of jobs that must be completed for a well-run restaurant. Erin was the chef de cuisine at an award-winning fine-dining restaurant, and she talked about taking turns sweeping up or taking out the garbage. She said her kitchen team benefited from knowing that she was willing to do some of the "grunt work" at the restaurant:

> I have a lot of respect in this kitchen because I won't ask anybody to do anything that I wouldn't do. I mop the floor and get my hands dirty just like

everybody else. And I think that I have gained a lot of respect because of that. So no one feels like, you know, I think that I'm better than anyone else. So that has helped me along the way.

This willingness to "get just as dirty as the rest of [the staff]" was listed as a positive by our participants. They attributed this to an attitude among women chefs where there was less focus on titles and more on the work that needed to be done. This illustrated their commitment to their restaurant "family" and their willingness to "lead by example" rather than delegating as they claimed men chefs were used to doing. They said men chefs they had worked under had not taken this approach because they viewed such tasks as being beneath them. Chelsea had even noticed this difference in her work as a culinary instructor. She said that younger men instructors, particularly those who had not been a chef for very long, were very tough on their students and had the attitude that "I'm the boss and you're going to listen to me." They also viewed themselves as being "too good" to do some of the less glamorous aspects of running teaching kitchens. In contrast, Chelsea said she and her female coworkers had a different approach:

> If I made these dishes, then I'm going to clean them. I'm not above this. I'm not above cleaning. I'm not above doing my dishes. The "my students are slaves" [mindset]. That kind of thing. I just find that very interesting. It's like this insecurity that comes out, "I'm going to be an asshole because I'm insecure."

Chelsea linked the willingness to take on more cleaning jobs as a sign that she and her women colleagues were secure about their place as chefs. For younger men chefs, they felt the need to hide behind their title and enforce a strict hierarchy as a way of faking their confidence in their role as kitchen leaders. Chelsea suggested that women did not have to engage in this type of behavior because they had earned their place in the kitchen.

The motherly approach to leadership also provided a calming influence on the kitchen. Professional kitchens are often male-dominated workplaces with machismo-filled cultures that include competitiveness, sexual joking and banter, and general "debauchery." This culture is usually so engrained that some have even questioned how well a gender-integrated kitchen could be able to function because it would challenge the sense of brother-hood created by men chefs (Fine 1987). In contrast, our participants suggested the addition of women leaders to male-dominated kitchens can provide a calming presence that reduces anger, competitiveness, sexual harassment, and other unprofessional behaviors and attitudes. Women, our participants claimed, were more likely to foster a comforting and more respectful workplace. Elisa provided an example of this when talking about a time when she had to have a discussion with one of the men chefs who worked at her restaurant. Bill had a short temper and would lash out when he was in a hurry and couldn't find an item he needed in the kitchen. When Elisa decided that his outbursts were damaging the sense of harmony in the kitchen, she pulled him aside:

> We talked. I said, "Bill, it's not good for you. It's not good for us. It's not going to help anybody. Nobody can help you better if you're angry and say bad words. So you have to say exactly what you need and ask the people for that and then they can help you. They don't know what to do when you're upset and say bad words. Everybody freaks out and it's worse. No more."

Because a calm demeanor helped the whole restaurant, Elisa focused on how his actions were harming the restaurant as a group. Elisa believed that, by focusing on how she and the rest of the staff could better help him, Bill was able to listen to her advice and alter his behavior.

Dana, the young executive chef who cited the double standard faced by women chefs in the opening of this chapter, commented that her restaurant's owners specifically wanted to hire a woman for the head position. When asked why, she said:

> When there's not a woman in the kitchen, there's just so much testosterone and grossness. I think it [having a woman in charge] calms things down. Everyone feels more comfortable. The wait staff thinks they can ask questions. It's not so scary. . . . Yeah, there's like a calmness. I guess guys feel like they have to act the fool all the time. I think there's a certain level of maturity that has to be brought in. Granted, I would never know what's that like. I've never worked in a kitchen with all guys because I am a woman. But that's what I've heard. I heard it [the kitchen environment before she was hired] was . . . not more hostile but maybe just more aggressive.

According to Dana and several others, the very presence of a woman in the kitchen impacts how the men behave. When unchecked, an all-men kitchen can foster a workplace where "grossness" such as sexual joking and aggressive teasing dominate. While Fine (1996b) found through his ethnography of restaurant kitchens that such interactions served as a form of one-upmanship and a way of creating solidarity among coworkers, our participants suggest there can be negative repercussions from such macho environments. Kate, a former chef and restaurateur, said that having women in leadership positions in the kitchen made the behavior more professional and avoided creating a "boys' club" in the kitchen that fostered competition and an unhappy workplace. In the example of Dana's restaurant, her predecessor had helped create a work environment that intimidated the wait staff and made them afraid to ask questions, which could harm the quality of service. Similarly, Chelsea spoke of working with men culinary students who were so intent on one-upping each other they failed to create a cohesive menu for the culinary school's student-run restaurant. Instead, Chelsea had to gently lead them back to the task at hand and remind them that their goal was to work together and create food that would please the customers—not see who could earn the most individual accolades.

Keeping this balance between mothering and managing is a challenge for women chefs, but many said that taking a more personal interest in their staff ultimately created a strong work team and a great sense of solidarity. Women chefs who could juggle these complex relationships thought that they had a greater chance at success than those pursuing a more authoritarian, masculine leadership style. This may speak to gendered expectations that women managers will be more caring than men, and that social sanctions exist when women violate these norms.

Women chefs did have to be careful when taking on maternal or big sister roles. Some respondents highlighted difficulties in enforcing boundaries when they were viewed as too approachable. Brenda, who had a negative experience working with a girly girl chef, admitted, "I'm a nice boss. I'm too nice." Through encouraging her staff to come to her with any problem, she sometimes found her staff to be "a little more open, especially with their complaints." While a more hierarchical man chef might intimidate his staff from speaking up, Brenda could sometimes find herself in the middle of workplace issues that ate into her work hours. She also recalled being asked to take on several last-minute requests, including baking several large cakes (usually a job that takes several days) because of her reputation for being "nice."

While caring for their staff and nurturing their talent was useful in creating a harmonious and creative kitchen, sometimes employees could take advantage. Natasha, who used her mothering nature to keep her younger male chefs in line, also had to draw boundaries with her staff lest she have to deal with unreasonable requests. She explained, "I think it's necessary to have that respect that you aren't just everybody's best friend, or else they'll just end up walking all over you. [They will] come to you saying: 'Please! I need this day off.' . . . It's just pathetic." Dana, who had been promoted up as executive chef from her restaurant's current staff, also struggled with maintaining boundaries with staff while simultaneously promoting a friendly, collaborative work environment: "You have to be able to listen to people's problems and know when to play and when to get back on track. That's the hard part. These are your friends who you spend most of your time with, but sometimes you can't be friends. That's really hard."

These comments suggest that acting as a mom or big sister is not without some challenges. After all, who is expected to (sometimes literally) clean up others' messes more than a mom? Women chefs who were seen in a maternal light perceive respect from their staff, but it could also come with the price in the form of having to manage "family" dynamics more than someone taking a more detached, hierarchical approach to leading a kitchen. As Kanter (1977) noted, motherly leaders were expected to provide comfort and deal with more personal issues than traditional bosses. Consequently, it can contribute to a gendered form of emotional labor in which women are giving to their staff at the expense of their own emotions at work.

Ridgeway (2011) argues that women who try to be cooperative leaders are engaging a tricky strategy given larger cultural conceptions of gendered leadership. At the same time, she is optimistic about what Alice Eagly and her co-authors refer to as transformational leadership styles. A transformational leader is one who garners respect by being more collaborative (Eagly, Johannesen-Schmidt, and van Engen 2003). Certainly, the women we interviewed appear to see great potential in their abilities to change the culture of the kitchen. A more nurturing style of leadership might indeed alter negative gender stereotypes about women in leadership roles. It should be noted, however, that this leadership style might not be as successful in other male-dominated settings. In construction work, police work, firefighting, or on Wall Street, emphasizing roles as family, mothers, or sisters might be perceived as a weakness or not appropriate for those masculine subcultures. But in professional kitchens, the women we interviewed appeared to want to resist and change those masculine chef roles. They didn't want to act like Gordon Ramsay, a celebrity chef whom they described as angry, dominant, and overly aggressive. Instead, the women chefs would draw on uniquely feminized aspects of their work (nurturing, teaching, etc.) to highlight or exaggerate what they see as women's unique leadership styles and, strategically employ different aspects of femininity.

GENDERED LEADERSHIP: ESSENTIAL OR ESSENTIALIZED?

Within our participants' responses about gender and leadership styles, they often used essentialized gender language to claim that women chefs can transform the workplace culture of professional kitchens. In their opinions, women have added to new professionalism in ways that draw from feminine strengths (i.e., not by being bitches or like men). Such statements not only allow women the psychological benefit of resisting gender-based stigma in the workplace, but they might also serve as a blueprint for how women chefs can help change the male-dominated kitchen culture.

Women's discussion of these leadership styles raises complicated questions for studies of gender and work. Building on Kanter's (1977) theory of tokenism, some gender scholars may argue that none of these leadership strategies are ideal because each is highly gendered. On one hand, the three leadership styles described rely on essentialized notions of gender and sex: that men are one way, and women are another and that these differences are universal and natural. For example, Dana's reason why the owners of her restaurant wanted to hire a woman to lead the kitchen was essentialized (i.e., the link between "testosterone" and "grossness") and used to explain how the two genders approach managing a kitchen. Dana admits that she has never actually experienced any of this hyper-masculinity at work as the very presence of a woman inhibits men's behavior.

Natasha, who saw herself as her staff's big sister, also used essentialized language when she claimed her maternal management style wasn't done purposefully because "that's just who I am" thus reinforcing the concept of natural differences between men chefs who bully and women chefs who mother. While, in these instances, women are claiming these natural differences provide them with benefits in kitchen management, too often, perceived natural differences between the genders have been used as reasons for denying women opportunities in the workplace. Using explanations of men and women's differences—even when used by women, and even when used to highlight women's strengths—rarely provides women with increased career opportunities, greater respect and legitimacy, or more successes in their workplace (England 2010; Irvine and Vermilya 2010). Kristen Schilt (2010) argues that anything that supports the gender binary ends up promoting gender inequality because society always devalues the feminine. This problem is exaggerated in work cultures that are male-dominated and where masculinity is valued more than femininity. Ultimately, the danger in essentializing lies in reinforcing the gendered status quo (Charles and Bradley 2009; England 2010).

What differentiates the chefs we interviewed from the women tokens in Kanter's research, whose personas at work were tied tightly to gender essentialist qualities, is an emphasis on feminine strength. Women chefs draw on a rhetoric in which they see themselves as different from and better than men. From their earliest days in the kitchen, women are often told they are different. Some women accept and redefine these claims of difference to highlight ways women chefs excel in the kitchen. Rather than trying to assimilate into masculine, Gordon Ramsay–esque management styles, our participants see women as being more effective leaders in the kitchen. According to our respondents, effective chef-leaders treat their staff well, show concern for employees' families, and decrease sexual harassment in the kitchen. Of course, it is not possible to determine whether the women we interviewed or women chefs in general are more effective, but it's clear that women themselves felt powerful in their leadership roles despite their descriptions of discrimination and bias. Even though the term "feminine strength" can be seen as a cultural oxymoron, the women we interviewed are resistant to dominant conceptions about masculine leadership.

It is easy to look at the numerous hurdles women chefs must overcome in order to enter and succeed in professional kitchens, but Dana describes these challenges as opportunities for women chefs.

I will say though that there is a definite double standard in how people react to a woman chef as opposed to a male chef. But I feel like it's that way in every industry. A male boss can say something and a female boss can say something, and it's perceived completely different. Same words, completely different. It makes us better though because we have to see things from both sides. We have to be aggressive and nurturing at the same time. Men don't have to worry about that. They can do whatever the hell they want and be fine with it. At the same time, who do you think is learning more? Who do you think people relate to more and respect more? Someone who can tell them what to do *and* be a nurturer when they have problems.

Dana's words highlight the potentially transformative power of feminine strength from her point of view. Instead of viewing herself as an "other" in the kitchen, Dana chose to see herself as a reflexive leader who considered the needs of the whole restaurant staff as an opportunity to learn. Her men peers, she suggested, would be able to draw from established tropes regarding masculine leadership and, therefore, miss out on this opportunity and not learn as much.

REFRAMING FEMININE LEADERSHIP: ACKNOWLEDGING FEMININE STRENGTHS

According to our participants, there was a fine line that needed to be walked regarding women leading professional kitchens. Just because a woman ascended the kitchen hierarchy to become a head or executive chef did not mean that she no longer faced scrutiny and challenges to her new-found authority. Adopting a more masculine, authoritarian leadership style would lead to being labeled a bitch, while overt displays of femininity in terms of dress (e.g., wearing makeup or jewelry) or behavior (e.g., friendliness, flirting) was also seen as incongruent with leading a kitchen. Some of the women chefs drew from more culturally acceptable models of feminine leadership by taking on the roles of moms or big sisters. These roles, while helpful in earning the respect and cooperation of staff, could still be perceived as problematic as they still drew from essentialized notions about gender and leadership.

One hopeful note from the interviews involved the acknowledgment that, while different (or perceived to be different), women chefs offered advantages as leaders. These advantages were directly related to the chefs' status as women and the participants found ways to reframe critiques of women leaders into discourses of feminine strength. Our participants rejected the idea that men are naturally better managers and suggested that women leaders are better because they manage employees by caring about them. They said that they (and other women chefs) can be strong leaders in the kitchen by caring about their staff and staff member's families, encouraging employees to have time for their own families, discouraging sexual harassment, and eliminating angry chef behavior. Instead of viewing these behaviors as evidence that women were too sensitive to lead a kitchen (see chapter 3), our participants reframed these behaviors as strengths that were common among good women chefs. Through accepting differences between men and women leaders and drawing from feminine strengths, our participants believed that they could alter professional kitchens (including those in restaurants and culinary schools) to be more democratic, humanistic settings.

5 · CHALLENGING "CHOICES"

Why Some Women Leave
Restaurant Kitchen Work

Melissa, a thirty-six-year-old pastry shop owner, was every qualitative interviewer's dream: she was friendly, open, and reflective when talking about her experiences as a professional pastry chef. During her interview with Deborah, Melissa talked a mile a minute about everything from her experiences with sexual harassment to the challenges of opening her own business. But, when Deborah asked her why there were so few women chefs, Melissa came to a halt. At first, she expressed confusion, saying, "I really don't know why more women don't cook." After a pause, she said "it's a hard job" to explain women's underrepresentation. However, after thinking some more, she made the leap to the issue of motherhood.

You don't have time for anybody else. You can't have a kid. I mean, [my female business partner] just had a little girl and every time I think about it I'm like: "Wow! I *couldn't* have a kid right now!" I mean, you just can't. I think that maybe that's a big part of it. Just depending on what you want for your life, all the women I know who are chefs are my age and probably not married yet. Or just got married. Because they haven't had time in their lives for anything like that, and, if they did think about it [having a child], it meant their job stopped. You don't get any benefits. If you do get benefits, it's not going to pay for you to be off three months. So, that aspect, maybe that holds women back? I don't know. I know it makes me think I don't want kids. Not right now, anyway.

When we began this project, we wanted to know why so many women who began working as professional chefs eventually left the career. Because much of the literature on restaurant kitchen culture mentioned the macho, highly competitive work environment and the ubiquitous sexual joking and teasing, we assumed issues of discrimination or sexual harassment would be at the top of our participants' reasons for leaving. To our surprise, few of the seventeen women (out of thirty-three) who had left restaurant kitchens behind mentioned discrimination or sexual harassment as the reason for their career change. Instead, the most commonly cited cause for these women to leave professional kitchens was the incompatibility of restaurant work with family lives and the difficulties in meeting the competing responsibilities of work and home. According to Melissa and the other participants, what makes the job "hard" wasn't the heavy lifting or hours running around a busy kitchen. The sexual harassment or discrimination women chefs sometimes face also wasn't the hardest thing for women chefs. It was the incredible time commitment required to be a successful chef and the lack of benefits that was difficult for women, particularly for mothers.

Being a chef is a difficult job for anyone—man or woman—however, there are certain cultural expectations for mothers that add even more stress to balancing work and home. During her interview, Melissa made a note of this by saying, "'Cause even guys who work in the kitchen that have kids, they don't have time. They don't go home. Whoever they're married to takes care of their children." While married men chefs may be able to delegate the majority of childrearing tasks to their wives, many working mothers face expectations to be both perfect workers and perfect mothers, which often ends with them feeling they have failed at both (Hays 1998; Hochschild 1990).

These competing responsibilities led several participants to opt out of paid work or change jobs to less demanding employment. Universally, these career decisions are framed as women's "choices" regarding family and work. For example, in Melissa's earlier comments she emphasizes that the decision whether to have children or not is based on "just depending on what you want for your life," The framing of this issue as women's "choices" about whether or not to remain working as chefs ignores many of the larger cultural and structural factors guiding these decisions, as well as the potential outcomes for women's career opportunities. When women in demanding jobs "step out," as some of our participants called it, or, in the terminology used by sociologists like Pamela Stone (2007), "opt out" of work for motherhood or for less demanding employment, it can have negative outcomes for their longtime career trajectories (Blair-Loy 2003; Roth 2006). Even if women see family as pulling them back home (or pulling them into less demanding occupations in their fields as was the case for some of our respondents), in many cases it is actually the structure of their workplaces that pushes women out due to inflexible and difficult work structures (Damaske 2011; Stone 2007).

As currently nearly three-quarters of all mothers are employed (U.S. Bureau of Labor Statistics 2013), it is important to examine how work and motherhood prove incompatible, as well as how women negotiate these competing responsibilities in demanding workplaces. Understanding this phenomenon may help us understand why, even though women are graduating from culinary schools in similar numbers to men, this does not translate into equal numbers in fine dining restaurants. In our interviews, we wanted to understand why some women leave restaurant work behind for other employment because this may shed some light on why the occupation remains male-dominated. Examining how and why women chefs leave the professional kitchen is integral to understanding the underlying processes that contribute to internal job segregation among chefs. Internal job segregation means that, in the same job title, men and women concentrate in different areas or specializations. We examine why women who have been chefs (including executive chefs, sous chefs, executive pastry chefs, etc.) in fine dining restaurant kitchens (the jobs that tend to have the most status within the gastronomic field) have chosen to work as catering chefs, chef instructors at culinary schools, and other jobs. Understanding the process of internal job segregation is important because it, along with occupational segregation, have been shown to be one of the most significant causes of the gender wage gap (Cohen 2013; Williams 1995).

Of the seventeen women who had left restaurant kitchens, all claimed that they had loved working in those work environments. Each of them had found some kind of work that was still in the culinary industry, suggesting that there are characteristics of the fine dining chef career and its environment that make it difficult for women to stay. In this chapter we examine how and why women decided to leave restaurant kitchen work and what benefits their current positions provide that their previous employment did not. We also discuss what allowed some of our participants to remain working in restaurants and how they were able to balance work and family responsibilities. Throughout their interviews we learned of the demands to be ideal workers and the rhetoric surrounding women's "choices" regarding work and family, and we emphasize the limitations of framing decisions about employment as freely made decisions.

WORK AND FAMILY IMBALANCE

The number one reason why our participants said they left restaurant kitchen work behind was that it was incompatible with family needs. Several participants stated it would be impossible to have it all and a woman chef would eventually have to pick family or career. Such findings aren't surprising, as numerous studies have cited the stress caused by work-family conflict, with some research suggesting that women face greater problems due to this imbalance, including higher rates of depression and anxiety (Milkie and Peltola 1999; Moen and Yu 2000; Voydanoff and Donnelly 1989).

Before continuing, we want to return briefly to the work conditions of professional chefs to illustrate how some of these factors make it difficult to combine kitchen work and family needs. First of all, being a chef can be a very physically demanding job that entails standing for twelve hours or more a day and lifting heavy pots and containers of ingredients. Being head or executive chef does not necessarily mean an end to this physical labor, particularly if one works at a small restaurant with limited staff. Camille, an executive pastry chef, explains:

> The thing about being in the kitchen is there's no retirement. There's no kind of moment in which you've been there for ten years and now you can say "Okay. I'm gonna start handing off this or that to my underlings." . . . There's no kind of [guarantee that] age and experience gets you an easier life.

As Camille suggests, being the boss still doesn't excuse someone from the long hours and numerous tasks of a chef. Shelley, a chef-owner, joked that she does "a lot of everything" at her restaurant, even filling in as dishwasher when needed. In addition to the physical work, head or executive chefs also need to create dishes, negotiate with suppliers, complete the endless paperwork needed to run a small business, manage staff, and make public appearances to promote the restaurant. This work all translates into incredibly long hours. Often these hours fall under what Harriet Presser refers to as nonstandard work that "occurs in the evening, at night, on a rotating shift, or during the weekend" (2003, 1). In many ways chefs are the epitome of non-standard workers as, Sara, a culinary instructor described:

> In the restaurant world, there is not a lot of stability. As a manager, I was expected to be there at all times. I would work a schedule sometimes where one day I would come in at 6:00 P.M. The next day I would come in at 12:00 P.M. The next day I would close. So your sleep schedule is completely off. You don't see your family as much. Having a new baby would be nearly impossible. You're also working fifty to sixty hours, which is fine, if you're single or you're married and you have a spouse working a similar job who understands. It is a very demanding job.

For chefs there are few options to these long hours as many fine dining restaurants are only open at night and, even if a restaurant served breakfast and lunch, working the dinner shift was a sign of status and that you were among the most skilled in the kitchen. In Sara's comments, she states that, while the long hours and varying schedules can be difficult, she claims they can be manageable—for someone who is single or who is married with an understanding spouse. This highlights one of the biggest difficulties for female chefs. Schedules and work conditions that may be considered acceptable at first may become unacceptable after having children.

These hours often do not align with childcare or school schedules, and our participants recalled how it is common to work most weekends and holidays. This was the experience of Rose, a pastry instructor, who had worked with some very well known chefs over the course of her career. She loved her job but after having children she experienced a change in priorities:

> Before I had my children, I worked in the hotels. I worked sixty, seventy, eighty hours a week, and that was all fine. Once I had my kids, I stepped out.

I couldn't go back. Being in the kitchen, in pastries, you can work very early in the morning such as 4:00 or 5:00 in the morning until about noon, which wasn't going to work because where would I get childcare? Or you work in the P.M. And you're always working weekends. And you're always working holidays. Once I had kids, I had to step out of it. And that's actually, I think, the only drawback to our profession: the fact that, once you have children, it's really hard. It's really, really hard to work because of the nights and the weekends. If you live around family, you can have your mom or somebody like that help out, but daycares are not going to work when they're open six to six [6:00 A.M. to 6:00 P.M.]. That was what stopped me. I knew at that point my career was kind of at a standstill now because my husband traveled all the time, so he's not going to be any help [small laugh].

While some of our participants suggested that working as a pastry chef offered better work hours that could be conducive to a more family-friendly schedule, this was not Rose's experience. She found it difficult to keep up with the demands of her job at a hotel because the hours worked by most chefs would not align with many daycare schedules. Even if daycares were available for the times Rose or other women chefs were at work, they may very well be cost prohibitive. Although the media pays disproportionate attention to superstar chefs whose restaurants, cookbooks, and product endorsements make them millionaires many times over, the majority of chefs do not earn very high wages. According to the U.S. Bureau of Labor Statistics (2013), the median yearly income of chefs and head cooks was $42,480. Particularly in expensive cities, these wages could make affording full-time childcare a challenge.

Restaurant kitchen work is also characterized by a lack of health benefits. According to a 2014 report, only 50 percent of fine dining restaurants offered any sort of employee health plan (Batt, Lee, and Lakhani 2014). The authors of the report also pointed out how these numbers do not reflect the complete picture of health care as the types of plans offered may not provide good coverage or may be too costly for many of the employees. There is also no data on how these plans address medical issues such as pregnancy, which can be poorly covered by insurance plans. In most workplaces, paid maternity leave would be unlikely for many women chefs. Of all our participants with children, only Erin, a chef de cuisine, had been satisfied with the maternity policies in place when she had her child. Her daughter was born while Erin was attending culinary school and working as a chef at this same institution. Because it was a corporate position, she had access to better benefits than the majority of chefs.

Lack of health benefits was a major obstacle for mothers who wanted to remain in restaurant kitchens. Marisel, a chef-owner and mother of four, discussed her desire to provide health benefits for her employees, but as the owner of a small business this would be cost prohibitive. Instead, she had an arrangement with a friend who was a doctor, and he would provide some medical care for her staff in exchange for free meals. While she admitted such an arrangement was less than ideal, she believed she was doing the best that she could for her employees.

Other benefits that can help make work more family friendly involve paid leave, onsite daycare, and flextime. However, according to our participants such policies were rare. There were also informal rules that discouraged employees from taking time off for sickness or other reasons. Jane explained how, in the workplace culture of restaurant kitchens, it was unacceptable to take time off:

> You can't say, "I've got to go" because there's nobody else to fill in for you. That's the thing about the industry is that you can't call in sick because there's no voicemail that will take care of it. It doesn't go to voicemail, it goes to somebody else's back. . . . You need to be there every day. You need to do all of those things. You can't just [leave] because you don't feel like it or you have a little scratchy throat, not come in. When I worked, you might be dying but you go in and the chef makes a decision about whether or not you go home. You don't call in and say, "I'm sick" (laughs). You just never call in sick.

Because so many restaurants tried to operate lean and employ as few workers as possible in order to stay profitable, there was rarely any backup available when employees got sick. This was particularly hard for mothers who may need to take time off for their own health or when children were ill. Asking for time off could bring even more scrutiny to women chefs. Even friendly or sympathetic coworkers could be critical of a mother calling in sick because of the extra work that it meant for them. Anna, an executive chef, recalled, "They may feel like, 'I'm sorry your baby has a cough, but I haven't had a day off in seven days.'" Chefs were encouraged to tough it out regarding their own health, but this advice was difficult to take when pregnant and working fourteen-hour days or when a child was sick.

Some of our participants said they had sympathetic bosses who tried to be accommodating with family issues, but others cited uncaring managers who demanded workers be willing to come in early or to stay late in order to meet restaurant needs. In demanding careers, there can be strong messages that it is unacceptable to take time off and that high flyers would never ask for reduced hours (Smithson and Stokoe 2008). Among our participants, those who needed time off were seen as not dedicated to being a chef.

Two participants discussed being passed over for promotions because of their status as mothers. Both Ellen and Joan were being considered for chef jobs, but their "obligations" and competing demands for their time from family responsibilities were cited as reasons to deny them promotions. These supervisors were looking for ideal workers and our participants did not fit this mold. According to Joan Acker (1990), an ideal worker is wholly dedicated to her job and willing to work long hours for the benefit of her organization. The problem with this notion is that it presupposes no outside responsibilities such as parenting or caring for elderly relatives. Because women are more likely to be tasked with caregiving responsibilities, the reliance on the ideal worker trope disadvantages women in the workplace. They are seen as being less committed to their jobs which results in discrimination in hiring and promotion processes because it is assumed that women will not be able to devote 100 percent of their time to their career.

The belief system that underlies this "motherhood penalty" is so engrained that women are penalized in hiring and promotion even if they are not mothers. Rose, for example, recalled being asked if she planned on having children when she applied for chef positions during the 1980s. The man who asked this question explained that he didn't want to hire a woman chef just to have her quit when she became pregnant.

Just the specter of future pregnancy or motherhood is enough to deny women jobs and promotions (Bobbit-Zeher 2011). Ironically, another woman chef, Jill, was denied a promotion because she did not have children in favor of a man job candidate who was a father. As cultural ideas of parenting tend to align women with the caring role and men with the breadwinning role, when women had children, it was expected they would not have the time to devote to being a chef because of family responsibilities. Men, on the other hand, were seen as ripe for promotion because they needed to be able to provide for their families financially and, therefore, would be hardworking employees.

TIME FOR A CHANGE

Despite the difficult working conditions and low pay of kitchen work, the chefs explained how they loved their jobs and did not want to leave cooking behind. Being a chef had become part of their personal identity and some of the participants, even after leaving restaurant kitchens, still used the title of chef to describe themselves. Many had tried to find ways to reconcile dueling responsibilities in order to continue working as chefs. The decision to leave restaurant kitchen work behind usually came after some sort of breaking point where a chef admitted she could no longer continue her job. For example, Ellen, who had left her job as a pastry chef to work in culinary sales at an upscale grocer, made the career change after being passed over for a promotion following the birth of her second child:

> Well, I had a second child. I got passed over for a promotion because I was having children and they felt like, "Well, you won't be able to [carry] out your time in the way you should." I said, "I'm done." The executive pastry chef . . . I had some issues with him. We had some run-ins. I decided I was done.
>
>   INTERVIEWER: Did the run-ins have anything to do with the fact that you're a woman?
>
> Yes, definitely. In those days . . . you have children, you have obligations. Yes, there are times where you might not make it into work. When you're in an operation like that you have to be there. We had a big event coming up and I had worked a whole week, seven days straight. It was probably 10 or 11:00 at night. I said, "I'm off tomorrow." [The chef] said, "No, you're coming in tomorrow. You will be here tomorrow." Threatening me if I didn't show up.

Ellen's statements illustrate the incredible double bind women chefs faced. If they had children, it was assumed that they would need extra time off—making them unfit as chefs. Once a woman had children, she was also expected to be the primary caregiver, and women chefs faced feelings of guilt when they did not live up to cultural expectations of good mothers. Throughout our discussion of the difficulties of combining work and family, we heard numerous references to the pressure to adhere to the role of ideal worker. At odds with these demands are pressures to also be ideal mothers. According to Sharon Hays (1998), the expectations of mothering have changed in recent decades with the rise of what she terms intensive mothering. Intensive mothering refers to a culturally constructed form of ideal motherhood in which mothers are intensely focused on the needs and cultivation of their children. Mothers are expected to be constantly engaged with their children, particularly young children and to make every effort to invest in their emotional, intellectual, and social development. Interactions with children go beyond caregiving to cultivating children to become their best possible selves. The time and energy demands of intensive mothering are great, and fulfilling the requirements of this type of mothering is near impossible when also expected to be an ideal worker at work, but this did not stop women from trying to do both. Christine, who had left her position as a production manager at an upscale grocer to become a culinary instructor, explained the lengths she went to in order to feel as though we was both a good mother and a good worker:

> I was working fifteen-hour days, six days a week. I would go in, and in order to make it work with my daughter, I would go in at midnight and my husband would take my daughter to school, to kindergarten, and when I was at [the store], I always made sure that two of my days off were weekdays so that she and I—this was before she got into kindergarten—so that she and I could spend the whole two days together. We'd spend lots of time together. I always made sure that I went in early enough to be off by like 3:00. I would go in at midnight and I would work until 3:00, 3:30, and then pick her up at school and do all the mother things then.

Several of our participants recalled making personal sacrifices, including not getting enough sleep in order to be good workers and good mothers. One participant, Elisa, described how she juggled restaurant ownership, being a good mother to her teenage son, and coping with a spouse with severe health problems by "split[ting] myself into so many parts for everybody." When asked about the sustainability of these arrangements, Elisa admitted, "I try not to think about it. I try to think: 'I have to do what I have to do.'"

Sometimes these efforts turned out to not be enough to remain in professional kitchens. Even though Christine thought she was making it work with her careful scheduling, her husband did not like these arrangements and the costs to their time as a family or to Christine's long-term health.

He urged her to find another job, but the final breaking point that convinced Christine to change jobs came during a particularly daunting Christmas season:

> The Christmas Eve before I started working here my daughter was in the pageant at church. . . . She must have been five. I kept calling and telling them, "I'm coming home. I'm coming home. I'm going to be there." And the next call was, "I'll meet you at the church." And then. "I'm going to be late." Finally, I was like, this is ridiculous. My daughter is way more important than you people and your stupid breads. So I left. I showed up at the church covered in chocolate and everything else, at the church, in my whites, ready to go to Mass. My priest was like, "So, you have made some interesting choices in the past couple of years. How are you feeling about that?" My husband was finally like, "This is not okay. You're exhausted." So right at the right time, this job came along. They approached me to see if I would be interested and my husband was like, "I don't care if you take a $10,000 pay cut and you are demoted to the bottom person on the totem pole. You have got to take this job for your health and for the safety of your marriage."

This event was the impetus for Christine's applying for a job as a chef instructor at a local culinary institute. While Christine was concerned that she would miss the adrenaline rush of working in a kitchen, after a few weeks working as a culinary instructor she felt the change was "amazing" and that she "should have done this ages ago."

CHANGING JOBS

What kind of work did the seventeen women who had left restaurant kitchens move into? And what kinds of benefits did these jobs provide that were missing from their former employment? While this is certainly not universal among women who leave restaurant kitchen work, all seventeen women in our sample still remained in the food industry. Nine of the women had become culinary instructors, while five women had opened their own business as caterers or running a pastry shop. The remaining three women all worked at upscale grocers in a variety of positions from café chef to product buyer. The benefits the women experienced included more personal time for family, greater salary and benefits, and more creative control of the food they were preparing. Lisa, who worked as a culinary instructor at a college, as well as at an upscale grocer, appreciated her current schedule due to concerns for caring for an elderly parent. She also experienced less gender discrimination working at a college and for a corporate business. She found teaching to be particularly rewarding without the harsh physical demands of restaurant kitchen work.

> Once you get into teaching and you realize how little physical work you have to do, it's kind of a relief. It's different stresses. A completely different set of stresses. You're on your feet eight to ten hours a day, not bad, not bad, considering that twelve to sixteen is the norm [when working in restaurants]. So, it's kind of nice. Lots more paperwork and dealing with all of those personalities and little intricate things during the day, those are the different stresses. Other than that, it's nothing like being in the business. To go back into that, makes you think twice. Do you really want to work sixty hours a week again? Do you really want to do that hot kitchen? We're in a comfortable, climate-controlled [place] here. It's so different but it's a balance. Most married people want to stay here because they can spend more time with their families. They're off every weekend so . . . we have holidays, scheduled holidays. A week in spring and a week in summer and then Christmas, so that's a blessing.

Participants like Lisa reported feeling relief and called their busy but manageable schedules a "blessing" compared to what it was like working in a restaurant kitchen. Jane, another culinary instructor who is married to a chef, knew she and her husband wanted to have children. The last pastry chef position she was offered only paid nine dollars per hour. Instead, she chose to leave restaurant kitchen work in favor of working at a culinary school. She explains some of the benefits:

> [I work] Monday through Friday, more or less. We work some Saturdays. I have insurance. I have paid vacation. Although I can only go when the school is closed, but still. We have 401K options and all that kind of stuff like a real job, which is one of the biggest complaints about the industry.

Jane's description suggests that working as a chef is still considered in some ways to be low status employment. We've discussed earlier in this book about how chefs have historically struggled to have their efforts recognized as that of trained professionals. For Jane, being a chef was not a real job because it offered no retirement benefits and few holidays, which is expected in much of white-collar professional employment. Jane's critique also highlights the disjuncture between the media fawning over chefs and the actual conditions of the job. For all the talk of chefs being the new rock stars, unless one is part of the handful of superstar chefs, many restaurant chefs actually have little prestige. Unless they work in large cities for well-known upscale restaurants and receive media attention, it is a difficult occupation that is often low-paid, especially given the hours involved. For Jane and the other women, working as a chef instructor offered the pragmatic benefits of a real job that gets credibility as well as stability.

Several of the chef instructors described high levels of job satisfaction and didn't think they would be able to return to kitchen work after experiencing the more professional work environment, better pay, and shorter hours characteristic of work as an instructor. Ironically, as more people became interested in becoming professional chefs this opened up new job openings for chefs who no longer wanted or were unable to work in restaurants. One of the chef instructors, Chelsea, expressed some concern about if she even could go back to kitchen work. Chelsea had worked as a well-respected pastry chef, but had taken her position as culinary school instructor after becoming pregnant with her son. She was grateful for a job that included shorter hours, especially after she and her husband divorced. She remarked that it would be difficult to move back into restaurant work and that her current job was somewhat limiting in its options for job mobility:

> I am really in a position right now where I don't know what I would do if I didn't do this [teaching]. I mean, I guess I could go be a pastry chef somewhere, but I haven't been a pastry chef here [in Texas]. I've only been here, doing this. There's not much of a lateral move that I could make here.

Although Chelsea enjoyed much of her job, she still felt that her current position was lacking in long-term opportunities, particularly being located in Texas. Much like women in other non-traditional jobs, leaving the fast track in professional chef careers can result in fewer opportunities for career advancement (Roth 2004; 2006) suggesting that, even with better jobs, there were still career tradeoffs for women with children.

Five women had moved into owning small businesses in catering or pastry shops. For these women, ownership permitted more control of their schedules and allowed the women to be creative without the constraints of restaurant work. This freedom to be more creative was especially important to women who had left corporate kitchens in national upscale restaurant chains or corporate-owned hotels that had set menus. In many ways, corporate restaurant jobs could be ideal for women chefs. They offered benefits, holidays, and generally paid more than many independently owned restaurants. However, these jobs also tended to come with long hours and little control over what foods were served. Brenda, who had left working as an executive pastry chef at a hotel to open her own bakery, said she knew it was time to leave corporate life behind when "You don't care what you're doing, but you can't wait to go home." At her previous job, Brenda worked a minimum of fifty hours a week often arriving at work between 6:00 and 7:00 A.M. and leaving as late at 9:00 or 10:00 P.M. The stress of working at such a high production venue left her exhausted and sometimes grappling with chest pains from the stress. Although she sometimes experienced boredom in her shop when business was slow, she appreciated that her new job gave her the opportunity to bake what she wanted and "play with the menus" in a way her corporate job had not. She also enjoyed the freedom to set her own schedule and stated, "If I need to close, I'll close." Similarly, Melissa had been the executive pastry chef for an upscale corporate restaurant for three years. Her pay was much higher than at other restaurant jobs, but the eighty-hour weeks expected of managers were stressful. In addition, the customers tended to err on the safer side when dining out, so Melissa received less personal satisfaction about the dishes she prepared. She explained:

> It's hard when you work at a place like that because you have, like three items that the customers expect to get [on the menu], so the other five that you may spend all your time and energy on researching and making may never sell because they come in for a chocolate soufflé. Which is great, but I felt like I was making pizzas all day. "Here's another soufflé." So, I did that for three years, and after that I decided that if I was going to work that hard, I wanted someone to appreciate what I was doing and to do it for myself and not for someone else.

After three years at the corporate restaurant, Melissa quit and took a year off from cooking. Eventually, she began making cookies and selling them to local coffee shops. At the time she was interviewed, she had started her own bakery that supplied restaurants and coffee shops with desserts. Although she still worked long hours, Melissa felt that at least she was able to bake what she wanted, and she found this creative freedom to be the best aspect of her current job.

While creating a new business offered several benefits to our participants, opening a small business wasn't always without stresses. Amber and her husband had opened up a meal delivery business. They felt, in the long run, this new path would be better for the needs of their young daughter. Each week Amber and her husband would draft a menu, spend several days shopping and preparing the food, and then deliver the food to their customers; however, the time spent trying to grow the business added several hours to their week. According to Amber, "The truth is that every day, if you're not cooking, you're trying to build the business, trying to do other things. Going and doing events . . . Sometimes we're lucky and we finish early, or relatively early, and sometimes we're working until midnight." This schedule was hectic, but, ultimately, Amber felt better about working long hours to build her own business rather than working to benefit someone else. She and her husband saw this as a family business and believed their hard work was part of building a future for their family. Amber hoped their business would be successful and that, by the time her daughter was an adult, she would be able to join in this family business as well.

Three of the participants went to work for upscale grocers in the area. These grocers contained small cafes and/or cases of prepared foods and required a chef. Other positions that were available for those with chef training included instructor for in-house cooking classes, cheesemonger, wine expert, and positions in sales and marketing. Some of these jobs paid better than many chef positions in restaurants, and many offered retirement and health insurance benefits. As an example, a recent job advertisement for chefs in an upscale grocer in North Carolina included the following:

EXPANDING GOURMET GROCERY CHAIN SEEKS
CHEFS AND PASTRY CHEFS FOR THEIR SCRATCH
KITCHEN CAFE AND CUSTOMER TAKE OUT.
5-day work week
40 hours weekly
Multiple Health Plan Options

Large Grocery Discounts on all purchases
100+ locations in Mid-Atlantic area
Tuition Reimbursement
2 Weeks Vacation; 5 Holidays; 2 Personal Days
Annual Bonus with unlimited potential—No Caps
Local Training (http://www.ashvegas.com/wanted-chefs-and-pastry-chefs-for-expanding-gourmet-grocery-chain)

For those who have spent years working long hours in restaurant kitchens, these hours and benefits can seem very attractive. Chefs would still be able to cook, but would do so under more standard hours and with numerous other perks that are unheard of within restaurant kitchens. There could also be chances for advancement within the corporate structure. If someone works as a line cook or even a sous chef at a restaurant, there is no guarantee they will ever ascend to the top executive chef position as there is tremendous competition for a relatively small number of jobs. Working for upscale grocers, in contrast, offered the opportunity for upward advancement both in and out of the kitchen.

FORGOING AND DELAYING CHILDBEARING

Because the difficulties in meeting work and mothering responsibilities were widely known in the industry, even by women who were not mothers, seven of our participants cited forgoing or delaying childbearing as the reason they could remain working in the gastronomic field. Alexandra, an event planner and a self-described workaholic, was fairly certain she would never have children. She described how her decision was based around her career goals:

> I'm probably not ever going to have kids because I work a lot and I enjoy what I do. I love my nieces but, if I was to have my own kids, would I be willing to give up three months to have the child and to do all that I need to? Probably not. Most of the female chefs in this industry have made that decision. They're not going to have a family because it would put them out of the scene for three months. The guys would rather we do take that three months so that they can take our position.

As Alexandra explained, working as a professional chef was an extremely competitive job. To even earn the title of chef, it takes many years working as a line cook then as a sous chef. Even if maternity leave was available, taking three months off to have a child would mean that her position in the kitchen was vulnerable and one of her men coworkers could take her place while she was away. Although underchefs are supposedly evaluated by "talent," additional factors such as who is perceived to be more devoted to their jobs can also influence career outcomes. Because men chefs, even fathers, would probably never have to leave the kitchen for caregiving responsibilities, they were able to prove their commitment to work and to being the ideal worker, and this would disadvantage women chefs in the long term. Alexandra, who had already worked her way up the kitchen hierarchy, did not want to slow the momentum of her career and had accepted that she would probably not have children.

Karen, who worked as a pastry chef, also discussed the damage to one's career if a woman left work, even briefly, for motherhood. At the time of her interview, Karen had recently returned from France, one of the many trips she took to compete in some very prominent pastry competitions. When asked about having children, she replied, "I think if I had had a family all of this [her career] would have been different. . . . This whole conversation. I probably wouldn't be sitting here talking to you. . . . I wouldn't have been able to get this far. A family would have held me back."

While women like Alexandra and Karen expressed no regrets for choosing to focus their energies on their career, Shelley, the chef-owner of a successful Italian restaurant, did feel she had made some personal sacrifices and she had mixed emotions about this. At the time of her interview, Shelley was about to turn forty-four and realizing that "this [her restaurant] is pretty much my life." While she had thought about having children when she turned forty, her commitment to her work meant that she had not met anyone that she wanted to marry and have children with. Although Shelley was very proud of the success of her business and received a lot of personal satisfaction from her professional accomplishments, she did express some regrets that she had devoted so much of her adult life to her work at the expense of her personal relationships.

Other women explained how they put their work first for much of their twenties, but had begun thinking about having children as they got older. Susan, who owned a bakery with her husband, explained how:

For us, we're doing career first because kids are not cheap. I think they cost more than a million dollars. If we have kids, we want [to provide for them] the same way [as] I grew up. We want to be able to buy food, clothes, good education, everything. . . . Our priority is to have a good career first.

Susan and some other women had decided to try and establish themselves professionally prior to having children. Their rationale was that, after a certain point, they would feel as though they had achieved enough as a chef that they could take some time to enjoy pregnancy and motherhood without damage to their businesses. Another strategy mentioned when asked about future family goals involved plans to eventually scale back their professional goals to make life more balanced between work and home after having children.

MAKING IT WORK

Of the fifteen participants who had children, six remained working in restaurant kitchens. For these women, they were able to continue to work in restaurants due to careful planning and through adapting either work or home life to be more compatible with their other responsibilities. Some of the women were able to do this because they worked in more adaptable work environments. Either they had supervisors who were sympathetic to the needs of parents, or they had reached levels of authority in their restaurants before having children that allowed them more power to shape their work schedules and duties. These conditions allowed some women to even bring their children to work with them. Camille, an executive pastry chef, recalled bringing her children with her to work when they were babies. She joked that she would bring them in their baby seats and set them on the counter "like a bag of flour" as she worked. Erin, a chef de cuisine, also recalled bringing her daughter to work with her. For Erin, the staff at her restaurant was like a "second family" and she felt comfortable bringing her daughter with her to work when she was young. This was beneficial as Erin was able to focus on work, but also spend time with her daughter. However, as her daughter became more mobile, she was unable to do this and had to make more complicated childcare arrangements.

Marisel, a chef and restaurant co-owner whose children ranged in age from late twenties to four years old, used to set up a playpen for her youngest child outside her office. While she acknowledged that this arrangement was unusual, it was what her family needed at the time. She also knew that she was very lucky to be in the position that allowed her to bring her son to work. She noted, "I'm the boss. Who's going to argue with me?" Marisel's attitude shows how, just as positions high in the kitchen hierarchy come with more responsibility, they also include the power to make more family-friendly workplace rules. Many women are unable to rise to top supervisory positions in kitchens in part because family responsibilities may encourage them to opt out of these career paths. They are, therefore, unable to reach those positions that would allow them to make the most difference in workplace cultures.

Another strategy employed by the six women was to try and reorganize or modify their work tasks to make them fit around their family's scheduling needs. As her children got older, this was the strategy that Camille was using most frequently. Because of her job as executive pastry chef, her schedule involved her coming to work earlier than the rest of the kitchen, baking the breads needed by the restaurant, and preparing the desserts that would be served that night. She would usually be able to leave before dinner service, but one of her jobs was to train the chefs who would plate her desserts each night. She joked that she "used to be a very dedicated employee" and would sometimes come in at night to help with the plating or other kitchen needs. Things had changed in recent years as "now I have two little kids and husband and I want to go home." No longer did she want to stay longer at work to make sure things were perfect, instead she rearranged her schedule while still accomplishing essential tasks. She explained how:

> I try to get everything done in what I feel is the appropriate amount of time. And instead of staying late, I come in early, Instead of "Okay, I'm going to come in and train this person for three days," maybe I come in and train them for two days and ask them to come in early one other day. I just try and work it around more of the kids' schedule.

Camille's joke that she used to be dedicated to her job underscores the focus on fitting into the ideal worker mold. Part of demonstrating commitment as an ideal worker means a willingness to work whatever hours are needed, including staying late or coming in on days off. Camille was no longer inter-ested in doing this and instead focused on what was the most efficient way to complete the duties of her job. She was lucky in that, by the time she had children, she was already working as an executive pastry chef and had proven her work ethic. Other women, particularly those working on the hot side of the kitchen, still faced pressures to work long hours. Among our participants, several would rearrange their work schedules sometimes com-ing in early, leaving around 3:00 to pick children up after school, and then return to work for that night's dinner service.

Some of the mothers would make their home life more flexible so that it fit with the schedule demands of being a chef. This could include cele-brating holidays or special events on different days so that it fit with work schedules. Other women came up with complicated childcare arrange-ments with their husbands, but this was usually only available to women whose husbands had compatible schedules. Some of the husbands had 9-to-5 jobs that would allow them to be home at night with the children while their wives were working. For example, early in her career, Erin would request shifts opposite those of her husband, who worked as electrician, so that they couple could save on childcare costs. This allowed them to save money, but Erin admitted that, with this schedule: "But the sacrifice is my family. I don't see them as often."

Joan and her husband, who is a chef-owner of a fine dining restaurant, would switch off children in parking lots when delivering them to and from school and after school activities. Such arrangements have been termed as "split shift shared parenting" in which one person parents while the other goes to work (Ehrensaft 1990). These arrangements generally worked well, although Joan mentioned how things sometimes got a little tricky at times, like each May, when she was both busy at her grocer job and her kids had numerous sports and end-of-the-school-year activities that needed to be coordinated.

The women we interviewed benefited from husbands who helped with the second shifts of childcare and other tasks, but several frequently drew from extended kin and friendship networks to help fill in the child-care gaps. The hours worked by professional chefs meant that there were few traditional daycare options available, so arrangements with family and friends to help with childcare and other emergencies were vital for their continuance as chefs. Marisel, the chef-owner mentioned previously in this chapter, shared childrearing of her two youngest children with her husband because he had a flexible schedule. But sometimes there were emergencies, which required juggling:

> Last night, for example, he [her husband] had an emergency so he worked late, which he normally doesn't [do]. . . . I was able to take them to gymnastics and one of the moms came back and was able to wait until my husband came home. . . . Usually if it's an emergency, it's my mom that [steps in]. But, if it's spur of the moment, it's usually another parent that will fill in.

Marisel recalled trying to plan for the large private party that was coming to her restaurant that night while also arranging care for her two youngest children with little notice. She was finally able to work something out with another parent and expressed relief that "Somebody up there is looking out for me!" Being able to rely on a large social network was beneficial because childcare arrangements could be adapted to the nontraditional work hours of female chefs (e.g., having a child spend the night with a friend) and required no payment other than a reciprocal assistance. However, a reliance on social networks could constrain mobility options. Most successful chefs need the ability to travel for short-term stages in order to gain experience working with established chefs, as well as the ability to change locations in search of better job opportunities (Cooper 1997). For women chefs with children, this was problematic as changing location could mean losing access to carefully cultivated social networks that provided support to the family.

WHO MAKES IT WORK?

Throughout this chapter we've discussed the pressure women chefs have faced in balancing work and family obligations and the routes they have taken (including job changes) to address these demands. It is important to note however, that, within demanding careers, both mothers and fathers bear significant pressure to be good workers and good parents. Yet, cultural conditions that place much of the ultimate responsibility for caregiving, particularly the wellbeing of children, on mothers still exist (Roth 2004; 2006). Women, even women heavily committed to their careers, face pressure to alter their behaviors, definitions of self, and career goals when they marry and begin to start a family. Our chefs were no different as, for example, Alexandra, the self-described workaholic who did not expect to have children, talked about the tension her job created in her romantic relationships:

> The guy I was with for seven years, and my two husbands, they met me when I worked in a kitchen, when I'm in chef whites and I'm covered [up]. The only thing you see are my hands and my face, no makeup, yet they still thought I was cute enough to go out with. [Then] they realized that I spend all of my waking hours [thinking] about food, about restaurants, and they're thinking, "Where is the wife who is supposed to be at home and cooking me dinner?" I'm like, "That's not me."

According to Alexandra, the men she was involved with met her while she was working as a chef and dressed in the boxy, unisex white jacket and were still attracted to a woman who did not display a typical feminine appearance. The relationship tension was not about how Alexandra looked, but how she acted. She was a chef first and did not adhere to the traditional wife role that included being at home and cooking her husband dinner at night. Alexandra was frustrated by their responses—the men knew from the outset of their relationship with her that she worked as a chef—but when she also took on the role of partner and wife the expectations changed in a way that made work and home life incompatible. Alexandra was expected to spend less time and mental energy on her career, and when she would not, this created tension in her relationships.

Differing expectations about marital roles are certainly not the only things that can lead a relationship to dissolve, but they can add serious strain to both relationships and careers. Joan, who we discussed earlier, is a selling manager at an upscale grocer. She has four children with her husband, who is the chef-owner at a fine dining restaurant. Joan had worked both in her husband's restaurant as well as several others over the course of her career before leaving kitchen work for employment at the grocer. Throughout the interview, Joan expressed mixed emotions about leaving restaurant kitchens. She was happy that her current job provided health insurance for her family and her schedule fit better with the needs of her children. However, she also made it clear several times that she could still "hold her own" in the kitchen and that, even now, she would be able to keep up in a restaurant kitchen. It wasn't that she was physically unable to fulfill her job duties, Joan emphasized, it was her choice to leave restaurant kitchens. Joan felt an obvious pride in being able to keep up with the physical demands of life in a kitchen, and part of Joan's reaction to changing careers may have been related to pressure she felt to be the parent to make concessions for the well-being of her family. There is research suggesting that it is more common for wives to alter their schedules than husbands in attempts to balance work-family conflict, particularly if it this means taking actions that will downgrade a career such as going to a part-time schedule (Webber and Williams 2008a; 2008b). Such actions may be related to the assumed gender roles of spouses and parents and the assumptions that wives/mothers should be the ones to make compromises regarding work and family. It could also be related to differences in earnings between parents, with mothers choosing to make concessions regarding their careers because they earn less than fathers.

Among our participants who changed careers, when there was work and family conflict, the women assumed that they would automatically be the partner who made changes. In order to have a family and a demanding job, it was up to the women to make things work. Ellen, the culinary instructor we mentioned earlier, had left restaurant work after being passed over for a promotion when she became pregnant with her second child. She noted how "In those days . . . you have children, you have obligations." Ellen was referring to the different level of responsibilities for mothers and fathers and how, as the mother, Ellen was automatically tasked with more of the childrearing responsibilities.

Many of the women seemed to accept that they were their children's primary caregiver unquestionably. None of the women in our study described any attempts to exchange and challenge these gender roles within their families. When husbands took on major childcare roles the women praised the men and described themselves as "lucky" to have such supportive husbands so willing to assist in childcare. This highlights the assumption that it is the natural role for women to rear children and men who share these activities are more than or exceptional in their willingness and ability to assist women in these responsibilities. When family members or friends help with day-to-day needs, women chefs tended to describe them as helping "me" in their role as mother rather than providing general assistance to the family (helping "us"). Such attitudes help account for the complex emotions experienced by women who love both their jobs and their families. Despite the rigidity of many kitchen jobs, none of the women suggested that their husband change his work schedule or job in order to be more available to the family. The taken-for-granted notion that fathers' careers take priority in work-family arrangements suggest that family decisions may be as problematic for women who want to stay at the top of the gastronomic field as the structure of the jobs and the masculine work cultures themselves (Stone 2007).

CREATING A MORE FAMILY-FRIENDLY WORKPLACE?

After discussing some of the difficulties in managing work and family responsibilities, we asked our participants what suggestions they had for making restaurant work more compatible with family lives. The most common answer was that there was nothing the participants would change about restaurants/the chef occupation that would make it more "family friendly." Part of this was due to fears that enforced changes would alter the unique workplace cultures of restaurant kitchens. Participants who maintained working in restaurant kitchens had developed an identity of survivors. They had faced the difficult conditions in professional cooking and been able to continue and even advance in this very competitive field. Much like women in the military, these women felt that some of the negative aspects of working in the industry were acceptable because it helped separate them from those who couldn't hack it as professional chefs (Williams 1989).

Some of our participants did have a few suggestions. They believed policies such as offering retirement funds or health insurance would be helpful to women chefs wanting to maintain a work-family balance. However, others didn't think it was realistic for small restaurants to offer these benefits because it would be too costly. Other work-family policies that are more common in the corporate world were also dismissed as not applicable to the work of chefs. The very structure of restaurant work—working at night and on weekends—made it difficult to apply policies like flextime or job-sharing. Many kitchens had such small staff that it would be difficult to find a way to alter hours or job-share with other employees.

A few women suggested higher pay would help keep women within the field but were careful to suggest that such policies would help all workers, not just mothers. This may be due in part to the increased scrutiny women chefs, particularly mothers, experience in professional kitchens. Any suggestion of special treatment, our participants feared, would just highlight that women did not really belong in the kitchen.

We should note that our interviews took place in 2008 and 2009, before the implementation of the Affordable Care Act in 2013, which was meant to make health insurance affordable and available to more American citizens. The ACA may actually contribute to decreasing internal job segregation among chefs and other male-dominated occupations. One reason that women chefs leave restaurants kitchens is to work in positions that offer health insurance. Perhaps more women will be able to stay in restaurant kitchens instead of opting out for other jobs that provide healthcare benefits.

One of the most important aspects of professional cooking that might help keep more women in the occupation may not be a policy or program, but instead relates to changes in the workplace culture that leaves more room for work and family. Rose, a culinary instructor who had spent years in restaurant kitchens, was definitely seeing a shift among her students and their priorities. She noted how, for many years there was the assumption that women chefs would drop out to have children and many owners used this as a means of denying women chefs any promotions:

> [I]n the back of all of [the owners'] minds is: "But she's a [female] chef. If I promote her up and promote her up and she has kids and her kids are sick, and the school calls and they have to go [pick the child up], who's going? It's going to be her that's going to go." And I think that's always been [the case].

However, in recent years, she has noted a shift in how men relate to their careers and their children:

> I think fathers nowadays are stepping up to the plate and being more an active part in their children's [lives]. And I think as pay has increased for women and women have better careers, it's not always going to be the males who have the best pay and stuff like that. And you're seeing a lot of women and men, husbands and wives in the restaurant business. . . . I've always found that, when

I worked for chefs who have children, they were much more understanding and much more respectful of me versus my single male chefs who just
didn't get it. . . . And they, too, want to be home with their kids. It wasn't like
forty-fifty years ago where men weren't supposed to show any emotion, and
that was the mother's job. Nowadays they're encouraged to spend time [with
their children]. And it shows. They'll tell you, "I want to go home and be
with my kid."

According to Rose, now there was less of an assumption that mothers
would automatically be the parent in charge of the majority of childcare.
There were also cultural shifts regarding masculinity and fatherhood that
were making it more acceptable for men to take on childcare responsibilities. In addition, there was less stigma about men wanting to spend time
with their children. As more men engage in childcare, discussions about
how "lucky" a woman is to have a supportive husband would change to talk
of how it is both parents' responsibilities to care for children. With more
family support in place, a greater number of women chefs can ascend to
positions of authority that can help them make real changes to the structure
and workplace culture of professional restaurant kitchens. As we noted in
chapter 2, several chef profiles of fathers featured children and family life as
a way of humanizing well-known chefs. If more men began admitting that
they, too, wanted more balance between work and family, that could open
the doors for all workers to lead more balanced lives. This could be helped
along as women begin to make more gains in the workforce. If more women
were able to reach pay parity with men, this could initiate more conversations about just which parent should work and which should spend more
time at home.

CHALLENGING "CHOICES"

Seventeen of our participants had left chef positions for other work in the
culinary sphere by the time of our interviews. The most popular reason
given for these career changes was the incompatibility of the demands of
working as a chef with the needs of family life. Of the women who remained
working as a chef, several had decided to delay childbearing or forgo motherhood due to the conditions of their work. Others were only able to

continue in the career because they had spouses with complementary work schedules and/or were able to draw from family and friend networks.

At the same time that women are expected to be ideal workers there are cultural norms that also require them to handle family needs as well. This double-bind makes it difficult for women to remain working in demanding careers. When women change jobs to less-demanding work, these actions are framed as women choosing to "opt out" or "scale back" their career ambitions. Like many sociologists, we see this choice rhetoric as problematic because it presumes individualized notions, unconstrained by structure. Choices about work and family are not made in a vacuum. They are impacted by organizational structure and culture, as well as by social beliefs regarding the roles of parents.

As more women leave these workplaces to find more family-friendly work, this choice rhetoric reinforces the idea that women who leave can't cut it and places the blame squarely on the shoulders of women workers. The conversation then becomes about women's choices and not how workplace norms and policies push women out of certain careers. Instead there needs to be attention paid to the ways work and family responsibilities— and the job of managing them—are disproportionately faced by women. Only after identifying structural and cultural factors that go much deeper than individual choices can we get a better view of what actually encourages occupational segregation and what can be done to support women (and men) in a variety of workplaces.

CONCLUSION

Where Are the Great Women Chefs?

In early 2014, the *New York Times* journalist Julia Moskin wrote an article entitled "A Change in the Kitchen," in which she discussed the new wave of women chefs ascending the ranks to become leaders in prominent restaurant kitchens. Her article cited the controversy surrounding the *Time* magazine "Gods of Food" issue and suggested the editors of *Time* were not paying enough attention to how much women chefs have accomplished. Moskin announced that we had finally reached the point where the idea that "one's sex has nothing to do with the real work of a chef" had been accepted. The author went on to suggest that women's place in professional kitchens would only grow in the future as increased corporatization of fine dining restaurants created more formal ways of hiring and promoting employees and older, traditional chefs retired from the industry and left room for new, less sexist chefs (both male and female) to lead.

Moskin's article raises a significant question with regard to our book: Does sex have anything to do with the real work of a chef? Our participants would argue that it does not and express a desire to be seen as "chefs" without the qualifier of "women chefs." However, their status as tokens within the larger gastronomic field means that it is difficult to separate their gender from their work. This is not to say that women chefs have not made gains and will continue to do so in the future. It is just that this process can be slow and filled with contradictions. Within the last year we have seen the creation of new organizations like the Toklas Society, which aims to represent women employed across the gastronomic field. Last year also included events like the one organized by chef Alexandra Feswick of Toronto's Samuel J. Moore restaurant to showcase the cooking of women chefs. The biannual magazine, *Cherry Bombe,* launched in 2013 to give focus to women and food, and the magazine has hosted networking events where successful women chefs gave panels on topics like "Getting Your Clog in the Door" and "Wait Until Your Mother Gets Home" to address issues relating to hiring and work-family balance.

But, at the same time we see these new women-centered organizations and culinary events, there has also been disapproval of women-only awards and social spaces, such as the criticism of Nadia Santini's Best Female Chef award with which we opened this book. Even as Barbara Lynch, who was excluded from the *Time* magazine "Gods of Food" issue despite owning seven restaurants and employing 260 people as part of her hospitality group, is given a profile in the *New York Times* about her success as a chef, there are also Q&A's like the one Elle.com did with Momofuku Milk Bar's Christina Tosi that focused—to the exclusion of the multiple bakeries she owns and awards she has won in the field—only on how she is able to stay so slim as a pastry chef. These contradictions suggest that women chefs are making waves and getting noticed, but there is still a lot to be done in order to receive the status of respected professionals.

FEMINIZATION THREAT, PRECARIOUS MASCULINITY, AND RELUCTANT CHANGE

At the same time that women are enrolling in culinary schools in record numbers and entering the kitchens of elite fine dining restaurants—some of which would not have even considered their applications a few year ago (or else relegated them to the salad station or what Moskin calls the "pink ghetto" of the pastry kitchen)—women still remain a minority in the upper management of these restaurants. Throughout this book, we've related this to the need for professional chefs to distance themselves from the unpaid, and often underappreciated, food work produced by women in the home. Because cooking is so highly linked to femininity, chefs experience precarious masculinity. Men chefs have to defend the merits of their occupation in order to retain and increase the social status provided by their work, and by extension, themselves. In many cases, it is not that men chefs are necessarily trying to mistreat women. They are trying to resist the negative impacts that can occur when a male-dominated occupation transitions from being man's work to women's work. When male-dominated occupations become less gender segregated, and especially if women eventually become the majority, there is often a reduction in status and pay within these jobs (Cohen and Huffman 2003; Mandel 2013; Reskin and Roos 1990; Tomaskovic-Devey 1993). Other fields such as construction, police work, or stock trading that are defined, a priori, as masculine have been able to retain their value as more women enter these arenas. These other fields do not experience as much risk when women do this kind of work. In contrast, chefs have to constantly engage in boundary work to address who exactly is a chef and whose cooking should be valued.

This feminization threat is especially worrisome for chefs, who already faced strong opposition in their movement from servant class to what Gary Alan Fine (1996a) calls "quasi-professionals." After several centuries metaphorically hiding in the kitchen, professional chefs have enjoyed the benefits that have come with newfound status and attention. Yet, the threat to their professionalism remains. Few of us have ever performed a surgical procedure; therefore, we respect and give status to surgeons because their work is viewed as specialized and requiring years of education and practice (Fine 1996a). Cooking, on the other hand, is done by many people daily— often for no pay and with little fanfare. Those who cook professionally have to constantly draw boundaries around their work in order to retain its value. Because women often make up the group performing the unpaid food labor at home, these boundaries have frequently been drawn in ways that exclude all women who cook both professionally and as amateurs.

These boundaries may be even more important now as the gastronomic field as a whole, and the chef occupation in particular, are undergoing profound changes. As the profiles of chefs have been raised, this has led to an upsurge in insecurity over who exactly is a chef (Rousseau 2012; Ruhlman 2007). These changes have meant increased competitiveness over who is worthy of the title. We already see this in some of the strong critiques of cooking celebrities, such as Rachael Ray and other women cooking show hosts. In discussions of these women, their status of nonprofessionals is highlighted as a way of drawing stronger professional boundaries around chefs.

FROM WOMEN'S WORK TO MEN'S DOMAIN

What are the mechanisms through which the chef occupation remains male-dominated? We traced the origins of gendered chef work by describing how chefs arose as an occupation and how the early exclusion of women was fundamental to the establishment of a professional identity. Cooking schools and exhibitions specifically banned women from attendance, while professional organizations highlighted the technical proficiency and artistic creations of men chefs when compared to the simple work of women home cooks. More recently, several major trends in the occupation, including nouvelle cuisine in the 1970s, the rise of superstar chefs in the 2000s, localism, nose-to-tail eating and butchery, and molecular gastronomy have emerged in ways that further gendered the occupation. Each of these trends further removes professional cooking from cooking done in the home and emphasizes the superiority of professionals (men) over amateurs (women).

Media discussions of successful, elite chefs emphasize the rare skills needed to be a gastronomic superstar. These accounts illustrate a shift in the occupation away from blue-collar production work to a more skilled, artistic profession. Yet, despite the emphasis on merit and art, gender remains salient and deeply entrenched within this rapidly changing occupation. The process of evaluating chefs has a gendered component and these different ways of assigning titles of greatness to chefs play a role in women chefs' ability to earn high levels of prestige in the occupation. This includes the framing of successful men chefs as provocateurs who challenge traditional cooking while women obtain more accolades when staying firmly within culinary boundaries, perhaps by relying on family or cultural traditions. Few women have received praise for being empire-builders, pioneers, or iconoclasts in any of these culinary trends. This media constructed dichotomy between home and haute cuisine and the genders associated with each helps maintain the gender hierarchy in professional cooking and raises serious questions about the supposed level playing field of creative careers. Creative fields are praised as meritocracies where "talent" is the basis for success, but if the markers of talent are gendered (or appraised through a gendered lens), women can be placed at a disadvantage.

Our interviews with women chefs indicated how organizational cultures are gendered in the culinary industry in terms of fitting in and moving up the hierarchy, establishing legitimate leadership styles, and negotiating work and family responsibilities. First, women we interviewed described the challenges they faced as they attempted to fit in to the masculine kitchen subculture. The women faced pernicious stereotypes that women lacked the physical and emotional strength needed to work in professional kitchens. Most women described male coworkers' tests they had to pass in order to be seen as legitimate professional chefs. Several reported sexual harassment that they tolerated and, in some cases, "gave back" in order to prove they could fit in within all-male work environments. Despite their descriptions of gender bias and discrimination, women were reluctant and even defensive regarding our questions about whether the culinary industry should change to be more women friendly.

Second, our interviews identified the stereotyped leadership roles that respondents enacted or that they observed among other women chefs. According to the majority of the chefs we interviewed, women in professional kitchens could choose to be bitchy by adapting a masculine style of management, or girly, which was used to describe women who relied heavily on their femininity and niceness in order to get what they wanted. Neither of these routes guaranteed the respect of coworkers as bitchy women were critiqued for being inauthentic and too harsh and girly women were seen as further proof that women lacked the physical and emotional strength to lead. Several of the women reported taking a third leadership route: that of mom or big sister to their male coworkers. Most said that they preferred this third leadership style because it relied on a form of feminine strength. As a mom or big sister, women chefs could take on a leadership role that was considered legitimate by men kitchen staff and several said they could transform their work environments from the stereotypical kitchen with shouting chefs who berate their staff to a more caring and communal workplace. Although women preferred this third management style, it—like the first two—relies on essentialist beliefs about men and women and raises the question of whether women chefs will ever be able to move beyond gendered notions of how they should perform their jobs.

Third, women we interviewed discussed the difficulties of balancing work and family responsibilities while working as a chef. About half of our respondents have left jobs in traditional restaurant kitchens for other employment: culinary school faculty, catering, working in upscale grocers, or owning a small shop. The main reason given for their exits was the incompatibility of restaurant work with family lives. The long hours, little time off, and lack of health benefits made it difficult for mothers to remain in the field. Women who were able to successfully combine work and home had significant social support from family and friends or had reached levels of authority where they were the ones making rules about work and family rather than the ones following them.

CHEFS ARE UNIQUE . . . BUT MAYBE NOT

Throughout this project, we came across numerous examples in chef memoirs, academic research articles, and from the women themselves insisting that being a chef is a job unlike any other. The long hours, intense work conditions, and the underlying pressure to balance food as a form of art with high production demands make it a unique occupation. Workplace norms are different for professional chefs as joking and teasing (some of this of a sexual nature), as well as angry outbursts, are not uncommon. The end result of these comments is that many people believe that professional kitchens—and the people who work within them—would be resistant to any sort of change. Many people enjoy the rush of cooking in a professional context. The trials by (literal) fire and camaraderie that develops have a strong pull for many chefs. These professional kitchens are seen as a kind of last bastion for outsiders who may not fit in within more corporate work contexts.

The uniqueness of the career and the culture of its workplaces were cited frequently in our interviews. The women chefs consistently said that there were no changes that could be made to professional kitchens that would make them friendlier to women. Even more importantly, many of the women argued that the occupation should not be changed as they, too, felt a strong sense of identity as a chef and had an affinity for these distinct workplaces. Any suggestion of formal policy or means of helping women chefs advance in their careers was met with the attitude that these changes would not work in the professional kitchen.

To some extent, these women are correct. Popular corporate responses to gender inequality, such as formal performance reviews that are used to base salary and promotions would not necessarily fit the work of chefs, which rely on creativity and teamwork. Such capabilities can be difficult to measure and a lack of a clear metric could actually disadvantage women who may have these reviews used against them because they do not fit the typical (masculine) mold of being a chef. Other workplace policies like flextime or job sharing that can be used to help employees balance work and family responsibilities may not work for chefs due to the hours they are expected to work. Benefits such as health care would be attractive to many chefs, particularly those with children. However, for many smaller restaurants, such benefits would be cost prohibitive.

Before these examples become too depressing, we want to take a moment and ask the important question: Are chefs really that unique? Conditions experienced by women chefs are not that different from that of other demanding male-dominated careers. In some professions, such as attorney (Pierce 1995; Wallace and Kay 2012), corporate manager (Kelly et al. 2010), geoscientist (Williams, Muller, and Kilanski 2012), and stockbroker, accountant, or financial advisor (Levin 2001; Roth 2004; 2006), workers are expected to be completely devoted to work, prioritize work over family, work significantly more than forty hours a week, and work after hours and on weekends. Likewise, among construction workers (Denissen 2010a; 2010b; Denissen and Saguy 2014; Paap 2006), coal miners (Tallichet 2000; Yount 1991), and firefighters (Yoder and Aniakudo 1997), women experience brutal work conditions, sexual and gender harassment, and workplace bullying. The work of chefs may be unique because of its connection to a feminine activity that occurs in the home, but it is not distinct from many of the gendered work conditions of other male-dominated occupations.

In fact, this focus on how being a chef is different from other jobs can actually help maintain these gendered divisions in the occupation. We are not suggesting that there are not unique elements to the occupation. We are saying that this focus on these elements helps create a form of inertia within the gastronomic field. It's not that "lunatics and madmen" are drawn to the occupation because such traits are required in a chef (Ruhlman 2001). It's that the long hours and work conditions of professional kitchens help shape employees to be this way. As our analysis has shown, fields emerge from historical forces and change over time and when influenced by powerful agents. This suggests that, if these conditions were altered, some of this "inevitable" behavior could also be changed.

Looking at the occupation in this way suggests that "wild" professional kitchens are the result of choices, especially by leaders, and are not the natural result of cooking professionally. For example, in many profiles of chef Thomas Keller, of the lauded Yountville, California, restaurant The French

Laundry, there is a focus on how calm and quiet his kitchen seems. Keller has even designed the kitchens in his restaurants to facilitate communication between staff so that no one has to yell, and he frequently judges the success of a dinner service by how clean his kitchen is at the end of the night. These examples suggest that kitchen cultures can stray from the macho, rowdy norm and still be incredibly successful.

Part of moving away from the loud, macho environments of professional kitchens helps, not only women chefs, but the entire occupation. Creating more professional work environments can only help chefs in their quest for greater respect, as chefs have long struggled to be seen as professionals and many have heralded the newfound attention and status provided the occupation. Creating more pathways for all kinds of employees to succeed is the mark of a fully accepted profession and a sign that chefs have moved into the realm of professionals rather than laborers. By questioning the inevitability of macho, unfriendly kitchens, we leave room for human agency and for organizations to become more welcoming to outsiders whether they are women, people of color, or gay men and lesbians.

CREATING GREATER GENDER EQUALITY

In order for women chefs to achieve greater success at work, we must acknowledge that the success of individual women chefs in their careers is linked to the position of women chefs in the larger gastronomic field. To achieve gains at either level, women must acknowledge their differences and find ways to capitalize on their strengths as chefs and potential leaders in the gastronomic field.

Women chefs can take advantage of the growing attention and status given to chefs to find ways to promote their work. Many of our participants have already begun doing this through their recognition and development of feminine strengths in the kitchen. Our work and others' indicate that women chefs can rarely be successful by becoming social men. If women act like men in their workplaces, they can be criticized for being inauthentic. Even if they truly adopt masculine leadership roles and become the epitome of the ideal worker, their gender still can be used to apply greater scrutiny to their performance and set them apart. A masculine work identity is always in danger as the slightest deviation from masculine work scripts, such as getting pregnant and requiring time off from work, means that one's status as a woman again becomes primary (Blair-Loy 2003; Byron and Roscigno 2014). In addition, if a woman proves successful in adapting to these masculine work cultures, her success would apply only in her individual case and there would be no greater transformation of the gastronomic field (see Kanter 1977).

Instead women chefs can accept and embrace that they are different from men. They can use these differences in making their kitchens stronger and better run. For example, in Moskin's *New York Times* piece she describes some of the workplace policies at Alice Waters' restaurant Chez Panisse including job-sharing programs for parents and six-months-off furloughs for head cooks, which allows more workers to get experience in leadership and makes it possible for employees to move in and out of the kitchen as situations in their lives change. More gender integrated workplaces have been found to offer higher levels emotional and informational support than more male-dominated firms (Wallace and Kay 2012). As women begin to make up a larger portion of the gastronomic field, they can pull from their feminine strengths to transform work arrangements and provide ways to engage and cultivate the talents of their staff.

These sources of difference can also be helpful in earning attention from powerful media agents in the gastronomic field, such as influential food writers and critics. Women chefs can use their status as statistical minorities to highlight how they are special and different from men chefs. We are not suggesting that women chefs play the "girl card" and change the way they act or present themselves in order to garner media attention. We are saying that media attention has become a major factor in determining a chef's success. As our research shows—and the *Time* magazine "Gods of Food" issue makes abundantly clear—food media is not immune to the same cultural schemas that shape how men and women are viewed in society. The world of elite cooking is a small one and women chefs are often not invited to be a part of this boys' club. Women need to find ways to attract this media attention and help shape their own portrayals in the media.

Women chefs can do this by banding together. Research on women's support groups in other male-dominated fields indicates that women sometimes criticize women-centered organizations because they feel that they do not help women actually move up in their workplace hierarchies, and involvement in these groups only serves to highlight "special treatment," implying lesser skills (Williams, Muller, and Kilanski 2012). There is also the risk that women-centered organizations can have a ghettoization effect in that women are "allowed" this small amount of territory within the gastronomic field and this is used as a way of restricting women's influence in the larger field. But when women come together in large numbers, they can help sponsor events that showcase their work. Such events can lead to garnering more media exposure highlighting the abilities of women chefs. With greater media attention can also come recognition from other agents in the gastronomic field, such as culinary organizations like the James Beard Foundation, which recognizes chefs and presents prestigious awards.

Women-centered organizations can also provide an outlet for women chefs. In many male-dominated fields, any critique of the structure or culture of an occupation can be considered whining and used as proof that a woman does not belong in this career. Our own interviews also bore this finding out. Even as our participants could name numerous conditions in the gastronomic field that disadvantaged women, many were loathe to discuss them at work in fear that they would be seen as complainers who were unworthy to work in professional kitchens. Having a social space that allows women to come together and discuss some of the challenges they face in their careers can be both psychologically and socially beneficial to women chefs. Because many women chefs may be the only woman working within a particular kitchen, it can be isolating and problems they experience can seem like personal issues rather than symbolic of larger structural or cultural problems within the gastronomic field. In these organizations, women chefs can learn that they are not alone and together discuss ways of addressing these issues at work.

If enough women come together and these groups include well-respected women chefs with influence within the larger gastronomic field, established chefs can help exert pressure to change the industry. Collective groups can ask hard questions of leaders in the gastronomic field, such as: "Why don't more kitchens offer maternity leave?" or "How come there are many women working as sous chef but so few as executive chef?" While individual women can be censured and ridiculed for bringing up gender issues at work, collective organizations can raise these issues and gain more momentum. This strategy can be especially effective when these organizations work with the media to publicly point out inequalities within the workplace (Jayamaran 2013).

Women can also help one another through mentoring. Mentoring has shown to be vital to success in demanding careers (Ecklund, Lincoln, and Tansey 2012; Roth 2006; Williams, Muller, and Kilanski 2012). Women who mentor other women can be a major resource in challenging the gender dynamics of the gastronomic field. There are numerous examples of these mentoring arrangements. For example, the *New York Times Magazine* did a profile of successful chef-restaurateur Barbara Lynch and her mentoring of *Top Chef* winner Kristen Kish. The article mentions Lynch's own troubled relationship with her former chef and mentor, Todd English, but goes on to describe how it was Lynch who persuaded Kish to enter the televised cooking competition that led to such positive exposure and career opportunities for the young chef. While not every woman chef can receive early career mentoring from the likes of Barbara Lynch, woman-to-woman mentoring offers a host of benefits to improving women's place in the gastronomic field. Mentors are an essential piece to the eradication of gender inequality because they can introduce mentees to important contacts in and outside of the organization, business, or workplace; teach mentees the informal ropes, including insider information about norms, roles, relationships, and subcultures; and help outsiders gain access to relatively closed networks.

This woman-to-woman mentoring has only become widely available in recent years. For a long time, women chefs had to be wary of hiring or mentoring other women. Just as in research about men and women Wall Street workers (Roth 2006), while it goes unquestioned when men hire or mentor other men, when women choose to work with other women, this can lead to criticism that women are not choosing employees for talent but rather are trying to push an agenda. Also, because women have had token status within professional kitchens for so long, there were fears that, by aligning oneself with another member of this minority group, if this person ended up being a less than stellar employee, their failures would be applied to all members of their group (Kanter 1977).

Today, while women are still a clear minority within professional kitchens, there are enough women in positions of influence that more mentorship is possible. Having high status women in management has been found to reduce inequality (Cohen and Huffman 2007). For example, in Bloomberg.com's analysis of the gender demographics of head chef positions within fifteen major restaurant and hospitality groups, they found the only group that had women as the majority of head chefs was the one headed by woman chef April Bloomfield. This suggests that, if more women in head chef positions choose to hire and promote other women, this can help shift the demographics of restaurant kitchens.

These associations with well-known chefs and their restaurants can also benefit women chefs who want to one day open their own restaurant. As Charlotte Druckman (2012) noted in her interviews with women chefs, one problem many women face is obtaining funding needed to open their own establishments. Druckman's participants suggested it is easier for men to obtain financial backing either through private investors or from banks or other financial institutions. When women are closely affiliated with other successful chefs, and when they have a track record of awards and positive media attention, these conditions can work together to make it easier for women chefs to become chef-owners. This can help women who aspire to become culinary empire builders like their men counterparts.

A final way to help women achieve more success in the culinary world is to push for more family policies that would allow women and men to manage the demands of being a chef and having a family. At the governmental level, more subsidized childcare could help parents balance work and family needs. Already a growing number of corporate restaurant groups have family leave policies in place and offer health insurance to employees and their families. Well-respected chefs in the gastronomic field, such as David Chang and Mario Batali, head some of these groups. For example, at Chang's Momofuku Restaurant Group, women employees have access to four weeks of paid maternity leave. When industry leaders like Chang and Batali institute work-family policies, they can influence others to follow suit.

As women achieve more powerful positions within the gastronomic field, they can also advocate for these changes. For example, Rebecca Glauber (2011) found that workers in gender integrated occupations were more likely to have flexible schedules compared to workers in male- or female-dominated fields. Women in more leadership roles can also help end the stigma of taking time off for family needs and let employees know that this policy exists not just on paper, but in practice as well. This transition can be accelerated as larger social shifts about work, family, and gender change among younger generations. To facilitate more women entering the occupation and succeeding as professional chefs, change must occur both inside and outside of the gastronomic field. Younger adults may be less willing to subscribe to more traditional beliefs about the different family roles of men and women. If these beliefs transform into more equitable divisions of household labor, research suggests these couples could benefit and have happier unions (Gerson 2010). Because both women and men indicate a strong desire for more work-family balance, having such policies will not be seen as ways to accommodate complaining women, but as necessary strategies to recruit and retain talented individuals.

SOME FINAL THOUGHTS ON OUTSIDERS IN WORKPLACES

As we were writing this book and engrossed in the world of women professional chefs, we became aware another major news story on workplace outsiders as Michael Sam and Jason Collins became the first openly gay men to be drafted by the NFL and NBA respectively. While both athletes found massive waves of support (Collins's jersey became the best seller at NBA.com), others were critical of the players for coming out in regards to their sexuality. Some argued that their status as out gay athletes would take attention away from the sport and damage their teams' morale as straight players would be made uncomfortable by having to work so closely with gay teammates. The result would be that teamwork would suffer and their teams would not perform as well.

While it might seem ridiculous to hear of gay men athletes being criticized that their sexuality is a detriment to teamwork, this story reminded us about similar statements about women who work in male-dominated kitchens: "Why is everything about gender? Why can't you just be a 'chef' like the rest of us?" Of course in every environment that requires teamwork there is the need for the individual to work toward becoming part of a group. However, when the need for group cohesion is used as a reason for exclusion and discrimination on the basis of ascribed characteristics like gender and sexuality, we are talking about something other than simply preserving group dynamics—these actions are truly preserving one group's dominance.

This example shows that while the work of chefs may be unique, the challenges faced by outsiders trying to fit in and advance in homogenous work environments are sadly common. Women chefs, like women workers in many fields, are encouraged to "lean in" at work (Sandberg 2013) and to find ways to fit within current occupational arrangements. While these options may work for a percentage of women at work, ultimately, such strategies can hamper the transformation of gender equality as they uphold traditional (masculine) ways of being at work. We hope that this book can help shed some light on the numerous ways that women in many different occupations can find ways to resist and even change gender inequalities at work. Unfortunately, our book is unable to examine how particular groups of women grapple with multiple forms of inequality. Our sample was neither racially nor sexually diverse. An intersectional analysis that involves interviews with particular groups of women (more women of color and lesbians, for example) would provide more insight into the complex ways that inequality occurs in the gastronomic field. And, because of the devaluation of femininity in this industry, men chefs who are stereotyped as feminine, or gay men who are presumed to be effeminate (Giuffre, Dellinger, and Williams 2008; Hennen 2008), might experience some of the biases we have described in this book. It would also be fruitful to examine how these different groups of chefs support or resist gender essentialism and gender neutrality.

As this work shows, even the most gender essentialized tasks like cooking can be co-opted by dominant groups. While women chefs have made headways into this career through time, talent, and action in recent years, there must be a shift in thinking of certain occupations as the "natural" places for men and women. Hidden behind statements like "Restaurant kitchens have always been this way" is the idea that transformative change to the occupation will not occur until more women work together to demand their place in professional kitchens. As women chefs work together to achieve even more success this increased diversity and inclusivity can only strengthen and promote the professional status of individual chefs and the occupation as a whole.

APPENDIX

METHODOLOGICAL APPROACH

Our study combines content analysis of restaurant reviews and chef profiles published in food media outlets (*New York Times, San Francisco Chronicle, Food & Wine,* and *Gourmet*) with in-depth interviews with thirty-three current and former women chefs from the central Texas area. Taken together, these data allow us to gain a sense of how men and women are evaluated by important legitimizing agents in the gastronomic field, as well as examine the lived experiences of women chefs who have worked in a variety of environments.

CONTENT ANALYSIS OF FOOD MEDIA

Fields are composed of not only producers and audiences, but also cultural tastemakers who help assign meaning and value to these cultural productions (Bourdieu 1993). To understand more about how chefs are evaluated and change position in the gastronomic field, we analyzed food media articles from New York and San Francisco newspapers and from national magazines that focused on chefs, their cooking, and their restaurants. In particular, we were interested in determining if there were gender differences in these discussions and in examining the ways in which the definition of being a great chef can be gendered. Our data came from the online archives of two newspapers: the *New York Times* and *San Francisco Chronicle* during the years 2004–2009. New York City has been recognized as one of the highest status and most competitive cities in which to work as a chef (Leschziner 2007). The *New York Times* is widely read for its food section and reviews of restaurants, and the approval of well-known food reviewers is given heavy weight in the uncertain formula of restaurant success. The *San Francisco Chronicle* highlights the Bay Area of California, which is credited as the birthplace of California cuisine, a uniquely American cooking style that focuses on seasonal ingredients prepared in ways to highlight the quality of foods produced in California. Alice Waters of the restaurant, Chez Panisse, in Berkeley, California, helped introduce California cuisine and she is one of the few women considered a master of a particular cuisine (McNamee 2007). Perhaps due to this history, or the Bay Area's geographic distance from the more established New York food scene, San Francisco could be considered a more woman friendly, yet highly competitive, culinary center (Leschziner 2007).

Articles from two food magazines: *Gourmet* (April 2004–October 2009) and *Food & Wine* (February 2006–December 2009) were also analyzed. *Gourmet* was launched in 1941 and has been described as "America's First Food Magazine," serving as a prototype for later food magazines (Rousseau 2012). Published monthly by Condé Nast Publishers, *Gourmet* began as more of a general lifestyle magazine before eventually focusing on cooking, recipes, food-related travel, and the overall American culinary scene. *Gourmet* has been credited as the first national magazine to regularly feature restaurant reviews. In late 2009, Condé Nast ceased production of *Gourmet*, although the name continues to be used for cookbooks and as an application for smart phones. *Food & Wine* magazine is published by American Express Publishers and was first introduced in 1978. It focuses on food and entertaining, travel, recipes, and chefs. Currently, *Food & Wine* has a circulation of almost one million and is known for co-hosting *Food & Wine* festivals and naming the Top Ten Best New Chefs in a special issue each year.

We began our media analysis by doing a search for restaurant reviews and chef profiles. From the four media sources, we included only articles that featured the name of a chef and gave significant attention to the food the chef created. This included content such as restaurant reviews in which a chef's food and their restaurant was critiqued. For this analysis, we included only articles in which a chef was identified and described as having at least some creative control over the kitchen. Articles in which no actual chef was named or there was little or no discussion of their work creating a menu were excluded.

We began our analysis by coding whether each review or profile included men or women chefs, or, in some cases, both. We also analyzed chef profiles, including interviews with chefs that contained discussion about the chef, their philosophy or approach to food, leadership style, and dishes they created. Through this process we were able to identify 2,206 reviews/profiles for use in our analysis. The majority of these data (1,439 sources) came from the *New York Times*, which has a weekly food section and is famous for its restaurant reviews. The *San Francisco Chronicle* provided 452 reviews/profiles for our analysis. From the magazines, there were 144 articles from *Gourmet* and 171 articles from *Food & Wine* that were included in the analysis.

Including this media data not only allowed us to look beyond Texas to national, and even international chef coverage, but it also let us examine the role of cultural tastemakers in legitimizing chefs and aiding in their career success. Our analysis examined the discourse surrounding the chefs. We employ the concept of discourse similarly to Josée Johnston and Shyon Baumann, who refer to "an institutionalized system of knowledge and thought that organizes populations" (2010, 38). For food writers, this system of knowledge relates to judgments of taste about chefs and their food creations, which can impact how the public views their cuisine and how chefs are awarded capital within the gastronomic field (Kamp 2006). In our data, this included descriptions of the chefs and their careers, personal histories, personalities, and cooking. In addition, we were interested in what sort of language was used to describe successful dishes and chefs to understand what attributes are rewarded by food writers and critics. We wanted to know if the description of great chefs differed by gender and if and how men and women chefs were discussed differently.

In order to analyze the restaurant reviews and chef profiles, we used the qualitative data analysis software NVivo (version 10). We imported the reviews and profiles into NVivo, which allowed us to systematically code the data into categories. We began by examining writing about men and women chefs separately and creating themes based upon how the food writers and critics discussed chefs, their restaurants, and their cooking. Both authors used NVivo to code the media data and we frequently compared our codes to discourage potential bias. Once basic coding was done of all 2,206 pieces of chef media, we used NVivo to see and read all quotes in a particular category (e.g., all of the mentions and quotes about a chef being a superstar) and continue our analysis. We then compiled the most common themes that applied to each gender and found examples from each.

IN-DEPTH INTERVIEWS WITH WOMEN CHEFS

We also interviewed thirty-three women chefs in the central Texas area. The Austin–San Antonio corridor possesses an emerging and diversifying restaurant scene with national media outlets, such as *Food & Wine* magazine and the website Eater.com highlighting this growth and recognizing accolades awarded to local chefs. In 2012, the BRAVO cable network aired *Top Chef: Texas*, a Texas-situated version of its popular reality cooking competition show. Austin, Texas, has recently hosted conferences for the International Association of Culinary Professionals and Les Dames d'Escoffier—two international organizations within the gastronomic field. The Austin Food & Wine Festival has continued to grow and now draws several well-known chefs to the area each year. San Antonio, Texas, is also home to a developing food scene and, in 2007, became home to a branch of the CIA meant to train new chefs in the cuisine of the American Southwest.

Selecting the Austin–San Antonio corridor provided the opportunity to speak with many women chefs who had a diversity of work experiences. Many of the restaurants have relatively small kitchen staffs that contain only a few trained chefs. Most of our participants were either the first women to work in the kitchen or were among the few who held chef positions at their establishments. This provided them a unique perspective on the permeability of a male-dominated profession as the local environment has transformed and become more professionalized.

When we began our research, we had to first come up with a working definition of who we considered to be a chef. We decided to include only women who identified as having worked as a chef in professional kitchens and whose positions included both creative control and management duties in their workplace. In order to identify women chefs in central Texas, we read numerous online restaurant reviews and pored over websites devoted to the local restaurant scene. Any time a woman chef was mentioned a note was made of her name and where she worked. We then contacted the women by phoning the restaurant at non-peak hours, explaining the purpose of our research, and asking for their participation. From our online research we also learned about a local culinary arts organization that included a number of women chefs. We contacted the president of this organization who agreed to help us identify potential participants. These women were contacted at their workplaces or via email and briefed about our study. We also recruited using snowball sampling by asking for the names of other possible interviewees from those originally contacted.

This procedure identified fifty women chefs working in central Texas. When we contacted their place of employment, we learned that five of the women had left those positions leaving no forwarding information. This brought the number of possible participants to forty-five, and thirty-three of these women (73%) completed interviews with one of the authors. Our interviews took place between 2008 and 2009.

As part of our research, we wanted to hear from a diverse group of women within the culinary world. We made a point to interview women who worked on what is called the "hot side" of the kitchen as head/executive chefs or sous chefs as well as women who worked on the "cold" side of restaurant kitchens as pastry chefs. While it has been established that most executive and head chef positions are held by men, more women worked in pastry chef positions. We wanted to examine if women had varying experiences based on type of job.

Because restaurant kitchens often report high levels of attrition (Batt, Lee, and Lakhani 2014) we also wanted to speak with women who had left restaurant work for other jobs. We believed this might help us understand why some women were choosing to opt out of restaurant work despite their investment of time and training for this career. Seventeen of the participants had left chef positions, although all still worked in the culinary industry as culinary school instructors, caterers, chefs and managers at gourmet grocers, and bakery owners. While these women do not represent all women who leave restaurant work—for example, their continued employment in the culinary industry suggests a positive regard toward working with food—they still can provide information on what conditions encourage women to leave restaurant kitchens for other types of jobs.

Table I.1 in the introduction lists the characteristics of the thirty-three participants and pseudonyms they were provided as part of this study. On average, the women had fifteen years of experience in the culinary industry. The participants ranged in age from twenty-four to sixty, with an average age of thirty-nine years. Twenty-four of the women identified as white, five described themselves as Hispanic or Latina, two participants were Asian, and two participants were Black. All of the chefs but one identified as heterosexual. Twenty-one were married or cohabitating at the time of the interviews and fifteen had children.

We conducted in-depth, semi-structured interviews with each participant. A copy of our questionnaire is provided at the end of this appendix. The interviews often took places at participants' homes, coffee shops, or even their places of business. The interview guides included questions about the women's motivations for becoming a chef, their chef training (both formally through culinary school and on-the-job), experiences working within restaurant kitchens, how they balanced work and family demands, and their overall impressions of recent changes to the occupation including their thoughts on how women fit into this new trajectory. Using an interview method allowed participants to speak in their own words and fully describe their lived experiences by providing a sense of context as well as numerous details of their lives. Face-to-face in-depth interviewing is especially adept at assessing experiences about which people feel ambivalence or when respondents offer contradictory descriptions, which is often the case when interviewing people about experiences of inequality. Interviewers can follow up with probing questions that permit the respondent to further clarify their perceptions and experiences. These types of follow up questions permit a closer analysis of respondents' everyday lives, which are often hard to capture on a survey that offers closed choice or "yes/no" answers.

We recognize that our sample is not representative of all women chefs. In particular, interviewing only Texas-based chefs provides some limitations to our sample. Because our participants were working in a state known for holding more conservative views, including views about women and their roles as leaders, this could mean the women would have experienced additional gender discrimination and mistreatment that would not have been the case in other places. However, on the other hand, because Texas is not as competitive of a cooking environment as other locations (e.g., New York City), this could also mean the women would have experienced less scrutiny and benefited from less pressure at work. During their interviews, none of our participants cited their location in Texas as being a major influence on how they were treated in the kitchen (although a small number mentioned there were fewer opportunities for chef jobs in smaller cities). Because many of our participants had experience working in other cities renowned for their restaurant scenes including New York City, Los Angeles, and Chicago, and they were able to speak about experiences at any of the professional cooking environments they had worked in, which helped address problems with using a Texas-based sample.

We transcribed the interviews and analyzed the transcripts using two techniques. We used open- and focused-coding techniques by hand, followed by an analysis using NVivo software (described earlier) to identify common themes within and across our groups of participants (Esterberg 2002; Miles and Huberman 1994). Open coding means reading the transcripts several times, highlighting and writing in the margins of the transcripts, and writing memos about themes and patterns that emerge inductively. Focused coding involves organizing the data by themes, identifying categories that are important for the research questions of the study, and comparing and contrasting different groups in the sample (e.g., pastry and line chefs, or chefs with few years and many years of experience). We analyzed the transcripts individually then compared the themes we identified in order to discourage potential bias. Once we had identified some initial themes via open and focused coding, we further analyzed the data using NVivo to find additional evidence of each theme and to generate new themes in a systematic way.

IN-DEPTH INTERVIEW QUESTIONNAIRE

Before we began our in-depth interviews, we asked each respondent to complete a brief written questionnaire that requested contact information, demographic information (e.g. race and ethnicity, sexual orientation, relationship status), and professional information (e.g. current employer and position, years in the food industry, whether the respondent attended culinary school, and previous positions in the food industry).

MOTIVATIONS

1. Is your work as a chef your first professional career? If not, what was your first career? How did you decide to change your career focus?
2. When did you first decide to pursue a career as a chef? What was going on in your life at the time? Was your decision influenced by any role models? How did people respond to this decision? Were you concerned being female could impact your career as a chef?

TRAINING

1. Please describe your training experience. What led you to choose this method of training/particular school or program?

2. Do you feel your training provided a good preparation for life in the kitchen? Why or why not? If you could, is there any type of your training experience that you would change?

3. Do you have a specialization? What led you to pick this particular specialization? Were you encouraged to go this route by any mentors/instructors/supervisors? If so, how do you think your gender impacted their recommendations?

4. During your training, how many other females were in your class/first job? Did you observe any differences between male and female students in terms of treatment? What about in expectations regarding their future careers?

WORK EXPERIENCE

1. How did you get to your current position? What is your typical day like (personal and professional)? What are your major roles/duties at work?

2. Describe the hierarchy at work. How many other females work at your restaurant?

3. Based upon your work experiences as a chef, have you felt that some jobs/duties are more difficult because you are female (strength, stature)? Could you describe a time when this happened? How did others in the kitchen react?

4. In general, how have male employees responded to you or other female chefs?

5. Are your supervisors male or female? Would you say that men and women work together well in the kitchen? How do male employees react to female supervisors? If there are ever conflicts, what seems to be the cause of the problem?

6. At this job or others, have you noticed any patterns in the jobs that men tend to hold and those that women tend to hold in the kitchen? What do you think causes these differences to exist?

7. Describe a time when your gender "mattered" at work (what happened, how you felt, and what resulted from this experience).

8. Have you ever experienced anything that could be defined as sexual harassment? What happened? How did you respond?

9. Have you noticed any differences working with male or female managers? How do men manage the kitchen? How about women?

10. What are your future goals for your career? How does your gender affect your plans?

11. What do you need to achieve these future goals? What are the major barriers to achieving these goals?

CHARACTERISTICS OF A CHEF

1. Describe the ideal chef. What are their major characteristics?

2. In your opinion, are there any gender differences that tend to make males or females more likely to have those characteristics?

3. How would a chef describe success? Would male and female chefs have different definitions?

4. In your own career, how would you describe your relationship to your job? What are your major commitments as a chef? And as a woman?

5. How would you describe your approach to food? Do you think male and female chefs have different approaches to food? If so, how are they different?

WORK-LIFE BALANCE

1. Who are your major sources of social/emotional support?

2. How has your career affected your personal life? Do you feel that you have had to make any sacrifices in your work or personal life?

3. If they have children: Were you working as a chef when you gave birth to your children? If so, did you take leave from your restaurant job? How long was your leave? How did you coworkers respond to your decision to start or expand your family?

4. Overall, how do you balance your career as a chef and the needs of your family? How do you manage situations such as childcare, housework, etc.?

5. Have you ever thought of changing jobs or of leaving the food industry? If so, why?

(For those who have left the occupation) What made you want to leave restaurant work for your current job? How is your life different now than when you were working in a restaurant?

6. Within your field, who has been the most supportive? What type of support do they provide?

WOMEN AS CHEFS

1. Overall, how would you describe how women are treated in the culinary world? What are the major barriers to female chefs achieving success in their profession?

2. Is there a particular type of woman who is more likely to succeed in this field? Are there particular jobs in which men and women tend to be more successful? Have you known any women who have left the field due to issues of treatment or discrimination?

3. What changes would you make to the industry to make it easier to attract and retain talented female chefs?

4. There has been a major increase in women entering the culinary field. What advice would you give future chefs about succeeding in this career?

REFERENCES

Acker, Joan. 1990. "Hierarchies, Jobs, Bodies: A Theory of Gendered Organizations." *Gender & Society* 4 (2): 139–158.

Balazs, Katharina. 2002. "Take One Entrepreneur: The Recipe for Success of France's Great Chefs." *European Management Journal* 20 (3): 247–259.

Bartholomew, Patricia S., and Jenene G. Garey. 1996. "An Analysis of Determinants of Career Success for Elite Female Executive Chefs." *Hospitality Research Journal* 20 (2): 125–135.

Batt, Rosemary, Jae Eun Lee, and Tashlin Lakhani. 2014. *A National Study of Human Resource Practices, Turnover, and Customer Service in the Restaurant Industry.* New York: Restaurant Opportunities Centers United.

Baumann, Shyon. 2002. "Marketing, Cultural Hierarchy, and the Relevance of Critics: Film in the United States, 1935–1980." *Poetics* 30 (4): 243–262.

Beagan, Brenda, Gwen E. Chapman, Andrea D'Sylva, and B. Raewyn Bassett. 2008. "'It's Just Easier for Me to Do It': Rationalizing the Family Division of Foodwork." *Sociology* 42 (4): 653–671.

Bellas, Marcia. 1999. "Emotional Labor in Academia: The Case of Professors." *ANNALS of the American Academy of Political and Social Science* 561 (1): 96–110.

Benard, Stephen, and Shelley J. Correll. 2010. "Normative Discrimination and the Motherhood Penalty." *Gender & Society* 24 (5): 616–646.

Bielby, Denise D., Molly Moloney, and Bob Q. Ngo. 2005. "Aesthetics of Television Criticism: Mapping Critics' Reviews in an Era of Industry Transformation." *Research in the Sociology of Organizations* 23: 1–43.

Bilderback, Leslie. 2007. *The Complete Idiot's Guide to Success as a Chef.* New York: Alpha Books.

Bird, Sharon R. 1996. "Welcome to the Men's Club: Homosociality and the Maintenance of Hegemonic Masculinity." *Gender & Society* 10 (2): 120–132.

Bird, Sharon, and Laura A. Rhoton. 2011. "Women Professionals' Gender Strategies: Negotiating Gendered Organizational Barriers." In *Handbook of Gender, Work, and Organization*, edited by Emma Jeanes, David Knights, and Yancy Martin, 245–262. Chichester, West Sussex: Blackwell/Wiley Publishing.

Blair-Loy, Mary. 2003. *Competing Devotions: Career and Family among Women Executives.* Cambridge, MA: Harvard University Press.

Bobbitt-Zeher, Donna. 2011. "Gender Discrimination at Work: Connecting Gender Stereotypes, Institutional Policies, and Gender Composition of Workplace." *Gender & Society* 25 (6): 764–786.

Bourdain, Anthony. 2000. *Kitchen Confidential: Adventures in the Culinary Underbelly.* London: Bloomsbury.

Bourdieu, Pierre. 1993. *The Field of Cultural Production.* New York: Columbia University Press.

Bourdieu, Pierre, and Loïc J. D. Wacquant. 1992. *An Invitation to Reflexive Sociology.* Chicago: University of Chicago Press.

Britton, Dana M. 1990. "Homophobia and Homosexuality: An Analysis of Boundary Maintenance." *The Sociological Quarterly* 31 (3): 423–440.

_____. 2003. *At Work in the Iron Cage: The Prison as Gendered Organization.* New York: New York University Press.

Britton, Dana M., and Laura Logan. 2008. "Gendered Organizations: Progress and Prospects." *Sociology Compass* 2 (1): 107–121.

Brundson, Charlotte. 2005. "Feminism, Postfeminism, Martha, Martha, and Nigella." *Cinema Journal* 44 (2): 110–116.

Bugge, Annechen Bahr, and Reidar Almas. 2006. "Domestic Dinner: Representations and Practices of a Proper Meal among Young Suburban Mothers." *Journal of Consumer Culture* 6 (2): 203–228.

Byron, Reginald A., and Vincent J. Roscigno. 2014. "Relational Power, Legitimation, and Pregnancy Discrimination." *Gender & Society* 1–28. Accessed April 22, 2014. doi: 10.1177/0891243214523123.

Carli, Linda L. 2001. "Gender and Social Influence." *Journal of Social Issues* 57 (4): 724–741.

Castilla, Emilio J. 2008. "Gender, Race, and Meritocracy in Organizational Careers." *American Journal of Sociology* 113 (6): 1479–1526.

Charles, Maria, and Karen Bradley. 2009. "Indulging Our Gendered Selves? Sex Segregation by Field of Study in 44 Countries." *American Journal of Sociology* 114 (4): 924–976.

Cohen, Phillip N. 2013. "The Persistence of Workplace Gender Segregation in the U.S." *Sociology Compass* 7 (11): 889–899.

Cohen, Phillip N., and Matt L. Huffman. 2003. "Individuals, Jobs, and Labor Markets: The Devaluation of Women's Work." *American Sociological Review* 68 (3): 443–463.

_____. 2007. "Working for the Woman: Female Managers and the Gender Wage Gap." *American Sociological Review* 72 (5): 681–704.

Cooper, Ann. 1997. *A Woman's Place is in the Kitchen.* New York: Van Nostrand Reinhold Company.

Correll, Shelley J., and Stephen Benard. 2006. "Biased Estimators? Comparing Status and Statistical Theories of Gender Discrimination." *Social Psychology of the Workplace* 23: 89–116.

Crittenden, Ann. 2001. *The Price of Motherhood.* New York: Henry Holt and Company, LLC.

Damaske, Sarah. 2011. *For the Family? How Class and Gender Shape Women's Work.* New York: Oxford University Press.

Davis, Mitchell. 2009. "A Taste for New York: Restaurant Reviews, Food Discourse, and the Field of Gastronomy in America." PhD diss., New York University.

De Beauvoir, Simone. 1953. *The Second Sex*. New York: Bantam Books.

Dellinger, Kristen. 2002. "Wearing Gender and Sexuality 'on Your Sleeve': Dress Norms and the Importance of Occupational and Organizational Culture at Work." *Gender Issues* 20 (1): 3–25.

_____. 2004. "Masculinities in 'Safe' and 'Embattled' Organizations: Accounting for Pornographic and Feminist Magazines." *Gender & Society* 18 (5): 545–566.

Dellinger, Kirsten, and Christine L. Williams. 1997. "Make-Up at Work: Negotiating Appearance Rules in the Workplace." *Gender & Society* 11 (2): 151–177.

_____. 2002. "The Locker Room and the Dorm Room: Workplace Norms and the Boundaries of Sexual Harassment in Magazine Editing." *Social Problems* 49 (2): 242–257.

Denissen, Amy M. 2010a. "The Right Tools for the Job: Constructing Gender Meanings and Identities in the Male-Dominated Building Trades." *Human Relations* 63 (7): 1051–1069.

_____. 2010b. "Crossing the Line: How Women in the Building Trades Interpret and Respond to Sexual Conduct at Work." *Journal of Contemporary Ethnography* 39: 297–327.

Denissen, Amy M., and Abigail C. Saguy. 2014. "Gendered Homophobia and the Contradictions of Workplace Discrimination for Women in the Building Trades." *Gender & Society* 28 (3): 381–403.

DeVault, Marjorie. 1994. *Feeding the Family: The Social Organization of Caring as Gendered Work*. Chicago: University of Chicago Press.

Druckman, Charlotte. 2010. "Why are There No Great Women Chefs?" *Gastronomica* 10: 24–31.

_____. 2012. *Skirt Steak: Women Chefs on Standing the Heat and Staying in the Kitchen*. San Francisco: Chronicle Books.

Eagly, Alice H., and Mary C. Johannesen-Schmidt. 2001. "The Leadership Styles of Women and Men." *Journal of Social Issues* 57 (4): 781–797.

Eagly, Alice, Mary C. Johannesen-Schmidt, and Marloes L. van Engen. 2003. "Transformational, Transactional, and Laissez-Faire Leadership Styles: A Meta—Analysis Comparing Women and Men." *Psychological Bulletin* 129 (4): 569–591.

Ecklund, Elaine Howard, Anne E. Lincoln, and Cassandra Tansey. 2012. "Gender Segregation in Elite Academic Science." *Gender & Society* 26 (5): 693–717.

Ehrensaft, Diane. 1990. *Parenting Together: Men and Women Sharing the Care of their Children*. Champaign: University of Illinois Press.

England, Paula. 2010. "The Gender Revolution: Uneven and Stalled." *Gender & Society* 24 (2): 149–156.

England, Paula, and Nancy Folbre. 1999. "The Cost of Caring." *Annals of the American Academy of Political & Social Science* 561: 39–51.

Epstein, Cynthia Fuchs. 1989. "Workplace Boundaries: Conceptions and Creations." *Social Research* 56 (3): 571–590.

Erickson, Karla. 2010. "Talk, Touch, and Intolerance: Sexual Harassment in an Overtly Sexualized Work Culture." *Research in the Sociology of Work* 20: 179–202.

Esterberg, Kristin G. 2002. *Qualitative Methods in Social Research*. Boston: McGraw Hill.

Fantasia, Rick. 2010. "'Cooking the Books' of the French Gastronomic Field." In *Cultural Analysis and Bourdieu's Legacy*, edited by Elizabeth Silva and Alan Warde, 28–44. London: Routledge.

Ferguson, Priscilla Parkhurst. 2004. *Accounting for Taste: The Triumph of French Cuisine.* Chicago: University of Chicago Press.

Fine, Gary Alan. 1987. "One of the Boys: Women in Male-Dominated Settings." In *Changing Men: New Directions in Research on Men and Masculinity*, edited by Michael S. Kimmel, 131–147. Newbury Park, CA: Sage Publications.

_____. 1992. "The Culture of Production: Aesthetic Choices and Constraints in Culinary Work." *American Journal of Sociology* 97 (5): 1268–1294.

_____. 1996a. "Justifying Work: Occupational Rhetorics as Resources in Restaurant Kitchens." *Administrative Science Quarterly* 41 (1): 90–115.

_____. 1996b. *Kitchens: The Culture of Restaurant Work*. Berkeley, CA: University of California Press.

Florida, Richard. 2002. *The Rise of the Creative Class*. New York: Basic Books.

Furia, Stacie. 2010. "Navigating the Boundaries: Army Women in Training." *Research in the Sociology of Work* 20: 107–126.

Gans, Herbert J. 1999. *Popular Culture and High Culture*. New York: Basic Books.

Gardner, William L., Dawn Fischer, and James G. Hunt. 2009. "Emotional Labor and Leadership: A Threat to Authenticity?" *The Leadership Quarterly* 20: 466–482.

Gerson, Kathleen. 2010. *The Unfinished Revolution: How a Generation is Reshaping Family, Work, and Gender in America*. Oxford: Oxford University Press.

Giffort, Danielle M. 2011. "Show and Tell? Feminist Dilemmas and Implicit Feminism at Girls' Rock Camp." *Gender & Society* 25 (5): 569–588.

Giuffre, Patti A., and Christine L. Williams. 1994. "Boundary Lines: Labeling Sexual Harassment in Restaurants." *Gender & Society* 8 (3): 378–401.

Giuffre, Patti, Kirsten Dellinger, and Christine Williams. 2008. "'No Retribution for Being Gay?': Inequality in Gay-Friendly Workplaces." *Sociological Spectrum* 28: 254–277.

Glauber, Rebecca. 2011. "Limited Access: Gender, Occupational Composition, and Flexible Work Scheduling." *Sociological Quarterly* 52 (3): 474–494.

Gopnik, Adam. 2011. *The Table Comes First: Family, France, and the Meaning of Food*. New York: Alfred E. Knopf.

Gorman, Elizabeth. 2005. "Gender Stereotypes, Same-Gender Preferences, and Organizational Variation in the Hiring of Women: Evidence from Law Firms." *American Sociological Review* 70 (4): 702–728.

Haas, Scott. 2005. "Why a Chef?: A Journey into the Darkest Regions of the Kitchen." *Gastronomica* 5: 37–42.

_____. 2013. *Back of the House: The Secret Life of a Restaurant.* New York: Berkeley Books.

Hamrick, Karen S., Margaret Andrews, Joanne Guthrie, David Hopkins, and Ket McClelland. 2011. *How Much Time Do Americans Spend on Food?* EIB-86, U.S. Department of Agriculture, Economic Research Service.

Hays, Sharon.1998. *The Cultural Contradictions of Motherhood.* New Haven, CT: Yale University Press.

Hennen, Peter. 2008. *Faeries, Bears and Leathermen: Men in Community Queering the Masculine.* Chicago: University of Chicago Press.

Hochschild, Arlie R. 1983. *The Managed Heart: The Commercialization of Feeling.* Berkeley: University of California Press.

_____. 1990. *The Second Shift.* New York: Avon Books.

Hollows, Joanne. 2003. "Feeling Like a Domestic Goddess: Post-feminism and Cooking." *European Journal of Cultural Studies* 6 (2): 179–202.

Hopfl, Heather. 2011. "Women's Writing." In *Handbook of Gender, Work, and Organization,* edited by Emma J. Jeanes, David Knights, and Patricia Yancey Martin, 25–36. New York: Wiley.

Hughey, Matthew W. 2010. "The White Savior Films and Reviewers' Reaction." *Symbolic Interaction* 33 (3): 475–496.

Hyman, Gwen. 2008. "The Taste of Fame: Chefs, Diners, Celebrity, Class." *Gastronomica* 8 (3): 43–52.

Irvine, Leslie, and Jenny R. Vermilya. 2010. "Gender Work in a Feminized Profession: The Case of Veterinary Medicine." *Gender & Society* 24 (1): 56–82.

Jayaraman, Sara. 2013. *Beyond the Kitchen Door.* Ithaca, NY: Cornell University Press.

Jeanes, Emma J., David Knights, and Patricia Yancey Martin, eds. 2011. *Handbook of Gender, Work, and Organization.* New York: Wiley.

Johnston, Josée, and Shyon Baumann. 2010. *Foodies: Democracy and Distinction in the Gourmet Foodscape.* New York: Routledge.

Jones, Steve, and Benn Taylor. 2001. "Food Writing and Food Cultures: The Case of Elizabeth David and Jane Grigson." *European Journal of Cultural Studies* 4 (2): 171–188.

Kamp, David. 2006. *The United States of Arugula.* New York: Broadway Books.

Kanter, Rosabeth M. 1977. *Men and Women of the Corporation.* New York: Basic Books.

Katila, Saija, and Paivi Eriksson. 2013. "He Is a Firm, Strong-Minded, and Empowering Leader, but Is She? Gendered Positioning of Female and Male CEOs." *Gender, Work, and Organization* 20 (1): 71–84.

Kelly, Erin L., Samantha K. Ammons, Kelly Chermack, and Phyllis Moen. 2010. "Gendered Challenge, Gendered Response: Confronting the Ideal Worker Norm in a White-Collar Organization." *Gender & Society* 24 (3): 281–303.

Kelly, Ian. 2003. *Cooking for Kings: The Life of Antonin Carême the First Celebrity Chef.* New York: Walker and Company.

Kuh, Patric. 2001. *The Last Days of Haute Cuisine*. New York: Penguin.

Lamont, Michele, and Virag Molnar. 2002. "The Study of Boundaries in the Social Sciences." *Annual Review of Sociology* 28: 167–195.

Leidner, Robin. 1991. "Serving Hamburgers and Selling Insurance: Gender, Work, and Identity in Interactive Service Jobs." *Gender & Society* 5 (2): 154–177.

Leschziner, Vanina. 2007. "Cooking Careers: Institutional Structures and Professional Self-concepts in the Field of High Cuisine." Presentation at the ASA Annual Conference. New York, NY.

Levin, Peter. 2001. "Gendering the Market Temporality, Work, and Gender on a National Futures Exchange." *Work and Occupations* 28 (1): 112–130.

Levine, Lawrence. 1988. *Highbrow/Lowbrow: The Emergence of Cultural Hierarchy in America*. Cambridge, MA: Harvard University Press.

Lizardo, Omar, and Sara Skiles. 2008. "Cultural Consumption in the Fine and Popular Arts Realms." *Sociology Compass* 2 (2): 485–502.

Lounsbury, Michael, and Mary Ann Glynn. 2001. "Cultural Entrepreneurship: Stories, Legitimacy, and the Acquisition of Resources." *Strategic Management Journal* 22: 545–564.

Mandel, Hadas. 2013. "'Up the Down Staircase:' Women's Upward Mobility and the Wage Penalty for Occupational Feminism, 1970–2007." *Social Forces* 91 (4): 1183–1207.

Marcus, Miriam. 2005. "Editor's Dish: Results of Starchefs.com 2005 Salary Survey." Accessed November 19, 2008. http://www.starchefs.com/features/editors_dish/salary_survey/.

Martin, Patricia Y. 2003. "'Said and Done' Versus 'Saying and Doing': Gendering Practices, Practicing Gender at Work." *Gender & Society* 17 (3): 342–366.

McLaughlin, Heather, Christopher Uggen, and Amy Blackstone. 2012. "Sexual Harassment, Workplace Authority, and the Paradox of Power." *American Sociological Review* 77 (4): 625–647.

McNamee, Thomas. 2007. *Alice Waters and Chez Panisse*. New York: Penguin.

Miles, Elizabeth. 1993. "Adventures in the Postmodernist Kitchen: The Cuisine of Wolfgang Puck." *Journal of Popular Culture* 27 (3): 191–203.

Miles, Matthew B., and A. Michael Huberman. 1994. *Qualitative Data Analysis: An Expanded Sourcebook*. Thousand Oaks, CA: Sage.

Milkie, Melissa A., and Pia Peltola. 1999. "Playing All the Roles: Gender and the Work—Family Balancing Act." *Journal of Marriage and the Family* 61 (2): 476–490.

Moen, Phyllis, and Yan Yu. 2000. "Effective Work/Life Strategies: Working Couples, Work Conditions, Gender, and Life Quality." *Social Problems* 47 (3): 291–326.

Moskin, Julia. 2014. "A Change in the Kitchen." *New York Times*, January 21. Accessed February 1, 2014. http://www.nytimes.com/2014/01/22/dining/a-change-in-the-kitchen.html?_r=0.

Paap, Kris. 2006. *Working Construction: Why White Working-Class Men Put Themselves—and the Labor Movement—in Harm's Way*. New York: Cornell University Press.

Parsa, H. G., John T. Self, David Njite, and Tiffany King. 2005. "Why Restaurants Fail." *Cornell Hotel and Restaurant Administration Quarterly* 46 (3): 304–322.

Pearlman, Alison. 2013. *Smart Casual: The Transformation of Gourmet Restaurant Style in America*. Chicago: University of Chicago Press.

Pierce, Jennifer. 1995. *Gender Trials: Emotional Lives in Contemporary Law Firms*. Berkeley: University of California Press.

Pinkard, Susan. 2009. *A Revolution in Taste: The Rise of French Cuisine, 1650–1800*. New York: Cambridge University Press.

Pollan, Michael. 2013. *Cooked: A Natural History of Transformation*. New York: Penguin.

Presser, Harriet. 2003. *Working in a 24/7 Economy: Challenges for American Families*. New York: Russell Sage Foundation.

Rao, Hayagreeva, Philippe Monin, and Rodolphe Durand. 2003. "Institutional Change in Toque Ville: Nouvelle Cuisine as an Identity Movement in French Gastronomy." *American Journal of Sociology* 108 (4): 795–843.

Reskin, Barbara F., and Patricia A. Roos. 1990. *Job Queues, Gender Queues: Explaining Women's Inroads into Male Occupations*. Philadelphia: Temple University Press.

Rhoton, Laura A. 2011. "Distancing as a Gendered Barrier: Understanding Women Scientists' Gender Practices." *Gender & Society* 25 (6): 696–716.

Ridgeway, Cecilia. 2007. "Gender as a Group Process: Implications for the Persistence of Inequality." In *The Social Psychology of Gender*, edited by Shelley Correll, 311–333. New York: Elsevier.

_____. 2011. *Framed by Gender: How Gender Inequality Persists in the Modern World*. Oxford: Oxford University Press.

Roth, Louise M. 2004. "Engendering Inequality: Processes of Sex Segregation on Wall Street." *Sociological Forum* 19 (2): 203–228.

_____. 2006. *Selling Women Short: Gender and Money on Wall Street*. Princeton, NJ: Princeton University Press.

Rousseau, Signe. 2012. *Food Media: Celebrity Chefs and the Politics of Everyday Interference*. London: Berg.

Rudman, Laurie A., and Peter Glick. 2001. "Prescriptive Gender Stereotypes and Backlash toward Agentic Women." *Journal of Social Issues* 57 (4): 743–762.

Ruhlman, Michael. 2001. *The Soul of a Chef: The Journey Toward Perfection*. New York: Penguin.

_____. 2007. *The Reach of a Chef: Professional Cooks in the Age of Celebrity*. New York: Penguin.

Sandberg, Sheryl. 2013. *Lean In: Women, Work, and the Will to Lead*. New York: Alfred A. Knopf.

Schilt, Kristen. 2006. "Just One of the Guys? How Transmen Make Gender Visible at Work." *Gender & Society* 20 (4): 465–490.

_____. 2010. *Just One of the Guys? Transgender Men and the Persistence of Gender Inequality*. Chicago: University of Chicago Press.

Shapiro, Laura. 2001. *Perfection Salad: Women and Cooking at the Turn of the Century.* New York: Random House.

Sinclair, Alicia C. 2006. "'On the Line': Identifying Workplace Stressors in the Restaurant Kitchen." PhD diss., Columbia University.

Smithson, Janet, and Elizabeth H. Stokoe. 2008. "Discourses of Work–Life Balance: Negotiating 'Genderblind' Terms in Organizations." *Gender, Work, and Organization* 12 (2): 147–168.

Spang, Rebecca L. 2000. *The Invention of the Restaurant: Paris and Modern Gastronomic Culture.* Cambridge, MA: Harvard University Press.

Stone, Pamela. 2007. *Opting Out? Why Women Really Quit Careers and Head Home.* Berkeley: University of California Press.

Stringfellow, Lindsay, Andrew MacLaren, Mairi Maclean, and Kevin O'Gorman. 2013. "Conceptualizing Taste: Food, Culture, and Celebrities." *Tourism Management* 37: 77–85.

Sutton, Ryan. 2014. "Women Everywhere in Food Empires but No Head Chefs." *Bloomberg News,* March 6. Accessed April 1, 2014. http://www.bloomberg.com/news/2014-03-06/women-everywhere-in-chang-colicchio-empires-but-no-head-chefs.html.

Swinbank, Vicki A. 2002. "The Sexual Politics of Cooking: A Feminist Analysis of Culinary Hierarchy in Western Culture." *Journal of Historical Sociology* 15 (4): 464–494.

Symons, Michael. 2000. *A History of Cooks and Cooking.* Urbana: University of Illinois Press.

Tallichet, Suzanne E. 2000. "Barriers to Women's Advancement in Underground Coal Mining." *Rural Sociology* 65 (2): 234–252.

Tanner, Julian, and Rhonda Cockerill. 1996. "Gender, Social Chance, and the Professions: The Case of Pharmacy." *Sociological Forum* 11 (4): 643–660.

Tomaskovic-Devey, Donald. 1993. *Gender and Racial Inequality at Work: The Sources and Consequences of Job Segregation.* Ithaca, NY: ILR Press.

Townley, Barbara, Nic Beech, and Alan McKinlay. 2009. "Managing in the Creative Industries: Managing the Motley Crew." *Human Relations* 62 (7): 939–962.

Trubek, Amy. 2000. *Haute Cuisine: How the French Created the Culinary Profession.* Philadelphia: University of Pennsylvania Press.

U.S. Bureau of Labor Statistics. 2013. "BLS Reports: Women in the Labor Force, A Databook." *Bureau of Labor Statistics, U.S. Department of Labor, Occupational Outlook Handbook, 2014–15 Edition, Chefs and Head Cooks.* Accessed February 15, 2014. http://www.bls.gov/ooh/food-preparation-and-serving/chefsand—head-cooks.htm.

U.S. Department of Education, National Center for Education Statistics, Integrated Postsecondary Education Data System, Fall 2006. 2007.

Vallas, Steven Peter. 2001. "Symbolic Boundaries and the New Division of Labor: Engineers, Workers and the Restructuring of Factory Life." *Research in Social Stratification and Mobility* 18: 3–37.

Voydanoff, Patricia, and Brenda W. Donnelly. 1989. "Work and Family Roles and Psychological Distress." *Journal of Marriage and the Family* 51 (4): 923–932.

Wallace, Jean E., and Fiona M. Kay. 2012. "Tokenism, Organizational Segregation, and Coworker Relations in Law Firms." *Social Problems* 59 (3): 389–410.

Webber, Gretchen, and Christine Williams. 2008a. "Part-time Work and the Gender Division of Labor." *Qualitative Sociology* 31 (1): 15–36.

_____. 2008b. "Mothers in 'Good' and 'Bad' Part-time Jobs: Different Problems, Same Results." *Gender & Society* 22 (6): 752–777.

Wharton, Amy. 1999. "The Psychological Consequences of Emotional Labor." *Annals of the American Academy of Political and Social Science* 561: 158–176.

Williams, Christine L. 1989. *Gender Differences at Work: Women and Men in Nontraditional Occupations.* Berkeley: University of California Press.

_____. 1995. *Still a Man's World: Men Who Do Women's Work.* Berkeley: University of California Press.

Williams, Christine L., Chandra Muller, and Kristine Kilanski. 2012. "Gendered Organizations in the New Economy." *Gender & Society* 26 (4): 549–573.

Wingfield, Adia Harvey. 2013. *No Invisible Men: Race and Gender in Men's Work.* Philadelphia: Temple University Press.

Yoder, Janice D., and Patricia Aniakudo. 1997. "'Outsider Within' the Firehouse: Subordination and Difference in the Social Interactions of African-American Women Firefighters." *Gender & Society* 11 (3): 324–341.

Yount, Kristen R. 1991. "Ladies, Flirts, and Tomboys: Strategies for Managing Sexual Harassment in an Underground Coal Mine." *Journal of Contemporary Ethnography* 19 (4): 396–422.

Zimmer, Lynn. 1987. "How Women Reshape the Prison Guard Role." *Gender & Society* 1 (4): 415–431.

INDEX

Page numbers in *italics* refer to tables and figures.

Abboccato restaurant (New York City), *71*
Achatz, Grant, 52, 54, 59
Achatz, Grant, Sr., 59
Acker, Joan, 6–7, 10, 11, 70, 169
Adams, M. J., 81
Adrià, Ferran, 48, 61, 63
Aduriz, Andoni Luis, 63
Affordable Care Act, 186
agricultural production, 25
á la carte ordering, 24
Aleixandre, Mari, 61
Aleixandre, Raul, 61
Alinea restaurant (Chicago), 52, 59
American cooking: challenge to French
   haute cuisine, 31–35; role of women in,
   30–31; turn toward, 36
Angell, Katherine, 31
anger, 97, 155, 158, 161
anxiety, 165
appearance as chef, 104–106
apprenticeship, 26
Arguinzoniz, Victor, 62
art skills. *See* creative skills
Arzak restaurant (San Sebastián, Spain), 60
Atala, Alex, 43
Austin Food & Wine Festival, 206
awards, culinary, 1, 26, 30, 62, 73–74, 75, 78,
   190, 198, 200
Aziza restaurant (San Francisco), 77

bakeries. *See* pastry shops/bakeries
Balazs, Katharina, 93
Barker, Karen, 63
Bastianich, Joe, 80
Bastianich, Lidia, 80
Batali, Mario, 80, 200
Baumann, Shyon, 31, 32, 205
Bazirgan, David, 49
Beard, James, 32–33

Beard Foundation, James, 10, 198; James
   Beard Award, 74, 198
Beck, Simone, 33
Bello, Anselmo, 54
benefits. *See* flextime/flexible work
   schedule; health benefits; retirement
   benefits
Bertholle, Louisette, 33
Bernstein, Michelle, 57, 80–81
Bird, Sharon, 118, 123, 127
bitchy. *See* leadership style
Blackbird restaurant (Chicago), 73
Bloomberg News/Bloomberg.com, 3, 199
Bloomfield, April, 200
Blumenthal, Heston, 54
Bobbitt-Zeher, Donna, 93
Bocuse, Paul, 30, 51
Boldrini, Massi, 50
Boston Globe, 33
Botsacos, Jim, 70–71
Bouchon restaurant (Las Vegas,
   Nevada), 72
Boulud, Daniel, 53, 71
Bourdain, Anthony, 1, 17, 37, 38
Bourdieu, Pierre, 6, 7, 44, 45, 75
Bras, Laurent, 73
Bras, Michel, 70
BRAVO cable network, 206
Bruckner, Dawn, 67
Bruni, Frank, 72
Busch, Pamela, 67

California cuisine, 34–35, 39, 68, 203–204
career changers, 38, 162–187
Carême, Marie Antoine, 21–23
carework. *See* family: carework
Carro, Hermance, 77
caterer, 164, 171, 175
Cav wine bar (San Francisco), 67

Chang, David, 43, 74, 200
cheesemonger, 176
chef, professional: birth of, 20–26;
    boundary work, 18; celebrity chef, rise
    of, 41, 196; characteristics, 211; chef
    vs. dish, 48–58; definition, 2, 14, 206;
    designations, 1, 2–3; empire builder,
    68–72, 75–78, 192; empowerment of,
    29–30, 122, 124, 129; evaluations and
    descriptions, 47–48; evolution of
    career, 18; gendered divisions, 7, 20,
    39–42, 104, 190; gendered history,
    18–20, 25–29, 30–31, 39–42; gendered
    nature of occupation, 7, 19–20; history
    of profession, 21–38; making career
    family-friendly, 167–168, 180, 185, 188;
    male-dominated occupation, 7, 14, 16, 39,
    47, 85, 132–134, 141, 191–192, 195, 197–198,
    200–201; management responsibilities,
    2, 3, 131, 132; military origins of career, 21,
    24, 26, 58; motivation, 209; occupation
    in transition, 5–6, 29–30, 192–194;
    orientation toward career, 68–82;
    reclassification of career, 35; "rock star"
    status, 5–6, 18; rule breakers vs. rule
    followers, 58–68; statistics, 3; status
    changes, 35–38; structure of career, 10;
    uniqueness of career, 194–196; white
    jacket and toque, 22; work interactions,
    10. See also female chef; gastronomic
    field; kitchen, professional; male chef
chef/cooking television show. See television
    show
chef de cuisine, 21, 96. See also head/
    executive chef
chef de partie, 2, 98
Cherry Bombe (magazine), 190
Chez Panisse (Berkeley, California), 34–35,
    36, 68, 197, 204
Child, Julia, 33, 34, 120
child care. See daycare; family
children. See family
Chodorow, Jeffrey, 81
Choi, Roy, 39
Chou, Melissa, 76–77
Chua-Eoan, Howard, 44
Claiborne, Craig, 34

coal mining career, 86, 107, 118, 195
Cohen, Amanda, 43
"cold" area of kitchen. See kitchen,
    professional: "hot" side/"cold" side
Colicchio, Tom, 72
Collins, Jason, 201
commis, 3
competitions, 26, 31, 41, 140, 178, 192, 206
Condé Nast Publishers, 204
construction career, 86, 94, 101, 107, 118, 157,
    191, 195
content analysis of food media, 11, 47,
    203–204
cookbooks, 22–23, 27, 30–31, 32–33, 54, 70,
    78, 81, 204
cooks, 2, 18, 50
corporate-owned restaurants. See
    restaurant: corporate
creative economy, 6, 27, 192
creative skills, 2, 14, 30, 45, 54–55, 75, 120,
    175–176
Crittenden, Ann, 20
crying (as weakness), 95–98, 101, 107
culinary cloning, 72
Culinary Institute of America (CIA), 4, 31,
    38, 206
culinary instructors, 39, 66, 92, 95, 103, 123,
    127, 150, 153, 154, 164, 171, 172, 173, 174, 184,
    186, 207
culinary school: attendance, 2, 38, 48; ban
    on women, 26, 31, 41, 192; demographic
    makeup, 4; gender discrimination, 91–92;
    legitimizing force, 10; women-run, 31
cultural capital, 46
cultural schema, 47, 66, 194, 197

Dang, Vanessa, 56, 57
daycare, 167, 168, 177–178, 179–180, 181,
    184–185, 200
Deen, Paula, 120
del Posto restaurant (New York City), 80
democratization, 39
depression, 165
Des Jardins, Traci, 78
DeVault, Majorie, 20
Diaz, Mary Ellen, 81
Dirt Candy restaurant (New York City), 43

discrimination, 10; age, 92; gender, 42, 85–86, 91–92, 118–128, 163, 173, 193; hiring, 5, 41, 92, 134, 158; race, 84
Dixler, Hillary, 44
domestic cooking. *See* home cooking/cook
Druckman, Charlotte, 82, 200
Ducasse, Alain, 73
Dufresne, Wylie, 61
Dükkan restaurant (Istanbul), 67
Durand, Rodolphe, 29

Eagly, Alice, 157
Eater.com, 44, 206
education, degrees, 4. *See also* culinary school; on-the-job training
El Bulli restaurant (Spain), 48, 61, 63
Ellerbe Fine Foods (Fort Worth, Texas), 56
El Paseo restaurant (San Francisco), 57
emotional labor, 142–143, 157
endorsement deals, 33, 36, 37, 70, 73
England, Paula, 9, 86
English, Todd, 81, 199
entrée/grill station, 2
Epstein, Cynthia Fuchs, 94
Escoffier, Georges Auguste, 23–25, 26, 29
Esquire magazine, 74
Evans, Rob, 69
event planner, 95, 102, 105, 114
executive chef. *See* head/executive chef
Extebarri restaurant (Spain), 62
Eyherabide, Lisa, 66

family: balancing work and—, 127, 161, 165, 170, 179–182, 185, 193, 211; carework, 27, 86, 93, 162–165, 169, 177–178, 193; family-friendly workplace, 185–187; forgoing/delaying childbearing, 177–179, 187; issue of motherhood, 162–165; labor, 20; restaurant as—, 149–150, 154, 157, 158; time spent with, 76–77, 81–82, 172–173, 175; work and—imbalance, 165–169, 201
family leave policy, 200
Fantasia, Rick, 25, 37
Fegen, Lance, 75
Felidia restaurant (New York City), 80
female chef: addressing sexualized workplaces, 114–115; as advocate, 103–104; banned from culinary competitions and schools, 26; career motives, 78–82; changing work/career/job, 170–177; competency, 56–57; cooking spheres, 1, 19–20, 60, 82, 98–101; exclusion from French haute cuisine, 20–26; fitting in/standing out, 84–129; focus on object produced, 55–56; focus on pleasing others, 76–77; forgoing/delaying childbearing, 177–179, 187; gaining respect, 101–105, 130–131, 133, 136, 140, 143–145; great female chefs, 82–83, 189–202; guidance from men, 79–81; home cooking comparison, 67; as leader, 57–58, 130–161; management styles (*see* leadership style); mistreatment, 85–86; physical/emotional stereotypes, 94–98, 103, 129, 149; qualitative methodology, 11, 14, 203–211; protected by males, 107–108; proving herself, 101–108, 134, 136; reasons for leaving restaurant kitchen, 162–188; representation in food media, 43, 55–58, 63, 68, 76–83; role in American cooking, 30–31; role in French gastronomy, 25–26; rule breakers vs. rule followers, 58–68; statistics, 3, 39; study of, 1–16; tests of toughness, 101–108, 129; uncomfortable with media attention, 77–78; women as chefs (questionnaire), 212. *See also* chef; family; gastronomic field; kitchen, professional; leadership style; male chef
feminism, 3–4; third-wave, 124
femininity: devaluation of, 8, 9, 86, 159; models in restaurants, 105–106; as a strength, 134, 152, 160–161; as weakness, 40, 129, 145–148
feminization threat, 8–10, 18, 27, 33, 86–87, 190–191
Ferguson, Priscilla Parkhurst, 7–8, 25, 27
Feswick, Alexandra, 190
fields, notion of, 6–8, 203. *See also* gastronomic field
Fine, Gary Alan, 51, 96, 104, 108, 156, 191
firefighting career, 86, 118, 157, 195
flextime/flexible work schedule, 168, 180–183, 185, 195
Folbre, Nancy, 9

Food & Wine magazine, 39, 47, 49, 56, 67, 69, 74, 75, 80, 82, 204, 205, 206; Best New Chef, 59, 73, 78, 204
food blogs/websites, 37. *See also* media attention
food critics/writers/tastemakers, 7–8, 27, 30, 34, 62, 82: gendered impact of evaluation, 46–47; as legitimizing force, 10, 11, 51, 197, 205. *See also* media attention
food movement, 82. *See also specific movement*
Food Network, 36, 88, 120
Four Seasons restaurant (New York City), 32
Frank, Ken, 76
Frazier, Paula, 77
Freitag, Amanda, 64, 65–66
The French Chef (television show), 33, 34
French Culinary Academy, 91
French haute cuisine: birth of, 20–26; challenged by American cuisine, 31–35; codifying and standardizing, 23, 32; exclusionary tactics, 26–29, 41; food preparation, 27–28; home cooking vs.—, 17–42, 66; rise of, 7–8; sanitation practices, 22; training, 49
French Laundry restaurant (Yountville, California), 69, 72, 195–196
French Revolution, 21, 23, 24
frustration, 96–97

game, metaphor of, 7
garde manger, 3, 98
Garrelts, Megan, 81
Gastronomica (journal), 28
gastronomic field: culinary hierarchy, 7–8, 31, 98–99, 107, 134, 138, 139, 153, 180; geographic location, 7–8; industry organizations as legitimizing forces, 10; organizational norms/arrangements, 10; salary, 4, 5, 9, 89, 93, 167, 173, 174, 176, 186, 194; structural inequalities, 4; theoretical model, 8, 9; women and—, 6–11. *See also* chef, professional; female chef; kitchen, professional; male chef
gender discrimination. *See* discrimination
gender disparities, 2; cooking and separate spheres, 19–20, 190

gendered evaluation, 5, 46–47
gendered leadership, 131–161
gendered organization, 6–8, 10–11
gender inequality/equality, 194; impact of critics' evaluations on, 46–47, 203; professional chefs and, 4–6, 93, 124, 126, 134, 196–201
gender integration/segregation, 5, 10–11, 99, 131, 164, 191, 197
gender neutrality, 118–128
gender stereotypes, 11, 16, 46, 83–85, 94–98, 133–134, 143–145, 157, 193
geoscientist (career), 195
girly girl/girl card, 103, 131–132, 145–148, 197. *See also* leadership style
Gitane restaurant (San Francisco), 66
glass ceiling, 133
Glauber, Rebecca, 200
globalization and new markets, 34
Go Fish restaurant (St. Helena, California), 58
Goin, Suzanne, 78
Gopnik, Adam, 40
gourmand, 27
Gourmet magazine, 34, 47, 69, 81, 82, 204, 205
Grace, Meg, 79
Gramercy Tavern (New York City), 67
Gras, Laurent, 51
Grimod de La Reynière, Alexandre Balthazar Laurent, 27
Guerard, Michel, 30
guilds, 24
Gusto restaurant (New York City), 57

Haas, Scott, 28–29
habitus, 45–46
Halikas, Peter, 50
harassment, 10; bullying, 195; handling, 113–117; lawsuit, 117; sexual, 41, 85–86, 105, 108–118, 119, 129, 135, 146, 159, 161, 195; teasing/teambuilding, 108–114, 129, 138, 154–156, 163, 194
Harrison restaurant (New York City), 64
haute cuisine. *See* French haute cuisine
Hays, Sharon, 163, 170–171
hazing, 85–86, 108, 114

head/executive chef, 2, 3, 98, 100, 113, 117, 121, 166, 207; gender demographics, 199–200
health benefits, 167–168, 173, 175, 176, 183, 185–186, 194–195, 200
hegemonic masculinity, 85
Hell's Kitchen (television show), 130
Hochschild, Arlie, 142, 163
home cooking/cook, 4, 9–10; —vs. haute dichotomy, 66, 82, 192; perception of, 18, 19; professional vs., 27–28, 31; women chefs comparison, 67. See also French haute cuisine: home cooking vs.—
Hopfl, Heather, 152
"hot" area of kitchen. *See* kitchen, professional: "hot" side/"cold" side
Hugo's restaurant (Portland, Maine), 69
human capital/knowledge capital, 7, 26, 46, 91, 93
Huynh, Michael, 54
Hyman, Gwen, 32, 37, 38, 40
hypermasculinity, 10, 15, 16, 86, 87, 98

ideal worker norm, 70, 165, 169, 170–171, 178, 180–181, 188, 196
immigration and new markets, 34
ingredients, local, 34–35, 36, 39, 62, 64, 68, 192
Inn at Little Washington (Virginia), 69
internal job segregation, 5, 101, 164, 186
International Association of Culinary Professionals, 206
investors, restaurant, 64–65, 70, 72, 200
An Invitation to Reflexive Sociology (Bourdieu and Wacquant), 7
Iron Chef (television show), 59
iron maiden, 133, 138

Jimenez, Atxen, 60
Jimenez, Nicolás, 60
jobs, masculine/feminine coding, 2, 5, 9–10, 18, 132–133
jobsharing, 185, 195, 197
Johnston, Josée, 31, 32, 205

Kahan, Paul, 73–74
Kamp, David, 39

Kanter, Rosabeth Moss, 94, 96, 98, 121, 133, 146, 152, 157, 158, 159
Keller, Hubert, 49
Keller, Thomas, 72, 195–196
Kelly, Ian, 21, 22
Kish, Kristen, 199
kitchen, professional: attrition, 100, 163–165, 170, 172–175, 184, 186–187, 207; "back of the house/front of the house," 27, 88, 144; boundaries, 86, 94, 156–157; competitive environment, 11, 21, 89–90, 100, 110, 155, 163, 177, 178, 203–204, 208; creating family-friendly workplace, 185–187; entering, 84–129; gender composition and harassment, 110, 154–156; "hot" side/"cold" side, 14, 88, 98–99, 100–101, 181, 207; hours, 77, 88, 109, 156–157, 165–167, 175, 180–181, 182, 183, 193–195; male-dominated workplace, 86–87, 104, 128–129; physical conditions, 3, 41–42, 87–91, 147–148, 165–166, 195; subculture/unique culture, 88, 104, 109–110, 129, 154, 158, 163, 168, 193–194, 196, 199; teamwork, 89–90, 106, 153, 201. *See also* chef; female chef; gastronomic field; male chef
Kitchen Confidential (Bourdain), 37
Koryurek, Defne, 67
Kuh, Patric, 32, 33
Kunz, Gray, 52

L20 restaurant (Chicago), 51
La Brea Bakery (Los Angeles, California), 120
L'Art de la Cuisine Française (Carême), 23
Lauren, Jamie, 65
Lawson, Nigella, 17
leadership: cultural schemas, 47, 134; establishing authority, 134, 135, 138–141, 148–151; feminine strength, 158–161, 193; gendered—, 131, 132, 137–138, 141–142, 156–160, 193, 196–197; in male-dominated workplaces/jobs, 131, 132–134; opposition to women leaders, 134, 135–136; skills, 11, 52–54; by tokens, 133–134, 152–153, 158–159; women's in professional kitchen, 134–137. *See also* leadership style

leadership style, 130–132, 160–161, 208;
    bitchy, 132, 133, 137–145, 160, 193; girly girl,
    133, 137, 145–148, 193; men's vs. women's,
    149, 151–156, 159, 160–161; mom/big
    sister, 132–134, 137, 148–158, 160, 193;
    transformational, 157
Lean In: Women, Work, and the Will to Lead
    (Sandberg), 124
"lean in" strategy, 42, 124, 201–202
Lee, Sandra, 41
Lefebvre, Ludo, 17
Le Guide Culinaire (Escoffier), 23
Le Pavillon restaurant (New York City), 32
Le Relais d'Olèa restaurant (France), 77
Leschziner, Vanina, 93
Les Dames d'Escoffier, 206
Levin, Peter, 105
Levine, Lawrence, 31
line chef/line cook, 2–3, 98, 177, 178, 209
Lucas Carton restaurant (Paris), 75
Lynch, Barbara, 55–56, 190, 199

macho environment. *See* male-dominated
    work/occupation
Madame le Chef (television show), 77
Magnolia Grill (Durham, North Carolina),
    63
Malarkey, Brian, 17
male chef: as businessman, 68–73, 75;
    cooking spheres, 19–20, 60, 82; cooks
    vs.—, 50, 86; as dedicated to career,
    68–71; fatherhood/family time, 76–77,
    82, 93, 169, 178, 187; magic of cooking,
    28; masculine style of leadership,
    132, 137–145, 151; perception of, 19;
    perfection/controlling obsession, 55,
    68–71; as regular guy, 73–76; training/
    craftsmanship, 48–51; as visionary, 22,
    51, 55, 72, 82–83; working hours, 68–69.
    See also chef; female chef; gastronomic
    field; kitchen, professional; leadership
male-dominated work/occupation, 5, 7,
    8–11, 132–134, 152, 159, 192–195, 196–198
The Managed Heart (Hochschild), 142
Manso, Maria, 63
Mari, Juan, 51, 52
Marin, François, 23

masculinity, nature of work, 9, 19–20,
    21, 23, 25–26, 28, 33, 39–44, 86–87.
    See also hypermasculinity; precarious
    masculinity
Mason, Sam, 54–55
Mastering the Art of French Cooking (Child,
    Beck, and Bertholle), 33
maternity leave, 167, 168, 178, 200
McCook, Molly, 56
media attention: chef vs. dish, 48–58;
    content analysis, 11, 47–48, 203–205;
    evaluations and descriptions of chefs,
    47–48; gendered impact of critics'
    evaluation, 46–47, 205; orientation
    toward career, 68–82; power of, 10,
    11, 34, 36–37, 41, 43, 44–46, 196–198;
    rule breakers vs. rule followers, 58–68;
    women's representation, 43, 197–198.
    See also food blogs/websites; food
    critics/writers/tastemakers
memory, food, 59–60, 67
Menon, François, 23
mentor: importance of, 58, 103, 199; as
    nurturer, 77, 148–150, 152–153
menu, 32, 34
meritocracy, 6, 39, 120, 125–126, 192
methodology, study, 11, 14, 47–48, 203–212
Meyer, Claus, 69
Mia Dona restaurant (New York City), 74
Michelin Guide, 1, 30, 60, 75, 93
Michy restaurant (Miami, Florida), 80
Mihal, Rudy, 53–54
military, 9, 21, 26, 58, 106, 138, 185. *See also*
    chef, professional: military origins of
    career
Mina, Michael, 52
misogyny, 103
Mitterer, Lauren, 63
molecular gastronomy, 40, 48, 54, 61, 82, 192
Molyvos restaurant (New York City), 70
mom/big sister. *See* leadership style
Momofuku Milk Bar (New York City), 190
Momofuku Restaurant Group, 200
Monin, Philippe, 29
Montalvo, Alicia, 65
Moskin, Julia, 189, 190, 197
motherhood penalty, 169

mothering, expectations of, 163, 169, 170–171, 177–179, 182–185, 188. *See also* family
mother's/grandmother's influence, 27, 40, 58–61, 67, 149

Newsweek, 30
New York Times, 11, 34, 41, 47, 48, 52, 54, 72, 73, 79, 80, 189, 190, 197, 199, 203, 205
Nicotra, Fortunato, 80
nonstandard work hours, 166–167, 185, 195
nose-to-tail cooking, 39–40, 192
nouvelle cuisine, 29–30, 36, 51, 192
nurturing. *See* mentor: as nurturer
NVivo (data analysis software), 205, 209

occupational segregation, 5, 10, 83, 99, 123, 131, 164, 188
Odyssey restaurant (Windsor, California), 53
officer de cuisine, 21
Olive Garden restaurant chain, 72
Oliver, Jamie, 77
Olson, Nancy, 67
on-the-job training, 2, 91, 163–180. *See also* stage
opting out, 163–164, 180, 188
Osteria restaurant (New York City), 71
"otherness," 138, 151, 160, 201–202
Outback Steakhouse chain, 72

paid holidays/paid leave/paid vacation, 168, 173–175, 177, 200
pantry station, 98–101. *See also garde manger*
Paris, France, 21
participants. *See* study: participants
pastry chef, 3, 14, 44, 55, 63, 65, 67, 76–77, 81, 84–85, 88, 90, 94, 100, 102, 104, 109, 115, 125, 140, 146, 147, 151, 152, 165, 166–167, 207
pastry instructor, 102
pastry shops/bakeries, 171, 175, 176, 207
paternalism, 107–108
Patterson, Daniel, 52
Pawlcyn, Cindy, 58
Pearlman, Alison, 32, 39

performance review, 194–195. *See also* promotion
personality, 51–55, 57–58, 73–74, 93, 121–123, 126
Pizzeria Mozza restaurants, 80
poisonnier, 3
police work, 157, 191
Pope, Monica, 120
precarious masculinity, 9–10, 18, 41, 87, 104, 190–191
Presser, Harriet, 166
Price-Bottini, Celeste, 57
professional vs. amateur cooking. *See* home cooking/cook: professional vs.
promotion, 93, 94, 100, 124, 133, 134–135, 146, 157, 169, 170, 184, 186, 194–195
Psaltis, Doug, 49
Psilakis, Michael, 74
publishing. *See* cookbooks
Puck, Wolfgang, 36

qualitative methods, 11, 14, 119, 203, 205, 208, 209
Quek, Justin, 49
questionnaire, study, 208, 209–212; chef characteristics, 211; motivations, 209; training, 210; women as chefs, 212; work experience, 210–211; work-life balance, 211

Ramirez, Amelia, 65
Ramsay, Gordon, 72, 130, 131, 158, 159
Rao, Hayagreeva, 29, 30
Ray, Krishendu, 36
Ray, Rachael, 41, 120, 191
The Reach of a Chef (Ruhlman), 38
Redzepi, Rene, 43
restaurant: casual, trend toward, 74–75; corporate, 116, 117, 135, 168, 175, 200; as a family, 149, 154, 157–158, 179; history of, 22, 23, 24–25, 29, 30; home vs.—, 24, 27–28; multiple, 70–73, 76, 78, 82, 190; owner, 78–79, 97, 100, 101, 113, 121, 166
restaurant reviews, 11, 44–45, 47, 82–83
restaurant worlds, 10, 14, 85, 91, 128
retirement benefits, 165, 173–174, 176, 185
Rhoton, Laura, 118, 123, 127
Ridgeway, Cecilia, 4, 141, 143, 157

Ripert, Eric, 69–70
Robuchon, Joël, 73
Roth, Frances, 31
Rousseau, Signe, 41, 45
Ruhlman, Michael, 38
Russian service, 25
Ryan, Tim, 38

sales/marketing position, 111–112, 125, 170,
    176, 183
Samuel J. Moore restaurant (Toronto,
    Canada), 190
Samuelsson, Marcus, 61
Sandberg, Sheryl, 124
San Francisco Chronicle, 47, 64, 65, 76, 78,
    203, 205
sanitation practices, 22
Santini, Nadia, 1, 190
saucier, 2
Savoy Hotel (London), 24
Schilt, Kristen, 159
seductress role, 133, 146. See also leadership
    style: girly girl
self-confidence, 124
self-determination, 122–123
Senderens, Alain, 75
separate spheres, 19–20, 23, 26
Sette restaurant (New York City), 66
sexism, 6, 103
sexual harassment. See harassment: sexual
Sheraton, Mimi, 57
Silverton, Nancy, 80, 120
Sinclair, Alicia, 108
Small, Karen, 77
Smart Casual: The Transformation of
    Gourmet Restaurant Style in America
    (Pearlman), 39
social capital, 7, 46, 48, 71, 91, 93
"social men," 106, 196
Social restaurant chain, 81
sous chef, 2, 3, 84, 90, 98, 99, 116, 164, 177, 178
split shift shared parenting, 181
Sportello restaurant (Boston), 56
stage, 66, 93, 182
Starchefs.com, 3
stock trading career, 158, 191, 195, 199

Stone, Pamela, 164
study, 1–16; content analysis of food
    media, 11, 14, 43–83, 203–205;
    interview questionnaire, 208, 209–212;
    methodology, 11, 14, 47–48, 48, 87, 118,
    119, 203–212; participants, 12–13, 87–129,
    206–212; sampling bias, 87
survivor discourse, 123–124, 185
Swinbank, Vicki, 60
Symons, Michael, 18
symbolic capital, 37
Szathmary, Louis, 35

Tailor restaurant (New York City), 54–55
Takahashi, Keiko, 57
talent. See creative skills
Tallichet, Suzanne, 106
Tante Marie Cooking School, 76
television show, appearances, 18, 33, 36, 70,
    71–73, 77. See also specific television show
"tests" of ability in the kitchen/ability to fit
    in, 86, 101–108, 129, 148, 193
The Taste (television show), 17–18
Time magazine, 41; "The Gods of Food,"
    43–44, 82, 189, 190, 197
Time Out New York (magazine), 5
tokenism, 85, 94, 96, 98, 120, 121, 133–134,
    152–153, 158, 159, 189, 199
Toklas Society, 190
Top Chef (television show), 72, 199
Top Chef: Texas (television show), 206
toque, 22
Tosi, Christina, 190
touching, inappropriate, 109–117
Tower, Jeremiah, 68
Trabocchi, Fabio, 68
trade organization, 25, 41, 190, 198
trade union, 25
training approach, 28, 46, 48–49, 50, 67, 89,
    90, 91–92, 101, 151–153, 210
Troisgros, Jean, 30
Troisgros, Pierre, 30
Trotter, Charlie, 70
Trubek, Amy, 23
Túbal restaurant (Spain), 60
Tycer, Scott, 69

upscale grocery stores, 111, 143, 170, 172–173, 176–177, 183, 193, 207
U.S. Bureau of Labor Statistics, 3, 39, 89, 167
U.S. Department of Education, 4
U.S. Department of Labor, 35

Vetri, Marc, 71
Vetri restaurant (Philadelphia), 71
Veuve Clicquot, 1
Villagevoice.com, 43
Vines-Rushing, Allison, 81

Wacquant, Loïc J. D., 7
wages/wage gap, 8–9, 86, 89, 93, 164, 167, 173. *See also* gastronomic field: salary

Wall Street career. *See* stock trading career
Waters, Alice, 34–35, 39, 68, 120, 197, 204
websites. *See* food blogs/websites
Williams, Jody, 57, 65
Windisch, Patricia, 56
wine expert, 176
Wingfield, Adia Harvey, 121
work ethic, 101–102, 120, 123, 126, 181
work-family conflict. *See* family
working clean, 151
World's Best Female Chef Award, 1, 190

Yau, Alan, 72

Zakarian, Geoffrey, 49

ABOUT THE AUTHORS

DEBORAH A. HARRIS is an associate professor of sociology at Texas State University. She earned her PhD in sociology from Mississippi State University. Her research interests include areas of social inequality, the sociology of food, and qualitative methods. Her work has appeared in several outlets including: *Journal of Poverty, Journal of Sociology and Social Welfare, Gender Issues,* and *Research in the Sociology of Work.* She lives in Austin, Texas.

PATTI GIUFFRE is a professor of sociology at Texas State University. She earned her PhD in sociology from the University of Texas at Austin. Her research interests include inequality, gender, sexuality, work and occupations, and qualitative research methods. She has published articles on gender and work, sexual harassment in the workplace, and gay-friendly workplaces in *Gender & Society, Sexuality Research and Social Policy,* and *Sociology Compass.* She lives in San Marcos, Texas.

CPSIA information can be obtained
at www.ICGtesting.com
Printed in the USA
LVOW03s1724230218
567708LV00001B/104/P